Marriage *and*
CIVILIZATION

marriage *AND*
CIVILIZATION

HOW MONOGAMY
MADE US HUMAN

WILLIAM TUCKER

REGNERY
Publishing, Inc.
Washington, DC • Since 1947

Cataloging-in-Publication data on file with the Library of Congress

ISBN 978-1-62157-201-5

Published in the United States by
Regnery Publishing, Inc.
One Massachusetts Avenue NW
Washington, DC 20001
www.Regnery.com

Manufactured in the United States of America

10 9 8 7 6 5 4 3 2 1

Books are available in quantity for promotional or premium use. Write to Director of Special Sales, Regnery Publishing, Inc., One Massachusetts Avenue NW, Washington, DC 20001, for information on discounts and terms, or call (202) 216-0600.

Distributed to the trade by
Perseus Distribution
250 West 57th Street
New York, NY 10107

To the memory of my parents,
Grace and Bill Tucker.
They stayed married.

CONTENTS

"It is a good thing when a man and woman choose to live together as husband and wife. It is a joy to their friends, a warning to their enemies, but only they know the true meaning of it."

—Homer, *The Odyssey*

"We didn't know much about each other twenty years ago. We were guided by our intuition; you swept me off my feet. It was snowing when we got married at the Ahwahnee. Years passed, kids came, good times, hard times, but never bad times. Our love and respect has endured and grown. We've been through so much together and here we are right back where we started 20 years ago—older, wiser—with wrinkles on our faces and hearts. We now know many of life's joys, sufferings, secrets and wonders, and we're still here together. My feet have never returned to the ground."

—The late Steve Jobs's note to his wife on their twentieth anniversary

MONOGAMY AND ITS DISCONTENTS

I n the 1950s, America was a land of *Leave It to Beaver*, *My Three Sons*, and *Father Knows Best*. After centuries in which men had sought their identities as soldiers, as swashbuckling adventurers, pioneers, outlaws, or hard-driving businessmen, a new male role had appeared at the center of the culture—the family man.

The family man was a man who was devoted to his wife and children and worked hard to support them. He didn't harbor vague dreams of running off on wild adventures or abandoning his wife for an affair with a wanton woman. He didn't try to drink away his troubles or hide out in a barroom. In short, he didn't feel trapped in his home.

It has been a mighty struggle to domesticate men. During the late nineteenth and early twentieth century, the great enemy of domesticity had been the "demon rum" and a good many families had been ruined by a man's propensity to take to the bottle. Betty Smith's iconic *A Tree Grows in Brooklyn* told the story of a father gradually drifting away

1

from the family to drink. Even as late as the 1990s, Frank McCourt's *Angela's Ashes* tells the exact same story of a father who drinks up his paycheck before making it home every Friday evening and eventually disappears from the family. Although it is now remembered as a remnant of American Puritanism or a hopelessly outdated effort at social engineering, Prohibition was actually a movement of middle-class women attempting to hold lower-class men to the responsibilities of supporting their wives and families.

In the late 1930s, James Thurber touched the national psyche with his story of the mild-mannered Walter Mitty, whose pocketa-pocketa dreams of heroism were regularly interrupted by the demands of his nagging wife. In a famous *New Yorker* cartoon, Thurber depicted a poor Walter-Mitty type coming home from work to find his whole house morphed into his wife about to envelop him.

The generation that came of age in the 1950s, however, was different. They had fought a war in their youth and sowed some wild oats and now they were ready to settle down. *The Man in the Gray Flannel Suit*, the iconic image of the decade, tells the story of a young World War II veteran who has fathered an illegitimate child in Italy but comes back to America, marries, and settles into suburban life. The perpetual narrative of the era was that marriage and family were the ultimate goal of life and could be attained by anyone.

The statistics backed it up. More than 75 percent of households were occupied by married couples. Illegitimacy was at a minuscule 5 percent, and more than 80 percent of white children were living with both natural parents. Among African Americans the figures were slightly lower but not outrageously different. Illegitimacy rates were around 10 percent, and 70 percent of children were living with two parents. The phenomenon of "single motherhood" was virtually unknown.

Certainly there were the inevitable affairs and infidelities, the dissatisfied husbands, the frustrated wives, the closet alcoholics, the mothers who suffered nervous breakdowns, the children who grew up hiding some family secret—all the vicissitudes of life. As Tolstoy had written seventy-five years before, "All happy families are alike; each unhappy family is unhappy in its own way."

Yet the overwhelming message from the popular culture—and the one the public took to heart—was the story that marriage worked. There was a girl for every boy and a boy for every girl. In 1955, the Academy Award went to Paddy Chayefsky's *Marty*, about a Bronx butcher, a "fat, ugly little man," who is still single after all his younger brothers and sisters have married and hangs out every night with his buddies who spend their time asking, "So waddaya feel like doing tonight?" "I don't know, Ang'. Wadda you feel like doing?" At the insistence of his desperate mother, Marty finally goes to a Saturday night dance hall she tells him will be "loaded with tomatoes." There he meets a lonely schoolteacher who has been ditched by her date. They find solace in each other, however, and soon the emotional spigots are gushing. "I can't shut my mouth," Marty marvels as he walks her home. "I can't stop talking!" When he gets back with his buddies, however, word has gotten around that he "really got stuck with a dog" on Saturday. Soon they shame him into giving up the idea of calling her for another date. When the usual banter begins again, though—"Whadda you wanna do tonight, Angie?" "I don't know, whadda you wanna do?"—Marty blows up. "I'm going to call her up and ask her out. And then I'm going to call her up and ask her out again. And then I'm going to get down on my *knees* and beg her to marry me." The movie ends with Marty dialing her number in the phone booth.

In ninety-four minutes, Chayefsky had laid out the credo of the society: a girl for every boy, a boy for every girl. Marriage and domesticity were for everyone, even a fat, ugly little butcher from the Bronx.

———

In 2012, Charles Murray, who had brought attention to the breakdown of the African American family in his 1984 book *Losing Ground*, published a new report charting the breakdown of the white working-class family entitled *Coming Apart*. Murray showed how the once proud, tightly knit Philadelphia neighborhood of "Fishtown" had collapsed. In the 1960s, a head of social services had complained, "[Fishtown] doesn't want us there. It refuses to admit it's a poverty area." No more. Today, welfare dependence and single motherhood are rapidly becoming the norm. In 1960, 85 percent of Fishtown adults ages thirty to forty-nine were living as married couples. Now the figure is 48 percent. In 1960, 81 percent of households had someone working full time in the work force. Today it is only 53 percent. Divorce rates have climbed from 5 percent to 35 percent, and children living in broken homes or with single mothers rose from 2 percent to 23 percent. Among men most of the new leisure time has been absorbed by sleeping and watching television.

Remarkably, Murray noted, although many of the *attitudes* that denigrate the importance of marriage originate among the intelligentsia and the upper middle class, *that* stratum of society has so far managed to keep its families intact. The result has become a yawning gulf of economic inequality. "Over the last half century," Murray concludes, "marriage has become the fault line dividing American classes." The rule is: those who form traditional families succeed; those who don't fail.

So what happened? How did a society that once proclaimed marriage and family were for everyone turn into a society where men abandon their family responsibilities and women elect to raise their children alone, despite the economic consequences? And what happens next? Does the disintegration of family formation continue to creep upward until it engulfs the middle class? Should we attempt to strengthen the traditional two-parent family or do we accept broken homes and single motherhood as a "new type of family"—one that seems to require the everlasting support of the government?

Underlying all these issues, of course, are those monumental questions that have never really been settled: What is the human family? Where did it originate? Is it simply a Western institution of recent vintage that can be easily discarded? After all, as the anthropologists like to remind us, 75 percent of the cultures ever discovered in the world do not practice Western-style monogamy. They allow polygamy, where men can take more than one wife. Islam, the world's second largest religion, still sanctions this practice and seems happy with it—although Islamic countries do have a strong tendency to be at war with themselves and their neighbors. Are we one step ahead of the rest of the world or are they one step ahead of us? Are human beings naturally polygamous or monogamous? Does it even matter?

The theme of this book will be to try to provide answers to these important questions as a route to understanding what is going on in modern America and the world beyond. The question of how monogamy and polygamy evolved in different societies has only recently come into focus and provides a remarkable perspective on how societies develop. This inquiry can be carried right back to the dawn of human evolution when our earliest chimp ancestors first wandered out onto the African savanna about five million years ago. Were they monogamous or polygamous? Does it make a difference? And if so, does that have any relevance to the questions that nag at us today?

The premise from which we will work is simple. Human monogamy—the pair-bonding of couples within the framework of a larger social group—is not entirely a *natural* institution. This is attested by the observation that 95 percent of all species are polygamous. Where monogamy has been adopted in nature, it usually involves pair-bonded couples living in isolation in a challenging environment. Birds pair off within a larger group, which is why in matters of romance we often feel more affinity with them than we do with our fellow mammals; while 90 percent of bird species are monogamous, 97 percent of mammal species are polygamous and individual pair-bonds are almost unknown. Only the beaver and a few others practice monogamy.

Yet the payoff that was somehow achieved by our earliest chimp-like ancestors was extraordinary. The adoption of social monogamy by early hominids created something unique in nature—a society where males cooperate at common tasks with a minimum of sexual competition. In almost all species, males spend most of their time fighting among themselves for access to females. The unique social contract of monogamy—a male for every female, a female for every male—lowers the temperature of sexual competition and frees its members to work together in cooperation. It is at this juncture that human societies—even human civilizations—are born.

Unfortunately, monogamy does not sustain itself "naturally." It requires rules—rules that must be continuously enforced by the members practicing it. Moreover, the benefits of monogamy are not distributed equally. There are clear winners and losers, and there will always be pressure against the system from individuals who are dissatisfied with it. Yet any society that responds too enthusiastically to these grievances or decides that the system is no longer worth defending will find itself slipping back into an older social order where male competition is far more intense and the peace of civilization is difficult to maintain.

All this can be illustrated with some simple arithmetic. In any animal or human population, there will always be approximately the same number of males and females. When it comes to mating, then, there should be a male for every female and a female for every male. Without the restrictions of monogamy, however, the more powerful males will collect multiple females, leaving the lowest status males with none.

When this happens in nature, the unattached males usually wander off alone to lives that are "nasty, brutish, and short," or else congregate in a "bachelor herd" where they engage in endless status competitions until one or more emerge as strong challengers to the reigning alpha males. A titanic battle then ensues and if the challenger wins he takes over the "pride," "pod," or "harem" of females (there is a name in almost every species). He becomes the new alpha and gets to sire progeny.

Monogamy presents a different picture altogether. If every male is guaranteed a mate, then the losers are *high-status males*. Their breeding opportunities are curtailed. The winners are lower-status males, who are no longer thrust into exile but are given the opportunity to mate. There are winners and losers on the female side as well. The winners are *high-status females* who now have exclusive access to a high-status male instead of having to share him with other females. This is particularly important if the male is a *provider*. A high-status female who can lay exclusive claim to the efforts of a high-status male provider tremendously increases her chances of raising successful offspring. At the same time, the fortunes of *low-status* females are severely constricted by monogamy. They no longer have access to high-status males, either genetically or provisionally, but must be contented with the resources of an inferior, low-status male.

Although all this may seem transparent, its application to the workings of societies both contemporary and historic produces remarkable insights. First of all, it poses the question, how did monogamy ever evolve if high-status males are the biggest losers? After all, it is usually high-status males that dominate a social group and set the rules. Second, it explains why the predominant pattern in many former civilizations—that of Ancient Egypt or Imperial China, for instance—was polygamy at the top while monogamy prevailed among the common people. The rulers of most ancient civilizations were unabashed in taking multiple wives and consorts—even whole harems. In a few instances—the Ottoman Empire, for example—this stark inequality became so pronounced that the society became basically dysfunctional. On a smaller scale, the same pattern holds in Islamic societies today.

The important point is this. Although monogamy is manifestly a more equitable and successful way to organize a society, it is always under siege and forever fragile. It requires rules that must be upheld by its members. If a society becomes lax or indifferent about upholding its norms, the advantages will quickly unravel—as we are plainly witnessing in the America of today.

———

This is a book written for the average reader. It is not a scholarly treatise or an original piece of anthropological research. It is an attempt by a reasonable, educated person to tackle some subjects that many scholars and academics in the field seem to find uncomfortable.

Unfortunately, any contemporary discussion of marriage and the family quickly veers off into arguments about same-sex marriage. Yet the issue does not have much relevance to this book. From an evolutionary standpoint, gay marriage is a non-starter. It is only a few decades old and has played no part in evolutionary or human history. Whether it emerges as a *symbol* of a society's respect for marriage or a symbol of its undoing remains to be seen. Conservatives argue that gay unions cheapen marriage and detract from its central place in society. But it could just as easily be argued the other way—if gay people *aspire* to monogamous marriage that only enhances its place in society.

The important thing for supporters of same-sex marriage is to draw a stark line between acceptance of gay marriage and acceptance of an "anything-goes" attitude toward marriage, which says that it makes no difference whether people tie the knot or live in sin, whether they marry a man *and* a woman or marry two wives or three wives (because polygamy is always lurking at the edge of these discussions), or whether they marry their dog or their cat or a favorite lampshade.

Far more fundamental than the issue of same-sex marriage is that we arrive at a biological, anthropological, and historic understanding of the role that monogamy has played in the evolution of human society. At present, the debate bounces back and forth between claims that family disintegration and single motherhood represent only a "new kind of family" or even a justifiable revolt against an oppressive "patriarchy" versus the assertion that God created marriage to be between a man and a woman and we'd better keep it that way.

This book will be an attempt to put the matter in an entirely different perspective—to assess the role that monogamous pair-bonding has played in the evolution of humanity and the flowering of civilizations. For that reason, we will begin our investigation in the nineteenth century when a stable Victorian society where monogamous marriage had triumphed became aware that Christian marriage was only a frail bark floating on a much larger sea of humanity that honored quite different marital customs. So let us turn to nineteenth century "armchair anthropology" and the speculations it produced about the origins of marriage and the human family.

PART I

THE SEARCH
FOR origins

CHAPTER I

WHERE DID THE FAMILY COME FROM?

Nothing fascinated nineteenth century anthropologists more than the question of how and when the human family evolved.

Since antiquity, monogamy had been the general rule of Western civilizations. Yet people always knew that other mating systems were possible. The Greek gods practiced a very loose monogamy that bordered on marital chaos. Many of the early Hebrew patriarchs took multiple wives. Although monogamy was established in the legal codes of Greece and Rome and reinforced by the Catholic Church in the Middle Ages, it was well known that other cultures—most notably Islam in the Middle East—did not acknowledge it.

This became even more uncomfortably clear as European explorers pushed out among the tribes of Africa, the South Seas, and the American Plains, revealing that the practice of polygamy was almost universal outside the Christian West. The first account of Captain Cook's voyages, published in 1771, became the benchmark for recognition that Western marriage customs were not at all common in the big wide world. Writing of New Zealand natives, Cook recorded: "Polygamy is allowed amongst these people, and it is not uncommon for a man to have two or three wives. The women are marriageable at a very early age; and it would appear that one who is unmarried is but in a forlorn state." Another observation, confirmed by others over the following decades and centuries, was that primitive tribes were almost constantly at war with each other. "Their public contentions are frequent, or rather perpetual," wrote Cook, "for it appears, from their number of weapons, and dexterity in using them, that war is their principal profession." Numerous subsequent encounters and anthropological studies would later confirm this.

For Christian society of the eighteenth century, of course, all this had an easy explanation. Such peoples were heathen, unenlightened in the ways of God and in need of conversion. With the discovery of the first Neanderthal skeletons in 1856 and the publication of *The Origin of Species* (1859) and *The Descent of Man* (1871), however, this easy explanation began to lose ground. Gradually it became clear that the earth was far older than previously imagined and that human origins went back a long, long way—perhaps even to some "missing link" between man and the apes. Polygamy's roots, then, might be found in distant prehistory as well, and perhaps even be part of our evolutionary makeup.

The first attempt to explain the origins of the human family in evolutionary terms came in 1861, two years after *The Origin of Species*. Johann Bachofen, a Swiss law professor, published *Das Mutterrecht* ("The Mother-right"): *An Investigation of the Religious and Juridical Character of Matriarchy in the Ancient World*. Bachofen began with the simple observation that remains the most powerful argument of those, including many of today's feminists, who see family as based in single motherhood. Bachofen argued that while maternity is always known, paternity is always a bit of a mystery. In the civilized world, married men understand the connection between intercourse and conception and lay their paternal claims. In a primitive world, however, the link between sex and paternity would have been more obscure. As a result, males would have had more difficulty laying claim to their offspring and the family unit would have consisted only of a mother and her children. The two-parent family was only formed, said Bachofen, when women became weary of rearing children alone and persuaded men to settle down and help. He buttressed his case for this early matriarchy with evidence from mythology and legend.

These speculations were expanded in the next decade by Lewis Henry Morgan, an upstate New York attorney and amateur anthropologist. Among Morgan's clients were several Iroquois tribes. He became fascinated with their system of matrilineal tribal clans, each of which took the name of an animal. These clans still form the subject of endless controversy, prompting arguments as to whether their animal names acknowledge man's kinship with the animal world or are of no more significance than the mascots of high school football teams. But in 1871, in a book titled *Ancient Society*, Morgan postulated that these clans were actually the vestige of "group marriage." Noting that the Iroquois still practiced polygamy, particularly sororate marriage, where a man marries a group of sisters, Morgan conjectured that in ancient times whole families of brothers had married whole families of sisters, forming the totem clans.

But he didn't stop there. Projecting this logic all the way back to the beginning of human history, Morgan asserted that, without knowledge of paternity or the restraints of later civilization, marriage would have been unknown and *everybody would have mated with everybody*. Lewis called this indiscriminate form of mating "the primal horde."

This vision of earliest human history as a vast sex orgy both titillated and horrified Victorian society. Morgan's theory was widely publicized and became standard anthropological theory. Still, Morgan's theory probably would not be remembered today if it had not caught the attention of the son of a prosperous British factory owner named Friedrich Engels. In 1884, as an addendum to his friend Karl Marx's *Das Kapital*, Engels published *The Origin of the Family, Private Property, and the State*, in which he brought back the claims of primitive matriarchy with a vengeance.

Just as Marx had "turned Hegel on his head" by positing the primacy of the material over the ideal, so Engels "turned Morgan on his head" and argued that, far from being an unholy era of social chaos, the primal horde had actually been a lost paradise in which men and women lived in a utopia of sexual abandon before the chains of patriarchy were forged.

"The overthrow of the mother right was the *world historical defeat of the female sex*," wrote Engels (emphasis in the original). Once paternity was recognized, "The man took command in the home also; the woman was degraded and reduced to servitude; she became the slave of his lust and a mere instrument for the production of children." Once women became "property," material goods were claimed as property as well and all the evils of capitalism quickly followed. The downfall of the primal horde, said Engels, was the anthropological equivalent of the expulsion from the Garden of Eden. It was for this reason that early Communism was often coupled with the idea of "free love."

Genteel Victorian society was generally repulsed by this vision of amoral sex and serious scholars soon went to work to refute it. The most notable effort was made by Edward Westermarck, a Finnish anthropologist teaching at the University of London. In 1891 Westermarck published a monumental, three-volume encyclopedia of customs called *The History of Human Marriage* that tapped the massive accumulation of knowledge on non-Western peoples gathered by European missionaries and explorers.

Westermarck chronicled almost every imaginable form of sexual behavior. In many tribes (particularly polygamous ones), it was not uncommon for a man to lend his wife to guests and other men. Prenuptial chastity was honored or required in some societies, dismissed in others. The *jus primae noctis*—the deflowering of a bride by another man—was commonly practiced and even welcomed by men in some societies because they feared female blood.

Yet despite this wide variety of sexual customs, in no society was there a "primal horde" where mating was indiscriminate. All societies honored some form of marriage.

> I do not hesitate to affirm that anything like promiscuity among the unmarried is an exception in the customs of unadulterated savages. We have seen that even among peoples who are notorious for their laxity it is a slur upon a girl's reputation frequently to change her lover.... I think it is perfectly obvious... that among the "simpler peoples" the standard of pre-nuptial chastity in a tribe is not proportionate to its degree of culture.... It seems to me, on the contrary, that in the lowest tribes chastity is more respected than in the higher ones. This is also what might be expected if marriage is the natural and normal relation between the sexes in mankind.

While Westermarck's investigations were, at best, preliminary, his researches were soon extended into the field by one of his students, who became the foremost anthropologist of the early twentieth century, Bronislaw Malinowski. A native Pole studying under Westermarck in London, Malinowski left to do field work in New Guinea in 1914 and lived for several months among the tribes of Mailu Island. With the outbreak of World War I, however, he became a citizen of a hostile nation and was unable to return to England. So he signed on for a two-year stay in the remote Trobriand Islands, living among native peoples as no anthropologist had done before, learning their language and exploring their customs. His research eventually filled volumes.

One of Malinowski's major interests, inspired by Westermarck, was the question of whether there was or ever had been a primal horde. As he wrote in 1927:

> [A]t first sight, the typical savage family, as it is found among the vast majority of native tribes... seems hardly to differ at all from its civilized counterpart. Mother, father, and children share the camp, the home, the food, and the life. The intimacy of the family existence, the daily round of meals, the domestic occupations and outdoor work, the rest at night and the

awakening to a new day, seem to run on strictly parallel lines in civilized and savage societies.

As for Morgan's primeval forms of marriage, they were nowhere in sight.

[F]orms such as "group-marriage," "promiscuity," "anoma-lous" or "gerontocratic" marriages have been assumed by some writers as an inference from certain symptoms and survivals. At present these forms are not to be found, while their hypothetical existence in prehistoric times is doubtful; and it is important above all in such speculations never to confuse theory with fact.

In short, if the primal horde had ever existed, it was probably only in the imaginations of armchair anthropologists. There was certainly no evidence of it now.

Malinowski's observations settled another point about primitive marriage—knowledge of the connection between sex and childbirth was not crucial to paternity. The Trobrianders, as it happened, were not aware of the connection with intercourse but believed women to be impregnated "by the wind." In one particular instance, the natives pointed out to Malinowski a particularly unattractive woman who nevertheless had two children—a rare single mother—and scolded him by saying, "See, your idea is wrong. No one would ever sleep with her." Yet the Trobrianders still placed a high value on intercourse, arguing that it "helped the child grow" in the womb. This explained why children often resembled their fathers. Lineage was traced solely through the mother, however, and the most important male in the child's life was the mother's *brother*, giving rise to the term "avuncular society." Yet while the father was treated as a harmless drudge in his own household, he often became the child's "best friend" in adulthood. Wrote Malinowski:

[I]n all human societies a father is regarded as indispensable for each child, i.e., a husband for each mother. An illegitimate child—a child born out of wedlock—is an anomaly, whether it be an outcast or an unclaimed asset. A group consisting of a woman and her children is a legally incomplete union.... Marriage is never a mere cohabitation, and in no society are two people of different sex allowed to share life in common and produce children without having the approval of the community.... The main sociological principle...is that children should not be produced outside a socially approved contract of marriage.

Altogether, Malinowski's work seemed to settle the question of whether marriage differed widely between advanced and primitive societies.

Still, this left unsettled the larger question, "How did the human family evolve in the first place?" If evolution did indeed occur, if we were descended from some form of ape, why was there nothing among modern apes that closely resembled human society? How could the transition have occurred? One theorist who was willing to speculate on this issue was Sigmund Freud.

In *Totem and Taboo* (1913), Freud presented his own version of the early route from polygamy to monogamy, basing his speculation on a mix of contemporary anthropology plus his investigations into myth-making and the unconscious. Our earliest forebears, he suggested, probably lived in polygamous harems like today's gorilla, with a single alpha male controlling a "harem" of four to five females. Eventually, the excluded males grew tired of this arrangement and banded together to overthrow the alpha male. They killed him, and made a feast of his remains. Then they distributed the females equally among themselves, establishing a more egalitarian and democratic monogamy. These revolutionaries, however, were soon stricken with guilt at their patricide. So they instituted a "totem feast" in his honor, reenacting their rebellion and paying homage to the fallen patriarch all at once. Freud traced primitive totem feasts to this ritual and included the Christian Eucharist as a reenactment of this prehistoric crime. One critic summed it up as a "psychological Just So Story."

As fanciful as it sounds, Freud was trying to address a very important question—how would human society have moved from primitive polygamy to modern monogamy? Polygamy was obviously the earlier system. As anthropologist Robert Briffault reminded his readers in 1927 in a three-volume set called *The Mothers*, mother-and-child constellations were everywhere in nature while the human father and two-parent families were a very recent invention.

Then a few stray facts interrupted this speculation. It had always been assumed that the tribal societies discovered in tropical Africa and the forests of Indonesia and North and South America, all practicing what is called "hoe agriculture," represented the earliest human societies. As explorers pushed farther into the forgotten corners of the world, however, they discovered a few remaining tribes that were still practicing hunting-and-gathering—the Bushmen of the Kalahari Desert, the Pygmies of Central Africa, the Aborigines of Australia. This led to an astonishing revelation. *All turned out to be monogamous!*

The discovery of monogamy among what now seemed to be the most primitive societies turned the whole picture of human family evolution on its head. Now monogamy was the *original* form of the human family. As Richard Wrangham and Dale Peterson wrote in 1996:

> In general, hunter-gatherer people evince some of the most delightful and admirable ethics found anywhere. They may possess only a few rough and worn objects and little food beyond what is about to be eaten, but whatever one individual has is usually shared. People cooperate, and they promote cooperation. When one man tries to make himself better than his fellows, he is scorned, so that no one can become the "big man" or a petty tyrant over others. Hunter-gatherer societies are capable, anthropologists agree, of an "extreme political and sexual egalitarianism."

That egalitarianism rested on monogamy.

Apparently, it was the invention of agriculture and the accumulation of property and permanent wealth that had caused primitive agriculturalists to take up polygamy, as wealthier men began to acquire more women. By the 1930s, European anthropologists such as A. R. Radcliffe-Brown were arguing that polygamy was in fact a backsliding, arriving only after hunter-gatherer norms had broken down. With the loss of communal hunting, male members could now be excluded from the tribe without great consequence.

And so by the late 1920s a potential blueprint for the evolution of the family was coming into view. Monogamy was the original form of human bonding while polygamy was a later development. Yet it was at this very moment that the search for human origins suddenly ended. At Columbia University, Franz Boas founded a new school of anthropology based on "cultural relativism." He postulated that, rather than bearing the marks of biological evolution, human beings are "species specific." The invention of culture has severed our ties with the animal world and its biological roots. Instead, we are shaped by our culture, which is a response to the demands of a specific environment. Human nature is almost completely malleable. There is nothing "advanced" or "primitive" about any culture. All are simply a response to whatever lay around them.

In 1925, Boas' prize student Margaret Mead spent nearly a year living among the Samoans. There she famously claimed to have discovered a sexual paradise where the natives practiced free love, uninhibited by competition or jealousy. In 1934, Ruth Benedict, another Boas disciple, wrote *Patterns of Culture*, which became the template for the new anthropology. Investigating the Zuni of the southwestern United States, the Kwakiutl of western Canada, and the Dobuans of Melanesia, Benedict concluded that all cultures were driven by environmental factors and none could be classifiable as "primitive" or "modern." There followed a whole parade of titles emphasizing that there was no general human nature but that people were simply shaped by their surroundings: *People of the Plains, People of the Mist, People of the Deer, People of the River, Four Ways of Being Human*. As Gene Lisitzky put it in the opening pages of *Four Ways of Being Human* (1956):

> When people say you can't change human nature, they would seem to mean that there is only one way of being human. Yet

anthropology...denies this. It does not deny that it is pretty hard (though by no means impossible) to *change* human ways once they are set. But, say the anthropologists, it seems to be fairly easy to *make* different kinds of human nature if you start early enough. There are therefore many, and not just four, different ways of being human. [emphasis in original]

There was a strange anti-evolutionary subtext to all this. It left the search for human origins pretty much off the table. As a result, the next great advance would come not from academia but from a young British secretary who as a girl had reveled in nature, read all the Tarzan books, and occasionally taken earthworms to bed. In 1957, on a short visit to Africa, Jane Goodall met Louis Leakey, the famous paleontologist, who was looking for someone to study chimpanzees in the Gombe Stream National Park. Leakey ended up hiring Goodall as a secretary and eventually selected her to perform the investigation. The study of human origins would never be the same.

CHAPTER 2

THE PRIMATE INHERITANCE

J ane Goodall spent the next forty years doing what no one had done before—living among chimpanzees in the wild as a "participant observer," studying their behavior in their native habitat, interfering with their lives as little as possible. Other investigators who had observed them in zoos came away with conflicting reports—chimps were violent or passive, neurotic or aggressive, oversexed or celibate. None of this reflected anything except perhaps the behavior of chimps in captivity. Goodall settled into the forest, set up a base camp, and, using bananas, lured a troop of chimps into her area until they became accustomed to her presence. Then she sat and took notes. What she discovered amazed even the most sophisticated students of ethology.

First of all, chimps are a band of brothers. This is practically unique in nature. In almost every other social species, related females form the backbone of the group. The presence of an alpha male, such as the alpha male lion with its pride or the silverback gorilla and its harem, often creates the impression that males are in charge. Yet it is the females who form the close kinship relations. Alpha males come and go, with the younger males being exiled as they reach maturity. But it is the females who provide the continuity from generation to generation.

With chimps, however, the males have taken over the group, forming a bond of kinship among themselves and marking out a territory in which females cohabit. It is the males who remain through adulthood while the females migrate out of the troop on maturity in order to avoid inbreeding. (This avoidance of incest among members of any small band that have grown up together is called the "Westermarck Effect," after Edward Westermarck, who was the first to notice it.) The adult males then carefully patrol their borders, guarding against incursions by other males—and occasionally foraying outward on aggressive expeditions as well. It is a powerful and vigilant assembly. As Nicholas Wade observes in *Before the Dawn*, if you have ever wandered into a group of closely related males, you know you are in big trouble.

Within the group, however, relations remain relatively peaceful and non-competitive. There is a clear status hierarchy among both males and females but it is determined mostly by social cues and displays of strength rather than physical combat. In Goodall's troop, one ambitious young male became the alpha when he learned to bang on a set of oil drums Goodall brought into camp, overawing his fellow troop members.

Most interesting is that chimps occasionally *hunt together*. This is unique among primates.

> During the ten years that have passed since I began work at the Gombe Stream we have recorded chimpanzees feeding on the young of bushbucks, bushpigs and baboons, as well as both young and small adult red colobus monkeys, redtail monkeys, and blue monkeys.

These were highly coordinated efforts:

> Four years earlier, when Figan had been a young adolescent, Hugo [Goodall's husband] and I had watched him creeping

toward another juvenile baboon in a large fig tree. It had been Rodolf, so far as we could tell, who had actually initiated that hunt; he had walked toward the tree and stood, his hair very slightly on end; if he had looked at the baboon at all, we had not noticed. Yet, as though at a signal, the chimpanzees who had been resting and grooming peacefully on the ground had got up and stationed themselves close to trees that would act as escape routes for the intended victim. And Figan, the youngest adolescent male of the group, had crept toward the baboon.

Such cooperative efforts have evolved among non-primates that are not large or strong enough to hunt alone. The TV series *This Planet Earth* featured a remarkable aerial shot of a pack of hunting dogs stalking a solitary moose. Approaching the animal single file, the dogs suddenly peel off left and right with military precision until they have surrounded the hunted animal. Then they closed in. That chimps have also mastered such techniques has enormous implications for human evolution. Meat constitutes 5 percent of the chimp diet. Among human hunter-gatherers, it is generally 40 percent. More strategic cooperation means greater access to protein—and an inclination toward group combat as well.

In the 1980s, the chimps in Goodall's Kasakela troop went on a deliberate raiding expedition against its neighboring Kahama tribe. Using stealth and outright attack, the Kasakela systematically killed all six male members of the Kahama group, requisitioning their females in the process. Even more shocking was that the Kahama group was made up of former members of the Kasakela group who had moved to a neighboring territory to found their own group only a few years before. The murderers all knew their victims. It was a good lesson for those who insist that "humanity is the only species on earth that kills its own kind." There is such a thing as chimp warfare.

If relations with the outside world include aggressive combat and the effort to capture other females, however, what happens within the troop is truly astonishing. The chimps practice sexual communism. *Every male gets to mate with every female.* When a female goes into heat—"estrus"—

her bottom turns a bright pink, advertising her fertility to all. Males from everywhere in the troop congregate and line up, roughly according to status, to take turns mating with her. This may go on for a week or more. Even the lowest-status male gets to take a turn. Moreover, the *females encourage this.* Just why this should be plays a very important part, as we'll see later, in understanding how human monogamy might have evolved.

Compared to ordinary polygamy, where a jealous alpha male carefully guards his harem from other males, the chimps' sexual communism is a stunning departure. But it provides a rich reward. With rivalry between males minimized, the closely related group—none of whose members have overpowering size or strength—is able to inhabit a wide swath of the forest, defending territory and protecting against rival troops and predators. To be sure, there is still sexual competition. Males have developed huge testicles and produce prodigious amounts of sperm in order to try to win the mating contest. But as far as sexual rivalry, mate guarding, or attempts to exclude other males, there is none. Every male gets to mate with every female.

Although no one ever suggested it, this one-for-all-and-all-for-one mating organization could have easily been called the "primal horde."

The discovery of "polymorphous polygamy," as chimp mating came to be called, completely rearranged our assumptions about human evolution. Freud and his contemporaries had assumed that human monogamy evolved out of gorilla polygamy. Now the chimp "primal horde" seemed as if it must have been the original template. Still, this left us with the question, how could chimp polymorphous polygamy have evolved into human monogamy? Perhaps the best way to approach this question would be to put chimps in the context of the other great apes.

1) The mating pattern for gorillas follows the familiar pattern of many other mammals. Gorillas live deep in the forests of Central Africa, far removed from any potential predators. They weigh between four hundred and five hundred pounds and are entirely vegetarian, munching up to

fifty pounds of leaves a day. The silverback gorilla collects between four and eight females in a harem. He sometimes tolerates the presence of one or two subordinate males, to whom the females often allow secret sexual favors. They are now threatened by loss of habitat.

2) The orangutan is the gorilla equivalent of Southeast Asia. The name means "man of the forest" and orangutans come about as close as any species has ever come to resembling human beings. (Queen Victoria was horrified by the similarity.) Orangutans stand between three to five feet tall, and weigh anywhere from 66 to 198 pounds. They can stand upright and shape rudimentary tools. In Sumatra they are threatened by tigers and spend most of their time in the trees, but in Borneo, where they lack predators, they often descend to the ground.

Orangutan mating patterns resemble the casual couplings of the most disorganized human societies. Their lifestyle has been described as "solitary but social." Except for mothers caring for their youngsters, neither males nor females move in groups but wander the forest alone. If a young male encounters a female in estrus, he will force copulation—"orangutan rape." The females do not like this and often seek protection from the more dominant males. At about age twenty males grow "flanges" on the side of their cheeks that expand to make their heads appear bigger. The size of the flanges usually determines dominance.

Males attract females by singing. Upon pairing off, a couple may travel together for as long as a week, copulating all the while, but soon part ways. Infants remain with their mothers until age five and males play no part in rearing the offspring. Orangutans reach sexual maturity around age twelve. Their rather indolent lifestyle has much limited the orangutan's range. Their habitat is rapidly diminishing as Borneo and Sumatra cut down rainforests and, like the gorilla, they are being pushed to the brink of extinction.

3) Baboons are much smaller than gorillas, orangutans, or chimps, standing only three feet tall and weighing less than fifty pounds. Despite their diminutive size, the savanna baboon has been able to abandon the forest, where the hamadryas baboon still lives, and move out onto the East African grasslands where they have survived in an environment filled with predators, particularly the leopard, which relishes baboon

meat. Baboons survive in the same manner that African antelope, wildebeest, and other grazing animals do—by forming large herds that offer protection in numbers. But there is a difference. Unlike these herbivores, baboons have developed a complex, hierarchical, almost military social system.

The fifty to two hundred members of a savanna baboon troop are arranged in concentric circles, with the older and dominant males alongside the fertile females. As they reach maturity, the younger males are expelled to the perimeter of the troop, where they form a kind of Praetorian Guard to protect the troop from predators. Over the course of the next several years, the young male baboon will engage in endless status quarrels as he gradually attempts to work his way back toward the center. Not all this involves fighting. Younger males often form alliances that improve their chance of advancement. Having a high-status mother also helps as she often influences her sons' progress. One way or another, however, it is a long and arduous journey from the periphery to the center where mating takes place, often consuming five to ten years. In his 1970 book, *The Social Contract*, playwright-turned-anthropologist Robert Ardrey chronicled this eloquently in an often-excerpted chapter, "Time and the Young Baboon."

For a while in the 1960s, before Jane Goodall's work became widely known, the savanna baboon was thought to offer the best analog for human evolution. Like the earliest human ancestors, these baboons have successfully made the transition from the forest to the savanna. In *Men in Groups* (1969), Lionel Tiger even speculated that human intelligence evolved from the experience of young males suppressing their sexual desires in the presence of dominant males.

4) But perhaps no other primate offers a more interesting insight into the possible pathways of human evolution than the gibbons of South Asia. Gibbons stand three feet tall, weigh twelve to twenty pounds, and have extra-long arms with which they cannonball through the forests of Sumatra and Southern China at speeds up to 34 mph. They are purely monogamous. Gibbons court each other by singing eerie, high-pitched songs that can be heard half a mile away. If a male and female like each

other's song, they rendezvous in the forest, do a brief mating dance, and then copulate up to five hundred times over the next forty-eight to seventy-two hours, forming a tight sexual bond. (An immediate period of intense sexual abandon is what characterizes all monogamous species.)

What differentiates gibbon couples from human beings is that they are purely antisocial. They do not want other couples around. As they settle down to raise offspring, their songs become duets. These gibbon duets serve a very distinct purpose. *They warn other males and females out of their territory.* Specifically, the male does not want other males poaching his mate and the female does not want other females around tempting her consort. As the young offspring mature, they join in to form a family chorus.

So with all this in mind, let us examine how human monogamy might have evolved out of any of these possible patterns.

The commonly accepted scenario for the beginning of human history is that sometime around 5 million years ago, the East African climate grew drier and the tropical forest receded, leaving treeless patches that eventually opened into the current vast savannas. Onto these open grasslands ventured our common ancestors who, if they were not identical to the chimpanzees of today, were much more chimp than they were human. Recent research suggests that they may have first survived in this sparse environment by digging roots deep out of the ground and that the sticks they used for this task may have been the first human "tool." They were only about three feet tall, no bigger than today's baboons.

The principal theorist in this field is Owen Lovejoy, professor of anthropology at Kent State University, known for his work reconstructing the skeleton of "Lucy," the 3.5-million-year-old hominid discovered in Ethiopia by Donald Johansen in 1974 and only recently surpassed as the world's oldest anthropoid. Lovejoy has been interested in the question of early human mating since the 1970s and has come up with a powerful thesis. He argues that the transition from polygamy to monogamy happened at the very *beginning* of hominid evolution and that it was the key to all the evolutionary steps that came after it. In other words, we never would have become human if we hadn't adopted monogamy.

Now it may seem wildly presumptuous to think that we can deduce whether three-foot-tall creatures wandering the African savanna 5 million years ago were polygamous or monogamous, but in fact there are several key indicators. The first is the size of incisors. When males compete for females in a polygamous society, the stakes are very high because a few males will secure all the females while the majority of males will be left with none. Therefore combat takes place. It is important that this combat not be lethal, however, since if males were killing other males in competition for females the species itself would be endangered. All species have developed some sort of ritualized combat in order to keep male competition from becoming lethal. Poisonous snakes will wrestle each other for dominance but will not use their fangs on each other. A defeated wolf submits by exposing his throat, a signal that the dominant wolf doesn't have to tear it out. Male hippopotami, believe it or not, determine status by which can produce the most amount of excrement—something akin to today's politicians. With chimpanzees, baboons, and other primates, status competitions are often settled by a display of teeth. For this reason, chimps, baboons, and gorillas have all grown long, threatening incisors that are particularly prominent in males.

When the first fossil remains of *Australopithecines* began showing up in South Africa, however, their incisors were no bigger than those of today's human beings. Lovejoy quickly seized upon this as a crucial indicator. As early as 4 million years ago, hominids had given up competing fiercely for females. Instead they had paired off. And unlike the solitary gibbon, these hominids practiced monogamy *within* a social group. This allowed them to live in larger groups for protection and cooperative hunting without being disrupted by sexual competition. Monogamous pair-bonding allowed males to live together in larger groups—unlike, say, the gorilla band, which is limited to one or two males and five or six members of the harem. It also produced another unintended benefit. It opened the door to human intelligence.

When we began standing upright, the female pelvis narrowed considerably, making childbirth more difficult. Yet increased intelligence means a larger and larger brain, which meant a larger head coming through the birth canal. Such a development would have been impossible except for one thing—all humans are born prematurely. There is a general scale correlating adult body size with the amount of time an animal spends in the womb—the larger the adult, the longer the period of gestation. On this metric, we should spend about eleven months in the womb. But we are all born at nine months, two months premature. This means we arrive in a more helpless state, requiring constant care and attention for a period that ultimately lasts at least one or two years. Such extended care would have been difficult or impossible for a lone female. Only a pair-bonded couple could offer such protection. Had it not been for monogamy, Lovejoy argued, the evolution of the human brain would not have been possible.

Lovejoy's thesis suddenly came into focus in 1978 when Mary Leakey discovered the 3.5-million-year-old "First Human Footprints" in East Africa. The trail, left in fresh volcanic ash along with the tracks of a dozen other species, shows an upright couple walking next to each other across freshly fallen lava. There are actually three sets of footprints. A smaller creature has put its feet in the prints of one of the larger ones. Leakey believed they were a couple holding hands, followed by a child. There could be nothing more dramatic than this first set of hominid footprints walking into history as a complete family.

———

The discovery of the first human footprints seemed to show that Lovejoy was correct that pair bonding between males and females had occurred near the beginning of human evolution. Yet that still hadn't answered the question, how and why did it occur? In order to provide an answer, Lovejoy joined an even older controversy—why the earliest hominids stood on their hind legs. He argued that both standing up and pairing off had occurred at the same time. As we shall see, here he was on shakier ground.

CHAPTER 3

CHIMP SEXUAL COMMUNISM

I was once at a party discussing anthropology with a professor of literature when I mentioned that one the greatest mysteries of human evolution is why we stood on our hind legs. The gentleman looked at me with alarm. "We stood up so we could build the Parthenon," he declared. But evolution doesn't work that way. Building the Parthenon certainly became possible once we stood up and freed our hands for greater control of the environment, but it is not the *reason* we originally stood up. Evolution does not work by foresight. There has to be a more proximate cause. So it is with the early human adoption of monogamy.

When Lovejoy reached the point of answering the question of *why* we switched from polygamy to monogamy, he decided to link it to the much older controversy, why did we stand up? His hypothesis went like this. At some point very early on, our proto-chimp ancestors extended their hunting range and, blessed with a surplus of meat, carried their kill to a central camp. In order to do this efficiently, they had to stand up.

When the hunter males returned, each one shared his spoils with a particular female who, in return, granted him sexual favors. This exchange of food for sex—which hasn't completely left us today—established a monogamous relationship between couples and became a pair bond. Lovejoy has called this the "provisioning theory."

Now before we criticize this as nothing but mere guesswork, it should be noted that the provisioning theory has a lot to be said for it. There is a very strong association between hunting, male cooperation, and the provisioning of females and offspring. Later on we will meet a remarkable tribe in South America that has adopted hoe agriculture and slid into polygamy and raiding other tribes for wives. But when the women grow hungry enough, they make the rounds of the village urging the men to go on a hunt. At that point, each woman picks a particular man, *not necessarily her husband*, to provision her on that expedition. In return, he receives sexual favors. In other words, a tribe that has already transitioned into early agriculture and polygamy *reverts to monogamy* when it once again takes up hunting. This is a remarkable confirmation of the thesis that hunting-and-gathering promotes monogamy. Whether this transition can be placed at the beginning of human evolution, however, is a different story.

In choosing the provisioning theory, it must be admitted, Lovejoy was venturing into a briar patch already thick with controversy. The debate had been kicked off in 1961 with Robert Ardrey's publication of *African Genesis*. Ardrey was a successful journalist and playwright who had gone to Kenya to research a book on the Mau Mau. While in Africa, he met Raymond Dart, the South African anthropologist who had discovered the Taung Child, the first and most spectacular example of *Australopithecus*, the earliest hominid then known to appear on the veldt. At the time, Dart was in a battle with Louis Leakey in Kenya over whose fossil finds represented the most direct line of human origins. But Dart also had some rather heretical ideas that were not being given much attention in the anthropological community. Ardrey, who had studied anthropology in college, became fascinated with Dart's ideas and followed them up in *African Genesis*.

Dart's major point of dissent was with Leakey's description of man as the "the tool-making animal." Many stone tools had been found with the Leakey family's *Homo habilis*, who lived 2.3 to 1.4 million years ago, and Leakey had developed the thesis that upright posture had evolved in order to free the hands for fashioning these objects. Not quite, said Dart and Ardrey. The first object picked up by our ancestors was a *weapon*. Chimps will stand up and brandish a stick when threatened by a large predator, Dart noted. So it made sense that when the first proto-chimps wandered out onto the savanna, they probably carried a stick for protection. Later they substituted the thigh bone of the antelope—an object found with unusual frequency at *Australopithecine* sites. This theory was eventually dramatized in the memorable opening sequence of the film *2001: A Space Odyssey*, released in 1968, where a proto-human picks up the thigh bone and realizes he can use it to kill larger animals.

All this seemed plausible and might have carried the day except Dart and Ardrey felt compelled to take their argument one step further. There were actually two species of *Australopithecine* on the savanna between 4.5 and 3 million years ago. *A. afarensis* was a "gracile" species, small and lithe. Its cousin, *Australopithecus robustus*, was more gorilla-like, although still only three feet tall. *Robustus* had a huge Mohawk-like bone on its crown, obviously designed to anchor powerful jaw muscles. He seems to have lived on roots and nuts, earning him the nickname "Nutcracker Man." Although more physically powerful, the larger *Robustus* seems to have been limited by its vegetarian and nuts diet, while the more agile *Afarensis* was eating more meat, probably from scavenging or hunting small animals. In any case, the two lived side by side on the savanna together for nearly two million years. Then *Robustus* vanishes.

A simple explanation might be that the two ended up competing for habitat and *Afarensis* won. This is what appears to have happened 100,000 years ago when Cro-Magnons invaded Europe and pushed aside the older Neanderthals. Shunning such a simple explanation, however, Dart and Ardrey decided on something far more dramatic.

They conjectured that *Robustus* disappeared because *the smaller gracile species killed it*. Ardrey called this Cain-slew-Abel scenario the "dark secret of human beginnings" and labeled *Afarensis* "the killer ape."

All this raises cries of protest from anthropology departments around the world. There was nothing in the record that required such a nefarious explanation. In particular, it proved far too much for the new breed of feminist anthropologists who were beginning to make their presence felt. They came up with a completely different explanation for human origins. The first hominids stood up, they said, not because males picked up a weapon but because females began inventing ways of carrying food from their foraging expeditions. They might have used large leaves to weave primitive trays or baskets. In 1977, *The Sciences*, a publication of the New York Academy of Sciences, carried a cover illustration showing a group of female *Australopithecines* emerging from the forest with satchels slung over their shoulders like so many suburban housewives returning from a shopping expedition. This became the "carrying hypothesis."

Faced with these competing explanations for human beginnings, Lovejoy decided to split the difference. The first hominids did not stand up to brandish a weapon, he conceded. They stood up to carry food. But it was the *males* who did the carrying. They hunted larger game, carried it back to females, shared it with them, and instituted monogamy in the process.

Once again, it must be admitted that Lovejoy's scenario has the flavor of a Just So Story. There is nothing that *compels* any of these changes. (The most recent explanation is far less portentous. It says the earliest hominids stood up in their new treeless environment simply because walking on two legs was faster than the chimp knuckle-walk.) It is true that chimpanzees share some hunted kill and males often bargain food for sex. One ethnologist reports seeing a male chimp discover a particularly banana-laden tree and parking himself under it, requiring each female to have sex with him before being allowed to climb the tree. But none of this has led to pair-bonding. Standing up in order to provision in order to bargain for sex in order to form a permanent pair bond has the definite flavor of foresight, which evolution does not allow. It seems as though something more immediate should be at work. Monogamy, after all, is not about eating or provisioning, it is about reproduction and sex.

Perhaps the key may lie in another aspect of chimp communism that Goodall discovered after years of observation. Although at first it seemed insignificant, Goodall gradually recognized its import, calling it "the forerunner of human marriage." It was the "the consort relationship."

Goodall found that, once all the obligations for mating with every male had been met, females—and particularly high-ranking females—liked to sneak off into the jungle with a favorite male. The couple would stay away two or three days, even as long as a week, building a nest in the trees, grooming each other, exchanging signs of affection, and copulating frequently. She nicknamed it "going on safari." As further research began to reveal secrets of chimp biology, it was discovered that females actually *delay* ovulation through the period in which they are mating at random so that they are more likely to conceive with their consorts. In this way, they preserve the aboriginal right of females of every species, which is to *mate with the male of their choice*. The public show of uninhibited sexual activity is actually a ruse to deceive the lower-status males. Biologically, chimp females are designed to conceive with a preferred mate. Genetic tests have later showed that nearly half the offspring in a troop are sired in these consort relationships.

So why do female chimps go through the exhausting ritual of mating with every male member of the troop if they really want to be mated with a dominant male? It is not a pleasant ritual. Goodall describes the ordeal of Flo, the most popular female, who was left battered and bleeding after mating with every member of the troop, over and over, for more than a week. Studies have estimated a female chimp mates *300 times* for every conception. Goodall even noted that young females are often reluctant to go out among the males during their first estrus and have to be urged on by the older females. In all of nature, after all, "female coyness" is an almost universal characteristic. Because they can generally be fertilized by one male, females are much more selective about mating, while males—who have ample sperm and can mate with numerous females—are much more eager and indiscriminate. Why do chimp females act so differently?

That was the question Sarah Blaffer Hrdy began asking in the 1970s as a young graduate student. Hrdy became intrigued by the phenomenon of infanticide among langurs, a species of colobus monkeys in the forests of Southeast Asia. The prevailing theory was that langurs occasionally killed their young because of overcrowding. After studying colonies in the wild, however, Hrdy realized that overcrowding was not the problem. Instead, she perceived a pattern now recognized as common to all polygamous species and tied directly to selfish gene theory and the instinctive understanding males have about fostering their own offspring.

When an alpha male takes over a polygynous harem, no matter how small, he probably has only two or three years before he is displaced by another male. But in species such as the colobus monkey, an infant may nurse with the mother for four years, during which time her hormonal balance will prevent her from becoming fertile again. If the alpha is to take advantage of his dominance, he has only one choice. He must kill the offspring of the previous alpha and put the females to work producing his own. Mothers may try to protect their infants but it is to no avail. It is one of the most heart-rending dramas in nature to watch an adult male ruthlessly hunting down a juvenile while the mother stands helplessly nearby.

Hrdy soon realized that while such infanticide was common among other primates, female chimps had evolved a strategy to prevent this. *They confuse paternity.* By carefully mating with every male member of the group, females give each reason to think that he *might* be the father. This accommodation allows them to live in relative peace in the midst of a large group of males once the infant is born. They are protecting against infanticide. All this of course demolishes the theory, going back to Bachofen and Engels, that males are unaware of their own paternity. They do not have to understand the nature of intercourse in any theoretical sense. It is all bred into their nature. Male "mate guarding," as it is known, is a universal behavior.

The whole polymorphous polygamous mating system, then, is a set of rules designed to keep lower-status males loyal to the troop. Even among chimps, these rules require constant enforcement. Goodall found that a consorting couple had to be very careful about disappearing into the bush, always taking separate routes back when returning. In the few instances where couples were caught on safari, they were savagely beaten by other males.

So we can now ask the question, what would happen to such a chimp troop practicing polymorphous polygamy if it were to move out onto the more challenging savanna environment?

CHAPTER 4

THE ALPHA COUPLE
AND THE PRIMAL
HORDE

In the manner of Sigmund Freud, let us conduct a thought experiment: What would happen *today* if a chimp troop moved out on the savanna and tried to survive in a treeless environment with predators everywhere? Would chimp sexual behavior be subject to change?

The first thing to note is that such a group would have to cling much more tightly together. Chimps are generally described as a "fission-fusion" band. For the most part they roam their territory alone or in small groups. Only very rarely does the whole troop convene together. A female in estrus or the discovery of a particularly well-laden banana tree may result in an assembly but chimps generally roam far apart. Attempting to wander out on the savanna would change this. Like the baboon troop, they would have to huddle in close proximity for protection. This would change considerably the sexual dynamic within the group.

Second, under these conditions, primal-horde mating would become extremely awkward and disruptive, if not impossible. In the relative sanctuary of the tropical forest, when a chimp female goes into estrus, all other activity stops and the males may spend close to a week following her around. On the savanna, however, there would be no such luxury. A chimp troop that spends whole days obsessed with a female in heat would have trouble finding food and leave itself extremely vulnerable to predators.

Third and most important, *the consort relationship would no longer be possible.* There would be no way to sneak off into the forest with a favored partner. A male and female that left the troop for two or three days on an amorous safari would leave themselves highly exposed to predators. Remember, these creatures—the first savanna primates—were barely three feet tall and the giant cats that prowled the savanna were bigger and more numerous than they are today. A baboon troop is constantly on guard against leopards and suffers periodic casualties. A single male and female couple would have no chance at all.

But the loss of the consort relationship, the source of more than half of chimp pregnancies, would be severely disruptive, *particularly to high-status males.* If they were forced to go back to standing in line with the rest of the troop, their mating success would be severely circumscribed. Given this situation, then, what two members of the troop, male and female, would have the *most* to gain from defying the social order and forming an exclusive pair bond?

Let us consider what the possibilities might be. Suppose a lower-status male tried to monopolize a high-status female. He wouldn't have much luck. The other males would gang up on him and the female would resist as well, since she wants to mate with a more dominant male. So that wouldn't work. What if a lower-status male tried to monopolize a lower-status female at his own level? His chances might be better. The other males might not object to the loss of a lower-status female. But the *female* would object because she would not want to be excluded from mating with higher status males.

There remains then one other possibility. What if the *dominant male and the dominant female* decided to pair off, making their consort relationship public, so to speak, and defying the mores of the troop? There would be a distinct advantage for both. The alpha male now has 100 percent assurance that he will be siring offspring with the dominant female. This is a significant improvement over the crapshoot where he must compete with all the other males in the promiscuous free-for-all. Granted, he might also want to mate with other females as well—but here we are encountering a story that recurs throughout human history. For the time being, he is improving his mating possibilities by monopolizing the most desirable female.

Meanwhile, for the alpha female there is also a vast improvement. *She now has the assurance that the alpha male will be siring her offspring.* She no longer has to undergo the ordeal of mating with every available male for more than a week. But there remains one problem. *What about infanticide?* There is still the chance that after she gives birth she might encounter a sub-dominant male who knows he is not the father and wants to make her available for his offspring. Living in a large, tightly engaged group, this now becomes a perpetual problem—*unless the alpha male stays with her.* For the alpha couple, then, pairing off improves mating success for both of them—*but only if he remains to guard his offspring after it is born.* Since he knows for certain that it is his offspring, however, he will be willing to guard them. And so a permanent, monogamous relationship is born.

The alpha couple, then, can achieve an advantage by pairing off. Moreover, the alpha male—precisely because he is the strongest and most domineering—would be able to fend off the objections of the other males. But what about the rest of the troop? What happens to them? Well, once the alpha couple has paired off, the beta couple now find themselves in the same position. They have the same advantages in forming a pair bond. Moreover, they have the example of the alpha couple to justify them. After that the gamma couple has the same advantage and so on down the line—much the way it happens in high school. In the end, everyone's reproductive interest is reasonably optimized. The important thing is this: *The solidarity of the troop is maintained.* It is now possible for the males to get along with each other with only a minimum of sexual rivalry—unlike polygamy where males are constantly competing for control of numerous females and the lowest-status males must be excluded.

For a group trying to live in close proximity, the example of the alpha couple becomes crucial. If the "king and queen" can be satisfied with each other, then everyone else can be satisfied as well. But if the alpha male collects a "harem," then other males can have the same aspiration and the free-for-all of unlimited sexual competition returns. This is another story that has recurred throughout human history.

Altogether, this is what is known in game theory as "Nash Equilibrium," after the contribution of the great mathematician John Nash, the subject of the book and film, *A Beautiful Mind*. Nash's thesis, still the mainstay of all game theory, says that a system can reach an equilibrium without *maximizing* the interest of every individual player. This occurs when the system reaches a point where *each player has achieved the best outcome they can under the existing rules*. For a large heterosexual group with the same number of males and females, monogamy satisfies Nash Equilibrium. Each player has optimized his or her outcome *under the rules of the existing system*. More to the point, *the only way any individual can improve his or her outcome is by breaking the rules*. But this causes other kinds of disruption and works to the disadvantage of the entire group. It can be prevented by other members constantly *enforcing* the rules.

This is why human societies everywhere and throughout all time have enforced some kind of rules on marriage and frown on extra-marital affairs. The stability of the group is at stake. If people start flaunting the rules of marriage, then the equilibrium is upset and growing numbers of males and females are left without mates. These individuals will become a disruptive force and the cohesiveness of the entire society is threatened. Monogamy does not *maximize* the interests of every participant. What is does is *optimize* everyone's individual outcome in a way that maintains the integrity of the entire society.

———

In the 1990s, two ethnographic researchers, C. P. Van Schaik and R. I. M. Dunbar, sought to identify the advantages that gibbons have achieved by pairing off and whether it might have any implications for the origins of human society. The result was a brilliant article titled "The

Evolution of Monogamy in Large Primates: A New Hypothesis and Some Crucial Tests."

The authors began by hypothesizing that male gibbons settle for one mate because they cannot control enough territory to provide for other females. This was the subject of Robert Ardrey's book, *The Territorial Imperative*, in which he advanced the idea that polygamous male animals compete for females by marking out territory and inviting as many females as possible to settle within it. Van Schaik and Dunbar carefully measured the territory controlled by gibbon couples and found that it actually included enough vegetation to support two or three additional females. Yet male gibbons settle for one. So there must be some other explanation.

They hypothesized three possible advantages that could come to the female from pair-bonding: 1) better protection from predators, 2) increased access to food resources, and 3) protection from having her offspring killed by *other* males. Van Schaik and Dunbar discovered, however, that gibbons have few predators, and male gibbons actually spend no more time watching for them than female gibbons do. They also found that the size of the territory ranged by female gibbons did not vary, whether they lived alone or with a mate. So access to additional resources does not seem to result from pair-bonding.

But what did seem to correlate was that monogamous gibbon pairs offered better protection for the offspring—and it all came down to those duets. Gibbons sing, they found, in order to warn off other gibbons— *both male and female*. (They certainly wouldn't sing to warn off predators since they would only be advertising their presence.) The male doesn't want other males poaching his female, and the female not only doesn't want female competitors, she doesn't want any other *males* coming around because of the possibility of infanticide.

How do we know this? Well, one telling piece of evidence is that if a male gibbon dies and leaves his mate alone, *she stops singing*. A solo performance would reveal that she no longer has a protector. This would risk intrusion and infanticide by other males. Instead, she keeps very quiet in the hope of not being discovered. Concluded Dunbar and Van Schaik, "We therefore infer that the risk of infanticide is the primary factor promoting the evolution of monogamy in gibbons (and probably other large primates as well)."

And if this is true for gibbons who live in solitary isolation in the forest canopy of Southeast Asia, how much more intense would such pressures be for a male and female couple living among a band of proto-humans huddled together on the African savanna?

The alpha couple was the unit that overcame the sexual communism of the primal horde. What emerged was something completely unique in nature, a society where males and females could live in close proximity and engage in highly cooperative effort but where sexual competition was still minimized. Let us now further explore this original pairing off between male and female that set us on the road to humanity.

PART II

THE EMERGENCE
OF HUMANITY

CHAPTER 5

WHY WE DIDN'T REMAIN CHIMPANZEES

It is often easy to overlook how unique the organization of human society is in nature. Of all the species ever identified, approximately 95 percent are polygamous. Polygamy is by far the more "natural" system of mating. In addition, chimps and humans are the *only* two species in nature where the band of male brothers forms the core of the group. Freud's fanciful hypothesis of the overthrow of the polygamous alpha male probably did happen at some point, only it happened among *chimpanzees*, not early humans. The result is that human beings are the *only species in nature* where males work together in the context of social monogamy. That is what makes us unique. It makes us human.

The system of chimp communism is not unknown in other species and might be a sign of heightened intelligence. Dolphins, for instance, which have a high of intelligence, practice it. But monogamy usually emerges only where the demands of the environment require special care and protection for the young. Birds have become monogamous because the egg is too heavy for the female to carry around in flight. She must lay it outside her body, which leaves it vulnerable to predators. Ninety percent of all bird species are monogamous, compared to only 3 percent of mammals. That is why, strangely enough, we feel more in common with "love birds" in terms of courtship and fidelity than we do with our fellow mammals. The surprising popularity of the movie, *March of the Penguins*, illustrated this. The female emperor penguin lays a single egg and the male loses 60 percent of his body weight protecting it from the Antarctic cold. What human can boast such fidelity?

A classic case for comparing monogamy versus polygamy between closely related species has come with the discovery of the Midwestern voles. Uncannily, the line of demarcation seems to be the same one that separated our earliest ancestors from the chimpanzees—a move from a more lush forest environment to a sparser, more dangerous open terrain.

On the plains of Middle America there are two distinct species, the meadow vole and the prairie vole. The meadow vole lives among fairly lush vegetation and is able to nest in the thick grass hidden from predators. Meadow voles are polygamous, with males mating with multiple females and providing no care for the offspring. The prairie vole lives in a much sparser environment and is vulnerable to coyotes and other predators. The prairie vole is monogamous with males staying loyal to one partner and provisioning and protecting the offspring.

Prairie voles pair off in the classic manner of monogamous species. When a male and female choose each other, they engage in a sexual marathon that may last up to thirty-six hours. This bonding is not just physical but hormonal. Researchers have discovered that this sexual experience releases copious amounts of oxytocin, the "attachment hormone" that floods into a female's system after she gives birth, binding her to her offspring. In monogamous species, oxytocin *first binds the female to her mate*. At the same time, male prairie voles have been found to have many more receptors for vasopressin, a hormone that binds them to a particular female. In 2004, researchers at the Yerkes National Primate Research Center of Emory University and Atlanta's Center for Behavioral Neuroscience succeeded in converting polygamous meadow voles to monogamous behavior by transplanting a single gene that increased the number of vasopressin receptors in the reward center of the male's brain. This shows that monogamous behavior has a genetic component as well.

This is in accord with the theory of natural selection. In moving into a more dangerous environment, the old polygamous behavior becomes a liability. A genetic mutation or recessive characteristic can emerge that amplifies monogamous behavior. The carriers of this new gene prove more successful and it spreads through the population. Within a number of generations, a formerly polygamous species has become monogamous. It happened with voles. It apparently happened with early hominids as well.

Fortunately for anthropologists, there is another clear way of telling whether a species, fossilized or living, is or was monogamous or polygamous. It is called "sexual dimorphism." This refers to the *size differential* between males and females. The more dimorphism there is between the sexes, the more polygamous the species. This seems to occur for two reasons: 1) a large size differential allows a male to control more females, and 2) intense competition among males puts a premium on growing large and strong, since the prize for reproductive success is so high. Gorillas have a 150 percent size differential between the silverback and the individual members of his harem. With chimpanzees it is only 125 percent and with humans it has been reduced to 115 percent. This is smaller than our close primate cousins but still not at the level of the monogamous beaver, for instance, where females are often larger than males. As the anthropologists love to tell us, we are a "slightly polygamous" species—a judgment that seems to be confirmed by human history.

So would all the early hominids that roamed East Africa in the late Pliocene have converted to monogamy? Not necessarily. The key indicator chosen by Owen Lovejoy is the reduced canine teeth, which indicates that males are no longer competing by display. Most hominids have this—and in fact the reduced canine has become the standard marker of whether a fossil primate has become a hominid. But the other marker— sexual dimorphism—gives a more ambiguous message. Several researchers have examined the bones of the *Australopithecines* and concluded that there is a large difference between males and females and therefore they must have been polygamous. This seems to defeat the theory that monogamy emerged at the beginning of human history.

Lovejoy has engaged in several controversies over the issue. After re-examining the bones of the *Australopithecines*, he claims there is only minimal dimorphism and that his theory is upheld. Yet I wonder whether this is really necessary. One of the things we will learn from human history is how easy it is for human societies, large and small, to slip back into polygamy, even after monogamy has been established. Therefore I wonder if it isn't possible that some early populations of hominids may have made this backsliding. Remember, the period we're talking about stretches over nearly 3 million years. "Nutcracker Man" seems like a particularly likely candidate. He did not hunt and seems to have grown large and strong in gorilla-like proportions. This could indicate a species had reverted to smaller, gorilla-sized groups where only the strength of the alpha male protected against predators and other males. It would also answer Robert Ardrey's question of whether Cain slew Abel. It is easy to see how such a species would eventually be pushed aside by larger bands of pair-bonded hominids competing for the same ecological territory.

Contrary to nineteenth century thought, evolution is not a matter of "Kill or Be Killed" or "Nature Red in Tooth and Claw." It is a matter of "Be Fruitful and Multiply." A band that converted from polygamy to monogamy would have a distinct advantage because it could welcome more members into the group. The "First Family," a 3.2-million-year-old group of *Australopithecus afarensis* discovered in Ethiopia by Donald Johanson in 1975, consisted of at least thirteen individuals, which is already larger than the average gorilla troop. Other groups later grew larger. It is more than likely that not every band of early hominids that wandered the savanna for 3 million years maintained social monogamy. It may have only happened *once*. But that group would have been able to achieve the advantages that led to the main line of human development.

Anthropologists now believe the Cro-Magnon group that crossed from the Horn of Africa into Saudi Arabia 75,000 years ago and eventually spread across Asia, Europe, and North and South America might have numbered no more than fifty to a hundred individuals. But their system of cooperation was so successful that they were able to populate the entire planet. Without question, they were practicing social monogamy. The troops of proto-humans that had earlier come to dominate the savannas of East Africa would have certainly followed the same line.

That this transition did occur is written in our anatomy. Human sexuality has become a private affair. Whereas the female chimp advertises her estrus through a bright red bottom, the human female shows very little sign that she is ovulating and in fact she is often unaware of it herself. Human females do not go into periodic "heat" but are sexually available more or less all the time. This is crucial for establishing a permanent bond. Jane Goodall noted that once a consorting female chimp's period of sexual activity had passed, there was very little to hold the couple together. Our less periodic sexuality resolves this problem.

The transition to social monogamy also required that humans develop what Desmond Morris called the "universal fig leaf." Every human being feels shame and embarrassment at exposing his or her genitals. Because everyone is no longer available to everyone as in the primal horde, a certain amount of modesty becomes necessary. No one has ever discovered a human society where people do not *wear clothes*, even if it was only a penis sheath or a scant girdle covering the vagina. The flip side of this, of course, is the unending parade of "dirty jokes" and sexual innuendo that are the staple of every human society. This is the price we pay for having layered personalities. We inhabit a world in which we may live and work with people all our lives without ever seeing them naked. So too there is always some prophet of primitivism preaching that we should all shed our garments and go around nude. But social monogamy requires that some parts of our personalities remain forever hidden from the public. As was written in the Book of Genesis, it was at the dawn of human consciousness that we discovered our own nakedness.

Finally, it is easy to see why every human society has created some form of marriage. It requires the couple to pledge their fidelity to each other, but it also *draws a line* between the bonded pair and the group. Marriage creates sexual privacy—a place where the couple can engage in the intense sexual activity that bonds all mated pairs. The old chimp impulse that everybody belongs to everybody else had to be suppressed.

People are always testing the boundaries—through premarital "hooking up," celebrity worship, voyeurism, gossip, and pornography—but for the most part it holds. Marital monogamy is designed to allow couples to pair off in orderly fashion, just as our primeval ancestors did several million years ago.

What then are the requirements that keep such a group together? The first and foremost is that the *alpha male should take only one mate*. We will see this over and over in human history. When an alpha male tries to take too many wives or consorts, it disrupts the harmony of the group. Think of the "wrath of Achilles," where the Greeks' best warrior is refusing to fight because Agamemnon the king has requisitioned one of his concubines at the outset of *The Iliad*. Over and over we will find that the tone of a whole society is set by the actions of the alpha couple. If the king and queen are happy with each other, then everyone in the kingdom partakes of their happiness. But if a sultan or emperor takes as many wives as possible, other males will try to do the same thing and the society takes on a competitive and violent edge. Everywhere polygamy is practiced, it creates conflict.

All this requires *self-restraint*. It is more than likely, for instance, that at some point in the earliest human history, an alpha male was presented with the possibility of taking another male's mate. He elected *not* to do so on the basis that: a) it would create conflict with the other male, b) it might create conflict with his own mate, and/or c) it might create general disruption within the tightly knit group. We might call this the *first act of human intelligence*, although such acts of forbearance are not unknown among chimpanzees. It has been observed for instance, that when chimps learn a simple game and then teach it to other chimps, they often deliberately lose a round in order to keep their partner interested in the game. In any case, this original act of self-restraint mirrored the moral choices that human beings have had to make from the birth of the species right down through *Anna Karenina*.

In the early days of anthropology, the model for the development of human intelligence was that we were the "tool-making animal" and that our brains developed from the challenge of coping with the natural environment. Charles Darwin himself first suggested this scenario. Over the last decade, however, anthropologists have arrived at a different conclusion. The consensus now is that the chief driver of human intelligence was the task of *getting along with each other* and surviving in the tight-knit environment of social monogamy. Intelligence and self-restraint would provide an advantage in achieving high status within the group *plus* the meta-task of keeping the group together.

In a seminal 2003 paper entitled "Ecological Dominance, Social Competition, and Coalitionary Arms Races: Why Humans Evolved Extraordinary Intelligence," Mark Flinn, David Geary, and Carol Ward of the University of Missouri argue the case for an "ecological dominance-social competition" model, "EDSC" (sorry for all the anthropological jargon), in which establishing functional relations *within* the group was the key to dominating the natural environment.

> The EDSC model predicts that changes in hominid social structure related to the increasing stability of male-female pair bonds and male coalitionary behavior should accompany brain size increase, not precede it.... Unlike gorillas, with one-male breeding groups, and chimps, with promiscuous mating and little male parental behavior, the evolving hominids were faced with the difficulties of managing increasingly exclusive pair bonds in the midst of increasingly large coalitions of potential mate competitors.

Under such circumstances, they concluded, growing intelligence would give an enormous competitive advantage to any individual. As a result, the group as a whole would migrate toward greater intelligence.

Perhaps the best way to grasp how far we have come from the first pairing of the alpha couple is to look at our other primate cousin, the bonobo or "pygmy" chimp, discovered in the 1920s in the jungles of Central Africa. Among the bonobos sexual contact is a routine form of discourse. As Frans B. M. de Waal writes, "Whereas in most other species sexual behavior is a fairly distinct category, in the bonobo it is part and parcel of social relations—and not just between males and females. Bonobos engage in sex in virtually every partner combination (although such contact among close family members may be suppressed). And sexual interactions occur more often among bonobos than among other primates." The bonobos are a matrilocal species in which the brotherhood does not form but males migrate outward. Females constantly reduce social tensions by engaging in every kind of sexual activity. As a result, bonobos lead remarkably peaceful and idyllic lives.

Inevitably, this has prompted contemporary idealists to ask why we can't live like bonobos. In their book *Sex at Dawn*, Christopher Ryan and Cacilda Jethá present bonobos as a lost paradise of sexual abandon to which humanity should return. The bonobos came up again in a lengthy piece in the *New Yorker* in which editor-in-chief David Remnick chronicled former President Bill Clinton's tour through Africa in 2006:

> [W]e visited the National Museum [of Ethiopia], which houses the bones of "Lucy." ... The museum was dingy and underfunded, but the guides were thrilled to open the place to Clinton, even though it was their day off. As he walked past the exhibits, Clinton listened a little and talked a lot.... [A]s he walked past some of the display cases he started talking about the wonders of the bonobo apes.
>
> "They have the most incredibly developed social sense," he said. "When one of them makes a kill, they share the food, unlike all the other apes." And then, Clinton said, with a laugh, "they fall down to the ground and have group sex! It's a way of relieving aggression!" Such behavior, he said, "would drive the Christian right crazy!"

Indeed, compared to the dark repressions and foul inhibitions of their primate cousins, bonobos have a remarkably mellow, laid-back, go-with-the-flow lifestyle.

There is only one thing to consider. Bonobos have remained chimpanzees. We evolved into something different. It is our sexual repressions that have made us human.

CHAPTER 6

HUNTER-GATHERER MONOGAMY

I n 1966, anthropologists Richard Lee and Irven DeVore organized a worldwide symposium on hunter-gatherers that brought together nearly all the major researchers who had done fieldwork on the few hunter-gatherer tribes that had been found in the remote corners of the globe. The conference was crucially important because the participants needed time to sit back and compare notes in order to draw broad conclusions. It also became crucial because most of the small hunter-gatherer bands that had been discovered were on the verge of being absorbed by civilization and forced out of their primeval social patterns. In the 1940s and 1950s it was still possible for lone adventurers like Belgian globetrotter Jean-Pierre Hallet or New York explorer Lewis Cotlow to wander off into some obscure corner of Africa or the Amazon jungle and find tribes that had never been in contact with civilization. (The blurb on Hellet's *Pygmy Kitabu*, "Incredible adventure...action all the way," was from *True: The Man's Magazine*.) But by the mid-1960s most of these lost tribes had been discovered and the opportunity to study hunter-gatherers in their native habitat was disappearing.

The organizers of "Man the Hunter," as the symposium was named, counted twenty-seven individual societies of pure hunter-gatherers around the globe. These ranged from the Pygmies of Central Africa to the Eskimos of northern Canada, from the Bushmen of the Kalahari Desert to tribes of the Amazon jungle. Their general conclusions were as follows:

1) It was clear that hunting-and-gathering society had played a profoundly important part in human evolution. "Cultural Man has been on earth for some 2,000,000 years; for over 99 percent of this period he has lived as a hunter-gatherer," began Lee and DeVore in their printed volume, *Man the Hunter* (1968). "Only in the last 10,000 years has man begun to domesticate plants and animals, to use metals, and to harness energy sources other than the human body.... Of the estimated 150 billion men who have ever lived on earth, over 60 percent have lived as hunters and gatherers; almost 35 percent have lived by agriculture and the remaining few percent have lived in industrial societies."

2) Despite our image of hunting-and-gathering as a hard-scrabble life, in fact it was rather leisurely. "It came as a surprise to some that even the 'marginal' hunters studied by ethnographers actually work short hours and exploit abundant food sources," they wrote. Even in the forbidding Kalahari Desert of South Africa, game was common enough that the Bushmen were able to lead relatively relaxed lives. "Several hunting peoples lived well on two to four hours of subsistence effort per day and were not observed to undergo the periodic crises that have been commonly attributed to hunters in general." Pre-Neolithic hunters, living amid the huge grazing herds of mastodons and mammoths that populated the earth, must have had an even more comfortable lifestyle. (This probably explains why early American settlers were always so terrified of having their children kidnapped by Indians. The common experience was that once they had lived in Indian villages, the children did not want to return to civilization.)

3) The problem that led to the near-extinction of hunting-and-gathering cultures was their inability to support large population densities. The "carrying capacity" of any given landscape for a hunting culture is

about one person per square mile. A settled agricultural society can support anywhere up to one hundred times that. As a result, since the Neolithic Revolution of ten thousand years ago, hunting-and-gathering groups have been constantly crowded off the land by even the most primitive agriculturalists. This was the experience of American Indians, who were originally willing to share the land because they thought they were encountering only another hunting society but soon found themselves confronting "more white settlers than they ever dreamed of," as Francis Parkman put it in *The Oregon Trail*. The Pygmies of Central Africa are the remnants of an earlier population that was pushed into the remotest jungle by West African Negroes who invented primitive agriculture and then spread across the continent. Even in South America, as expert Donald Lathrap noted in one essay, hunting tribes that once occupied the broad fertile valleys have been forced into the jungle— hardly the best territory for hunting—by more successful agriculturalists.

4) Finally, despite the popular conception of "the Cave Man" as a fierce and uncouth barbarian who practiced "marriage by capture," hitting women over the head and dragging them back to his lair, in fact the hunting-and-gathering lifestyle seems to be relatively peaceful and equitable. Rather it was *early agriculturalists* who became fierce and warlike, constantly raiding neighboring villages, engaging in headhunting, torture of enemies, and even cannibalism. The Pygmies of Central Africa are regarded as sub-human slaves by neighboring agricultural tribes. The hunters of the deep Amazon live in terror of the settled riverine tribes that have pushed them deeper and deeper into the jungle.

And herein lies the great paradox at the beginning of visible human history. It is the earliest settled agricultural people that have become warlike while the earlier hunter-gatherers seemed much more content to pursue their hunting and live at relative peace with their neighbors. Why? Because the earliest agricultural societies reverted to polygamy after almost 5 million years in which monogamy seems to have prevailed.

That monogamy was the mating pattern of hunting-and-gathering seems clear from everything we know about the remnant of these earlier societies. Consider for example the Hadza, a small group of hunter-gatherers living in the Rift Valley just south of the equator in Tanzania.

After living among the Hadza in the early 1960s, British anthropologist James Woodburn made the following report:

> In the synchronic census I encountered 115 spouses of monogamous marriage and of these 112 were living with their spouses. The remaining three were married according to Hadza informants; that is, informants believed that the separations were temporary and that the couples would resume cohabitation.

Woodburn found these marriages to be relatively unstable.

> The calculated divorce rate is 49 per 1,000 years of marriage, though this is only a very rough approximation.... The rate for England and Wales, 1950–52 was 2.8 and for the United States, 1949–51, it was 10.4.

Of course this was the 1950s. Divorce rates in the United States have tripled since then, putting them in the neighborhood of the Hadza. Even at this seemingly high rate, however, Woodburn found the *institution* of monogamous marriage to be at the core of the tribe's social structure.

> In comparison with other Hadza relationships, the noteworthy aspect of the marital relationship is not its instability, but on the contrary its stability and strength. A marriage is broken by divorce on average only about once in twenty years of married life. In general, most Hadza men settle down and live for many years with a particular wife; to sustain the marriage they do not leave her for long on her own and they fulfill onerous obligations...to her and also to her mother.
>
> Once they marry for the first time, usually by their early twenties, very few men live for long unmarried. After the death of a wife or permanent separation from her, the husband will soon remarry. In the ten camps of the synchronic census, there was only one man who had previously been married

who then lacked a wife. On the other hand there were thirteen previously married women who at the time of the synchronic census were unmarried. Of these, eight were past the menopause.

A few men have more than one wife. This complicates their residential arrangements.

Polygamy, then, is not unknown—there is certainly no law against it—but it is exceptional and not common enough to be disruptive. Monogamy is definitely the norm whereby most members of the group live. This pattern has been found over and over among those few hunting-and-gathering people at the edges of the globe. Jean-Pierre Hallet found the Kitabu Pygmies to be "fierce monogamists" and marveled at their passionate adherence to the practice, contrary to most of the rest of Africa.

What motivates this morality? It is the fierce egalitarianism of these small, highly interdependent bands. As Lee and DeVore put it in their introduction:

> If individuals and groups have to move around in order to get food there is an important implication: the amount of personal property has to be kept to a very low level. Constraints on the possession of property also serve to keep wealth differences between individuals to a minimum and we postulate a generally egalitarian system for the hunters.

Modern anthropologists have put a slight slur into this pattern by calling hunter-gatherers "monogamists by necessity," suggesting that it is only the lack of resources that forces these most primitive groups to cling to monogamy. But it is obviously the egalitarian spirit and the cooperative requirements of hunting that play a crucial role.

There is one more important implication to hunter-gatherer monogamy. Claude Lévi-Strauss, the great French anthropologist, arrived at the predicate that it was the *exchange of wives* between tribes that ultimately promoted inter-tribal relations and allowed alien groups to live next to each other in relative peace. But the exchange of wives—

that is, the out-migration of women to other tribes and in-migration of new women from alien tribes—is only possible if a tribe is practicing monogamy. If it is polygamous, the demand for wives becomes *unlimited*, since each man can take any number of wives. And that is where inter-tribal warfare begins.

So what happened? The Neolithic Revolution appears to have begun in the eastern Mediterranean region about ten thousand years ago. Nomadic hunter-gatherers began settling down in permanent encampments and gradually gave up hunting for agriculture. The hybrid grains—wheat, millet, rye—were invented and soon enough food could be grown to support larger and larger populations. This agricultural revolution also appears to have occurred in the Indus Valley and in China as well, radiating outward in each case. It still continues today as the last remaining hunting-and-gathering tribes are gathered into the folds of sedentary civilization.

What were the results as far as marriage customs and the relations between the sexes are concerned? There were two major trends, which will be the subject of most of the rest of this book:

1) As the accumulation of greater wealth became possible, *inequalities* became more pronounced. One obvious and readily available inequality was that a man could take more than one wife. Some societies—the vast majority of *cultures*, according to the anthropologists—succumbed to this pattern. Others, however, eventually legislated against it, creating the very artificial situation where, even though there may be vast differences in wealth between individuals, a man can still take no more than one wife. This distinction ended up drawing a bright red line between primitive tribes and advanced civilizations.

2) The relationship between the sexes changed. With hunting-and-gathering, there was a very even division of labor between the sexes. As another conclave summoned in 1980 called "Woman the Gatherer" would establish, 60 to 70 percent of the food intake in hunting-and-gathering societies actually comes from women's activities. Meat is only the *preferred* food. This creates a balance between the sexes that makes monogamy a very productive enterprise. With the adoption of agriculture, however, things changed. In some cultures, men eventually took it

up and became productive. In others, however, they have disdained farming as "women's work" and contribute only occasional labor such as clearing land. Often they devise elaborate ceremonies to honor their place in society, even though they are no longer productive. My favorite is bungee jumping, which was invented by tribes on the South Sea island of Vanuatu fifteen centuries ago and still continues today. The purpose of this death-defying pastime, according to the men who practice it, is to assure the success of the women's yam harvest. In still other cultures—those that face particularly sparse environments—men became much more productive by herding animals while women, unable to draw sustenance from the soil, became unproductive. Once again, the economic balance between the sexes that fosters monogamy was upset.

It is to the consequences of these various changes that we will turn to next.

CHAPTER 7

THE END OF HUNTER-GATHERER MONOGAMY

I n 1964, Napoleon Chagnon, a freshly minted Ph.D. anthropologist from the University of Michigan, found himself crawling alongside a Protestant missionary through a last patch of underbrush before entering a village deep in the Amazon forest.

> My heart began to pound as we approached the village and heard the buzz of activity.... The excitement of meeting my first Yanomamö was almost unbearable as I duck-waddled through the low passage into the village clearing.
>
> I looked up and gasped when I saw a dozen burly, naked, sweaty, hideous men staring at us down the shafts of their drawn arrows....
>
> We had arrived just after a serious fight. Seven women had been abducted the day before by a neighboring group, and the local men and their guests had just that morning

recovered five of them in a brutal club fight that had nearly ended in a shooting war. The abductors, angry because they had lost five of their seven new captives, vowed to raid [this village]. . . .When [the missionary and I] arrived and entered the village unexpectedly, the [Yanomamö] feared that we were the raiders. On several occasions during the next two hours the men in the village jumped to their feet, armed themselves, nocked their arrows and waited nervously for the noise outside the village to be identified. My enthusiasm for collecting ethnographic facts diminished in proportion to the number of times such an alarm was raised.

So began a forty-year relationship between Chagnon and the tribes he came to call "the fierce people." Chagnon's book of the same title has sold a million copies since it was published in 1968, yet it also set off a controversy that has split the anthropological world in two, neatly summarized by the title of Chagnon's 2013 memoir: *Noble Savages: My Life among Two Dangerous Tribes—the Yanomamö and the Anthropologists.*

According to today's anthropological textbooks, people living in advanced civilizations have more in common with hunter-gatherers in terms of marriage customs than we do with people living in the in-between stages that were once called "primitive tribes." Both we and the hunter-gatherers practice monogamy while the people in between—whose resource base is variously described as "shifting cultivation," "slash-and-burn agriculture," "hoe agriculture," "horticulture," and "gardening"—practice polygamy.

Because of the influence of cultural anthropology, no real effort is ever made to explain this pattern. It's all just "different people responding to different environments." Tropical soils are thin and do not withstand intense cultivation without advanced farming methods. The easiest thing to do in many regions is to clear new land and let the old lie fallow for several years. Another characteristic of these cultures is that most of the agricultural work is done by women. This means that the more wives a man accumulates, the more land he can cultivate. It was not until domestic animals were hitched to the plow in what is called "advanced agriculture" that larger villages, towns, and cities started to appear. Once men became the principal laborers again, having additional wives was no longer an advantage and might even become a burden.

As for hunter-gatherers, if anything the anthropologists tend to downgrade their monogamy by referring to it as "resource-driven," while that of advanced civilizations is "normative." The implication is that hunter-gatherers live so close to the margin of subsistence that no one man can afford to support more than one wife, whereas the increased wealth of horticultural societies makes polygamy possible. This explanation is considered "non-judgmental," in contrast to the "cultural bias" against polygamy expressed by early European explorers and later Christian missionaries.

Another culture bias of Western colonial administrators was to outlaw tribal fighting. For the most part, this had a good effect. One native warrior told an early anthropologist that he was glad the colonial authorities had stopped the fighting because now he could go into the bush to relieve himself without worrying about being surprised by enemy warriors. But it also had the effect of misleading anthropologists. When the next generation of anthropologists came along, they encountered these pacified societies and assumed they had been like that all along. When they saw evidence of violence, they hypothesized that pacific primitive horticulturalists had become warlike only as a result of their encounter with Western Civilization.

Another interpretation—given that many tribes remained unpacified—was that although primitive tribes spent much of their time fighting, it was a more ceremonial than lethal form of warfare. Then scholars started calculating the proportion of tribal members that died in such conflicts and found it far exceeded the ratio of deaths experienced by advanced civilizations in their world wars.

Even in the face of such evidence, Chagnon found his colleagues extremely reluctant to accept what he had observed among the Yanomamö:

> A few of my colleagues object to my decision to view the Yanomamö culture in the context of warfare. But I did not arbitrarily choose this focus.... Ironically, I had started out to study something quite different—how much and what kinds of foods they ate....
>
> Strange as it may seem, some cultural anthropologists do not believe that warfare ever played any significant role in our evolutionary past or that it might have been commonplace in contemporary tribal societies prior to their contact with the outside world.... Other anthropologists admit that violence occurs in the tribal world but think we should not talk about it. I recall a female colleague, early in my career who seriously urged me to stop describing the warfare and violence I witnessed, saying, "Even if they are that way, we do not want others to know about it—it will give them the wrong impression."

In 1996, Lawrence H. Keeley, professor of anthropology at the University of Illinois at Chicago, wrote *War Before Civilization*, an attempt to put all this into perspective. Keeley's book, subtitled *The Myth of the Peaceful Savage*, was dedicated to dispelling the Rousseauian notion that life among early human cultures was peaceful and idyllic. Keeley chronicles all the prehistoric evidence of combat and mass slaughter—and there is a depressing amount. Mass graves of victims have been found going back seven thousand years. At many gravesites in Neolithic Europe nearly half the bodies have arrow wounds and other marks of violence. A fourteenth century site found in South Dakota contains the bodies of five hundred men, women, and children, all scalped and mutilated. Even the three-thousand-year-old "Iceman" found in the Italian Alps in 1991 was carrying a knife with DNA from four other human beings on it and apparently died from an arrow in his back.

But Keeley's long examination of tribal warfare also uncovered something very interesting. Drawing on the work of University of Buffalo anthropologist Keith Otterbein in his 1970 book, *The Evolution of War*, Keeley listed fifty societies gathered into four categories and compared how frequently they engaged in war. Here are the results:

Warfare Frequency

Economy	*Continuous*	*Frequent*	*Rare/Never*
Intensive Agriculture (modern civilization)	47.1% (8)	47.1% (8)	5.8% (1)
Shifting Cultivation (horticulture)	85.7% (12)	14.3% (2)	0% (0)
Animal Husbandry (herding)	88.9% (8)	0% (0)	11.1% (1)
Hunting-Gathering	20% (2)	50% (5)	30% (3)
Total	60% (30)	30% (15)	10% (5)

Advanced civilizations do indeed go to war, as no one needs to be told. But they do not engage in the *continuous* warfare that is endemic among tribal cultures. What is most striking, however, is the relatively *peaceful* nature of hunter-gatherers. In general, they do not wage war on their neighbors. They *do* go to war over *resources*. Keeley documents two nineteenth century California hunting tribes that battled for thirty years over a water hole. But, while hunter-gatherers constitute only 20 percent of the sample, they represent 60 percent of the societies that *never* go to war and only 6.7 percent of the societies that engage in continuous warfare.

Could it be that this pattern of warfare and the practice of polygamy (which is the practice of horticulture and herding tribes) are related?

The hallmark of a polygamous society is that there is always a shortage of women. The Nash Equilibrium is upset and men compete more aggressively for women, since there are never enough to go around. In organized polygamous societies the problem is resolved by having men *buy* their wives. The "brideprice" is the hallmark of a polygamous society, whereas the dowry—an extra incentive attached to an older or unattractive daughter—is the hallmark of a monogamous society. There are no "old maids" in a polygamous society, since women can become second or third or fourth wives of powerful men.

In his 1981 book, *A Treatise on the Family*, Nobel Prize–winning economist Gary Becker argued that families of young women become the biggest supporters of polygamy because they possess an inherently scarce resource. Love matches and independent liaisons are frowned upon because they risk reducing the brideprice. In order to preserve their market value, young women must be veiled or sequestered and kept out of contact with young men. Because of the difficulties in finding brides, older men with lesser means are forced to look among younger and younger cohorts. Child marriages become common. Given the degree of sexual inequality and the great age differences that result, the personal bond between husbands and wives is not strong and there is very little companionate marriage. For primitive tribes, however, there is always one way of resolving this dilemma—raiding neighboring villages for their women.

Academic anthropologists often have great difficulty dealing with this. In *Marriage, Family, and Kinship*, a book published in 1983 by the Human Area Relations Files at Yale University, for instance, Melvin and Carol R. Ember conducted a study that looked for correlations between polygamy and male-female imbalances. "[I]t appears that the cross-cultural evidence is consistent with the old notion that polygyny may generally be a response to an imbalanced sex ratio in favor of females," they wrote. What creates the imbalance? "It appears that an imbalanced sex ratio in favor of females may be produced by warfare that results in a high mortality rate for males." They parsed the data looking for correlations between high rates of warfare and polygyny and sure enough, there it was. "[W]e find that a high male mortality rate in warfare is fairly strongly associated with polygyny.... In sum, it seems that the cross-cultural evidence presented here is consistent with the theory that societies with a high male mortality in warfare are generally likely to have an imbalanced sex ratio in favor of females and, presumably for that reason, are likely to practice polygamy."

In theory, then, warfare kills a lot of men and leaves a surplus of women. The only way to make sure everyone is married is to allow polygamy.

Yet somehow it never occurs to the authors that the causality may work the other way around. Societies that are polygamous to begin with go to war precisely *because* they have created an imbalance by letting each man take more than one wife. This creates a demand for more women that can only be resolved by stealing women from other tribes. Thus warfare and polygamy become mutually reinforcing. Many anthropologists resist making this link, despite the evidence.

This is the kind of resistance that Chagnon encountered in his study of the Yanomamö. When he asked his informants why they were constantly raiding other villages, they told him they sought to capture more women. When he wrote this in *The Fierce People*, however, cultural anthropologists said he had it all wrong—they went to war for *protein*. Chagnon did dietary studies and found the Yanomamö had plenty of meat and did not lack protein. When he told his informants the explanation offered by his colleagues, they laughed. "We like meat," they told him, "but we like women more."

Yet while Chagnon proves his point that women are the subject of these endless wars through sophisticated protein studies and the testimony of the natives themselves, somehow he never draws the obvious conclusion—that *polygamy* is the root of the problem. Instead his arguments with the cultural anthropologists have veered off into questions of "human nature." Are people "naturally aggressive" or "naturally peaceful." They are probably neither. But the practice of polygamy does create tensions that cause small societies to be continuously at war with one another.

In the 1960s, novelist Peter Matthiessen was part of an expedition that lived among the Kurelu, a horticultural New Guinea tribe that had never had contact with civilization. He described his experience in *Under the Mountain Wall: A Chronicle of Two Seasons in Stone Age New Guinea*. The Kurelu lived in a state of perpetual warfare. The prize, once again, was women. Almost every afternoon they and a neighboring tribe would meet on a wide mountain meadow like neighboring towns preparing for a football game and square off in battle. Once in a while a tribe would excuse itself saying it had something else to do—giving the whole thing a farcical air—yet once the hostilities began, they were deadly serious. Men were killed, prompting cries for revenge, and on and on it went in a cycle that had lasted since anyone could remember.

The cruelties Matthiessen documented were almost unspeakable. When caught in the forest, children were slaughtered as readily as adults. In one instance a woman was surprised on a jungle path by a hostile warrior. Wanting to save herself, she lay down and invited him to have intercourse with her. Apparently bored with the ease of the conquest or not feeling particularly attracted to her, he thrust his spear into her vagina and killed her.

Under such circumstances, the best women could do was go with the strongest party. In another account of warrior culture, Gilbert Herdt's *Guardians of the Flutes*, the author recounts what one of his informants regarded as a very funny story. One day he burst into a neighboring village and found a group of women and children undefended. After slaying several of them, one attractive young woman rushed up to him and said, "Do not kill me, I will help you clean your nose." As he spoke the word "nose" he grabbed his genitals, indicating her real meaning, since the words "nose" and "penis" are almost identical in the native language. The warrior took the woman for a wife.

———

Friedrich Engels was definitely on the right track when he associated property and wives—except that he got it backwards. It wasn't that men first claimed women and then invented private property. It is that men acquired property and therefore increased their demand for women.

Although primitive horticulturalists may seem wretchedly poor to us, they are actually a step up from the impoverished hunter-gatherers. Once primitive farming began, tribes began to live in fixed settlements and accumulate land and other property. This led to differences in wealth, which allowed some men to claim and support more than one wife.

The other crucial element, of course, was that the *collective effort of hunting was lost*. When hunting-and-gathering bands went after big game it was crucial to have every adult male on board. And Stone Age hunters did indeed go after big game, bringing down wooly mammoths, mastodons, even giant cats in their march across Asia, Europe, and North America. Moreover, it is the common experience of all tribal cultures that *meat is shared*. The best hunters may claim larger portions but everyone gets a share. This is not the case with early agriculture, where crops are rarely shared from one family to another. If there is any tribal solidarity left, it exists only in the collective act of raiding other tribes.

This transition from hunting to primitive agriculture could not have been easy because it involved a major disruption in the relationship between the sexes. The reason we know this is because in many parts of Africa and the South Seas, the transition still has not been made. Men refuse to partake in agriculture because it is "women's work." Instead they spend their time "leaning on their spears" or bungee jumping or engaging in warfare.

One form of horticulture found commonly in Africa is called the "warrior-matriarchy." In this type of group, men and women live completely apart in men's and women's huts. Children are raised exclusively by the women but at some point in early adolescence the young men undergo an elaborate initiation—often involving the disclosure of secrets or some physical ritual such as circumcision—whereupon they become members of the male portion of the tribe. In a sense, many African American neighborhoods have now duplicated this pattern—except that instead of initiation rituals being conducted by adult males, they are orchestrated by ruthless teenage gangs.

An intermediate version of this transition from hunter-gathering to polygamous early agriculture can be seen in the Tiwi of Australia, an Aborigine group that is a cousin to Bronislaw Malinowski's Trobriand Islanders. When encountered in the 1950s by anthropologists C. W. M. Hart, Arnold Pilling, and Jane C. Goodale, the Tiwi were living on Melville and Bathhurst Islands in complete isolation from other tribes. The Tiwi were nomadic and still practiced some hunting and gathering, but because there was no longer any large game, hunting was not done in groups. Under these circumstances, the Tiwi had transitioned to polygamy.

As a result, Tiwi society had become extremely inegalitarian, with all women claimed by older men. Girl babies were betrothed at birth—sometimes even in the womb—with fathers allocating them to friends and important leaders in order to cement alliances. Younger men could not even think of marrying in their twenties and usually didn't contract their first bride until they were approaching forty. But at that point, the floodgates open. One marriage would follow another and many ended up with as many as twenty wives.

The only compensation for younger men was that they might marry *older* women, since Tiwi society ordained all women must be married at all times. Widows would marry at the gravesite of their deceased husbands, with younger men taking them as brides. At one point, the researchers found two younger men living together, each married to the other's mother!

Because of this configuration, *all* the tension within the society involved older men guarding their wives against seduction by younger men. There were few assignations in the camp, but with men and women leaving for the bush every day—the men to hunt, the women to gather—there were frequent furtive rendezvous. As a result, the researchers found, almost every night in camp the bickering involved senior men accusing younger men of romancing their wives. When such accusations came to a head, a "duel" was arranged wherein the older man was allowed to throw spears at the younger man while the younger man could not fight back but was only allowed to dodge the missiles. The matter was settled when the older man drew blood.

All this was only possible because village opinion was entirely on the side of the older men. As Hart, Pilling, and Goodale wrote:

> [These disputes] became a case not of simple seduction but of subversive activity, because it was a threat to the whole social structure of the tribe, centered as that was around old men married to young women. When confronted by such action, a Tiwi elder said (as people of other cultures might), "What would happen if everybody did that? We'd have complete anarchy and free love."

The only reason the Tiwi were not raiding neighbors is because they had none.

Even more remarkable was that, like Malinowski's Trobrianders, the Tiwi did not connect intercourse with childbirth but believed that women are impregnated by the wind. Yet even though they were unaware of physical paternity, Tiwi men fiercely guarded their mates. "Because any female was liable to be impregnated by a spirit at any time, the sensible step was to insist that every female have a husband *all the time* so that if she did become pregnant, the child would have a father [emphasis in original]."

We may shake our heads at such a system where senior men are allowed to monopolize the women, but we tolerate the same hierarchical privileges in many of our institutions. College faculties and law partnerships operate on the same principle, with neophytes going through a long period of unrewarded apprenticeship before they finally achieve tenure or partnership, at which point they inherit the same outsized privileges.

An even more illustrative example of the transition between hunting-and-gathering and horticulture can be seen in the Sharanahua Indians, an Amazonian tribe studied in the 1960s by Janet Siskind, a professor of anthropology at Rutgers and recounted in her book, *To Hunt in the Morning.* The Sharanahua are typical horticulturalists, living on the edge of a riverbank deep in the jungles of Peru. The women keep garden plots and the men do occasional heavy labor but also hunt in the jungle. Marriages are polygamous and, predictably, the men spend much of their time raiding other tribes for women and being raided in return. Every once in a while, however, the women persuade the men to organize joint hunting expeditions. When they do, an extraordinary thing happens:

> At times, when there has been no meat in the village for three or four days, the women decide to send the men on a special hunt. They talk together and complain that there is no meat and the men are lazy. The young married women and the unmarried adolescent girls...start at one end of [the village] and stop at each house, surrounding each man in turn. One or two women tug gently at his shirt or belt while they sing, "We are sending you to the forest to hunt, bring us back meat."

While the men are off hunting, the women make a corn drink, steam manioc, and gather firewood. Then once the daily chores are done:

> [T]he women bathe in the river, put on their best clothes and spend an hour or more painting careful designs on their faces....
>
> Throughout the morning while the women work and decorate themselves, a certain amount of questioning and conversation goes on concerning which man each woman is "waiting for." The expression "waiting for" describes the fact that each woman has sent someone to hunt for her....
>
> [T]wo women never wait for the same man. . . .
>
> During the special hunts there are important shifts in the pattern of distributing meat. Meat is given directly outside of the household, rather than to a wife, a mother-in-law, or a mother within the hunter's household.... The shift in the distribution pattern equalizes available hunting skills as men hunt for households other than their own....
>
> The choice of partners in the special hunts is usually a choice of lovers.... The teasing and the provocation of the special hunt games are symbolically sexual and, despite the

discretion of most love affairs...some flirtations are obvious, and they coincide with the partnerships of the special hunt. The women...told me of their own love affairs and those of others, and they usually chose one of their lovers as a partner.

Put at its crudest, the special hunt symbolizes an economic structure in which meat is exchanged for sex.

What is happening, however, is more important than that. What we are witnessing is the transition from hunting-and-gathering to hoe agriculture *in reverse*. Once the tribe goes back to hunting, *it reinvents monogamy*. Men and women pair off in exclusive relationships involving sex. The men hunt as a group but the men and women choose each other (the women probably having more say in the pairings), with women primping themselves so they will be attractive to the hunters. It confirms Owen Lovejoy's association between monogamy and provisioning, although it seems likely that monogamy preceded provisioning, since the earliest hominids did not begin hunting for more than a million years. The spoils of the hunt are then distributed in an egalitarian manner and everyone's interest is optimized.

There may be mild disagreements, quarrels, and competition within the group but there is an *inherent stability* to all this—a girl for every boy and a boy for every girl. Only when men begin taking more than one wife do they set against each other, trying to resolve the dilemma of the scarcity of women by raiding other tribes. Yet the stability of hunter-gatherer monogamy was lost when the game finally disappeared and the human race was forced to invent new ways of survival. To those we will turn next.

CHAPTER 8

HERDING AND HORTICULTURE: THE TWO ROADS TO POLYGAMY

The evidence of nature is that polygamy is the normal way for mammals to mate, and the return to polygamy among men was made all the easier by how much more successful hoe agriculturalists were than hunter-gatherers in sustaining population growth. But there is another ecological lifestyle that emerged when game became too scarce to support hunting and that is the *herding* of domesticated animals. This allows for more population growth than hunting-and-gathering but not as much as horticulture. And as with horticulture, societies based on herding tend toward polygamy. Both are based on an exaggerated inequality between the sexes. In horticulture, women dominate the economy as men pine for their masculine role as hunters. In the sparse environment that can sustain herding, men dominate, as women are no longer able to gather much in the way of fruits, seeds, and nuts or cultivate crops. Given the economic drivers, we might think of herding polygamy as "male driven polygamy" and horticulture as "female driven polygamy."

West Africa is the world epicenter of polygamy. It is almost universally accepted, widely celebrated, and in most tribal cultures a man can take as many wives as he likes. Writing in the 1920s, Robert Lowie, another student of Franz Boas, reported:

> It is true that from Africa there are reported instances of an extraordinary multiplicity of wives. Even disregarding such anomalies as the Dahomi court, where all the Amazons are by a fiction considered wives of the king, we find well-authenticated cases of men with five, twenty and even sixty wives, and these at least so far as the first-mentioned figure is concerned are described as fairly common.... From remarks incidentally dropped by [various authorities], it seems certain that only the wealthy and the eminent men have polygynous households. Thus, among the Kikuyu of East Africa, Mr. and Mrs. Routledge [authors of *With a Prehistoric People, London, 1910*] found monogamy "quite usual"; two or three wives were common; and the rich had six or seven. It is clear than even so moderate an indulgence in polygyny on the part of the socially distinguished would make it very difficult for many young men to acquire a mate at all.

Although much of West Africa is now urbanized and no longer depends on primitive agriculture for its sustenance, the custom of polygamy has been carried over into relatively modernized societies. Jean-Bédel Bokassa, the mad dictator of the Central African Republic in the 1970s, had seventeen wives, a harem of mistresses and fifty-five official children. The current CEO of Exxon in Nigeria is reported to have seventy-six wives. Jacob Zuma, president of the relatively modern and prosperous state of South Africa, currently has four wives but has been married six times and has fathered twenty children. He is reported to have appropriated millions of dollars from his ruling African National Congress, founded by Nelson Mandela, in order to build a palace large enough for his harem.

Nor is there any indication that Africans see much problem with polygamy. In 2006, Professor Ambe Njoh, a native of the Cameroons teaching at South Florida State, mounted an elaborate defense of polygamy in *Tradition, Culture and Development in Africa*, a book generally defending African native practices against the incursion of Western values. Dr. Njoh listed seven reasons for practicing polygamy:

1. There is an undersupply of marriageable men in Africa due to higher infant mortality rates among boys.
2. "Polygyny serves as a strategy for economic development in agrarian societies. Such societies usually require a large number of field hands [i.e., wives]."
3. "Multiple wives significantly increase a man's chances of having a male offspring."
4. "Polygyny ensured that a widow (and her children) could be inherited and cared for by her brother-in-law even if he was already married."
5. "Polygyny constitutes a source of wealth and social prestige in traditional Africa.... [P]olygynous families are (were) almost always wealthier than the monogamous ones.... [B]ridewealth usually entails huge expenses...making polygyny an expensive undertaking, which only the wealthier men can afford."
6. "Polygyny guaranteed men an alternative source of sexual gratification during a wife's pregnancy."
7. "[P]olygyny serves as an effective strategy to control population explosion. Contrary to popular belief, women in polygynous households experience a level of fertility that is considerably lower than their counterparts in monogamous marital relations."

Contrary to Dr. Njoh's assertion, there is no indication of a shortage of males in West Africa. According to the *World Fact Book*, the sex ratio in the Cameroons, for instance, is 1.02 males to females, slightly above the world average of 1.01. For Nigeria, the most populous country in

West Africa, it is 1.05. Polygynous wives can have a slower rate of birth but because more women marry the rate of population growth usually evens out. The argument that there are "no old maids" is a common defense of polygamy.

At the village level, a particularly successful man who takes several wives will build a hut for each and provide them with land to garden or farm. But providing for these extra wives and children is not entirely his responsibility. What makes the system work is that *the women are largely self-supportive.*

In Africa *farming is largely the province of women.* Men have never quite gotten over the loss of their hunting privileges and still shun farming as "women's work." Every agronomist who ever went to Africa trying to improve crop yields has eventually come away lamenting that "Farming would be a lot more productive in Africa if men were willing to do the work."

Feminist anthropologists, on the other hand, see African women as a model of independence and self-sufficiency, living free of the support of men. The "market mammies" that dominate the agricultural trade across the continent are held up as an ideal. These women drive trucks, hauling their produce across hundreds of miles, and often "marry" wives who stay at home and take care of their children. Ester Boserup, a Danish anthropologist who has written widely on the subject, says this:

> Africa is the region of female farming *par excellence.* In many African tribes, nearly all the tasks connected with food production continue to be left to women. In most of these tribal communities, the agricultural system is that of shifting cultivation: small pieces of land are cultivated for a few years only, until the natural fertility of the soil diminishes. When that happens, i.e. when crop yields decline, the field is abandoned and another plot is taken under cultivation. In this type of agriculture it is necessary to prepare some new plots every year for cultivation by felling trees or removing bush or grass cover. Tree felling is nearly always done by men, most often by young

boys of 15 to 18 years, but to women fall all the subsequent operations: the removal and burning of the felled trees; the sowing or planting in the ashes; the weeding of the crop; the harvesting and carrying in the crop for storing or immediate consumption.

Boserup reproduced a map created by H. Baumann, a German expert on African subsistence farming, in 1930, which showed that only in a region of Nigeria and a small section of Ethiopia do men do most of the cultivation. "Before the European conquest of Africa, felling, hunting and warfare were the chief occupations of men in the regions of female farming," continued Boserup.

Gradually, as felling and hunting became less important and inter-tribal warfare was prevented by European domination, little remained for the men to do. The Europeans, accustomed to the male farming systems of their home countries, looked with little sympathy on this unfamiliar distribution of the work load between the sexes and understandably, the concept of the "lazy African men" was firmly fixed in the minds of settlers and administrators.

Even as urbanization and wage labor have advanced, this pattern has persisted:

Older men can often stop working by leaving it to their usually younger wives or to their children, while many old women are widows who must fend for themselves. More boys than girls go to school and more young men than young women are away from the villages, working for wages in towns or plantations or attending schools. Since in African villages virtually all the women and many girls even very young ones, take part in the work, the agricultural labour force tends to become predominantly female.

Since women are so productive agriculturally, it would behoove a man with lots of land to "employ" many of them. And that is exactly what happens. As Boserup relates:

> In Africa...polygamy is widespread, and nobody seems to doubt that its occurrence is closely related to economic conditions. A report by the secretariat of the UN Economic Commission for Africa (ECA) affirms this point: "One of the strongest appeals of polygamy to men in Africa is precisely its economic aspect, for a man with several wives commands more land, can produce more food for his household and can achieve a high status due to the wealth which he can command."

But how, you may ask, can a man command much wealth if he doesn't work? The answer is "tribal politics." Across most of the continent, land is held in common by tribes instead of being individually owned. But tribal governments are still dominated by men and therefore they divide up access to the land among themselves with the most powerful and influential men taking much larger portions.

> An elderly cultivator with several wives is likely to have a number of...boys who can be used for [the] purpose [of felling trees]. By the combined efforts of young sons and young wives he may gradually expand his cultivation and become more and more prosperous, while a man with a single wife has less help in cultivation and is likely to have little or no help for felling.... A polygamic family is "the ideal family organization from the man's point of view."

The result is a high rate of polygamous marriages. One study in the 1950s found it to be at least 10 percent in most African countries with a median of 24 percent and rates as high as 51 percent in Sierra Leone and 61 percent in Nigeria. Even at the median rate of 24 percent, and assuming that most of these polygamous marriages involved only two women, that means that in the 1950s at least a quarter of the male African population was permanently excluded from marriage, leaving a volatile class of unattached males.

That is one price African men pay for polygamy. Another is that married men do not have much claim over their children, or, in a way, over their wives. Descent in Africa is generally matrilineal (meaning traced through the mother's line) with young men often taking their mother's names. When a woman chooses to leave a marriage, she simply takes her children and leaves—and it is a general rule among society that when women have exclusive claim on their children, divorce becomes much more common. In Africa marriages do not usually last long and by the time they have reached age forty the majority of men and women have been married three or four times. In traditional Chinese society, on the other hand, where children belonged to the father's family, divorce was practically unknown and wives would often kill themselves rather than quit a bad marriage and leave their children behind.

Interestingly, Boserup found that in societies where men do take up farming—not rejecting it as "women's work"—monogamy again becomes the norm:

> Polygamy offers fewer incentives in those parts of the world where, because they are more densely populated than Africa, the system of shifting cultivation has been replaced by the permanent cultivation of fields ploughed before sowing.... [In] farming systems where men do most of the agricultural work, a second wife can be an economic burden rather than an asset. In order to feed an additional wife the husband must either work harder himself or he must hire labourers to do part of the work. In such regions, polygamy is either non-existent or is a luxury in which only a small minority of rich farmers can indulge.

Ironically, Boserup discovers that in parts of Africa where Muslims live side-by-side with tribal cultures, "many women are said to prefer to marry Muslims because a Muslim has a religious duty to support his wife" instead of living off her labor.

Islam was born in a herding society and for marriage it makes a difference. Nomadic herding cultures seem to have arisen at about the same time
that Neolithic farmers were settling down into fixed agricultural communities. The Dodoth, a sub-tribe of the Masai, represent a traditional herding culture surviving in East Africa. For the Dodoth cattle are wealth and
where there is wealth there can be gradations in wealth. A man who has
many cattle is considered wealthy and a man who is wealthy can have more
than one wife. It comes as no surprise that the Dodoth practice polygamy.

It is a different kind of polygamy than in West Africa, however,
because tending animals is a man's occupation. While women may milk
the cows and even make butter to sell, their contribution to the family
diet is small. Women are valued instead for their household work and
reproductive worth. Since there is no cultural prohibition against it, men
collect as many wives as possible. And unlike in West Africa, men have
strong paternal claims, because descent is traced through the father's *and*
the mother's line. Households are patrilocal, meaning the wife moves in
with the husband's family, and young men are put into long apprentice-
ships that have them usually defer marriage until their late twenties.

But there is another type of herding society, and that is one of
nomadic polygamists, such as the Islamic nomads who burst out of the
Arabian Peninsula in the seventh century and the Mongol Hordes who
conquered China and overran much of the Eurasian land mass. "Nomads
plus religion equals power" is the way Ibn Khaldun, the fourteenth century Islamic historian described the rise of his own civilization. "Polygamy plus horses equals conquest" would apply equally well. Polygamous
societies are always unstable and one way to relieve the tension is to turn
those forces outward into conquest. Genghis Khan is generally reckoned
to have had more progeny than any man in history, and the Prophet
Mohammed, who founded what is essentially a Religion of Nomads,
codified polygamy into sacred law.

But before we get to this, let us consider how the great cultures of
East and West reestablished hunter-gatherer monogamy and used it to
build civilizations that grew beyond the wildest dreams of any tribal
societies.

PART III

THE ANCIENT WORLD

CHAPTER 9

MARRIAGE AT THE DAWN OF CIVILIZATION

n the January 2012 issue of the *Philosophical Transactions of the Royal Society*, three West Coast scholars—Joseph Henrich of the University of British Columbia, Robert Boyd of UCLA, and Peter Richerson of UC Davis—published an article entitled "The Puzzle of Monogamous Marriage." The authors point to the following paradox:

> The anthropological record indicates that approximately 85 per cent of human societies have permitted men to have more than one wife (polygynous marriage), and both empirical and evolutionary considerations suggest that large absolute differences in wealth should favour more polygynous marriages.
>
> Yet, monogamous marriage has spread across Europe, and more recently across the globe, even as absolute wealth differences have expanded. Here, we develop and explore

the hypothesis that the norms and institutions that compose the modern package of monogamous marriage have been favoured by cultural evolution because of their *group-beneficial effects*—promoting success in inter-group competition. In suppressing intrasexual competition and reducing the size of the pool of unmarried men, normative monogamy reduces crime rates, including rape, murder, assault, robbery and fraud, as well as decreasing personal abuses. By assuaging the competition for younger brides, normative monogamy decreases (i) the spousal age gap, (ii) fertility, and (iii) gender inequality. By shifting male efforts from seeking wives to paternal investment, normative monogamy increases savings, child investment and economic productivity.... Polygynous societies engage in more warfare. [emphasis added]

To put this in perspective, they go on: "The 15 per cent or so of societies in the anthropological record with monogamous marriage fall into two disparate categories: (i) small-scale societies inhabiting marginal environments with little status distinctions among males [i.e. hunter-gatherers] and (ii) some of history's largest and most successful ancient societies."

In other words, Western European, American, and East Asian societies live in relative peace and prosperity because they honor and enforce monogamous marriage, as did the earliest human societies. Meanwhile, the reason other societies remain relatively poor and plagued by internal violence is because they have reverted to polygamy and continue to practice it.

The authors point out that monogamy in many ways runs *against* human nature. It definitely runs against the interests of higher-status males. The monogamy practiced by hunter-gatherers is "ecological," forced on them by the struggle to survive. The monogamy practiced by successful modern civilizations is "normative," sustained by societal rules and the benefits they bring. These cultural norms are likely to be questioned and even ridiculed by those who are restricted by them. But the payoff comes in a more stable and just society.

Given the power of the forces working against it, however, what is remarkable is that normative monogamy ever succeeded at all. As the authors note: "Historically, the emergence of monogamous marriage is particularly puzzling since the very men who most benefit from polygynous marriage—wealthy aristocrats—are often those most influential in setting norms and shaping laws. Yet, here we are."

Conscious of the triumph of polygamous hoe agriculture societies over hunter-and-gatherers in Africa and the perpetual mayhem that polygamous nomadic societies have visited upon the more settled monogamous civilizations of Asia and Europe, the authors note that the triumph of civilized monogamy over polygyny is by no means foreordained.

> Competition among less complex societies need not favour normative monogamy. Some circumstances, such as those in which subsistence economies are dominated by female or child labour, would appear to favour greater polygynous marriage. When inter-group competition relies on large numbers of motivated young men to engage in continuous raiding and warfare to obtain resources, slaves, territory and concubines, groups with greater polygyny may generate larger and more motivated pools of males for these risky activities. If these larger pools of men more effectively expand their territories, populations and resources at the expense of groups that constrain this pool, cultural group selection could favour greater polygyny.

In other words, polygamous societies can temporarily prove more powerful, as occurred when Islam and the Mongol hordes overran portions of Europe, China, and India that were practicing monogamy. Yet the authors go on to enumerate the "civilizing" aspects of monogamy that may prove more beneficial in the long run:

1. The pool of unattached men is reduced so that they do not form a potentially disruptive residue in society

2. Crime is reduced since most crimes are committed by unmarried males. (In addition, longitudinal studies show that fewer crimes are committed by the same men when they marry.)

3. Political coups and factional fighting become less common because there are fewer single men willing to enlist in rebel armies

4. Society becomes more productive because men work more when they are married

5. Children do better because men invest in them instead of using their resources to obtain more wives

6. Spousal relations improve because men and women are more dedicated to each other instead of merely entering an economic/reproductive relationship

7. Child marriages disappear and the age gap between husbands and wives narrows. There is reduced inequality between men and women and spousal abuse declines.

8. Young women are no longer hoarded and sequestered by their families in order to protect the value of the bride-price. Marriages become elective and more stable.

They conclude with the following observation:

[I]t is worth speculating that the spread of normative monogamy, which represents a form of egalitarianism, may have helped create the conditions for the emergence of democracy and political equality at all levels of government. Within the anthropological record, there is a statistical linkage between democratic institutions and normative monogamy.... In Ancient Greece, we do not know which came first but we do know that Athens, for example, had both elements of monogamous marriage and of democracy.... In this sense, the peculiar institutions of monogamous marriage may help explain why democratic ideals and notions of equality and human rights first emerged in the West.

━━━━━━

We do not have any clear record of how and why monogamy was able to emerge as the predominating norm in the earliest civilizations that emerged four thousand years ago. But we can get a glimpse of the struggle in the oldest known story in world literature, the Mesopotamian *Epic of Gilgamesh*.

The *Epic of Gilgamesh* was discovered on clay tablets in Iraq in the 1850s and was first translated and published in the 1870s. Since then several other versions of the story have been discovered at widely different sites from widely different eras, indicating the story obviously had long standing in the civilizations of the Tigris and Euphrates Valley.

The story tells of Gilgamesh, an early Sumerian king, living somewhere around 2500 B.C. He was born of a mortal father and a goddess mother and his reign has been long and productive. One of his great achievements has been the building of walls around his city of Uruk to protect his people.

His success and valor have made him intemperate, however, and he insists on constantly competing with the young men of his city in exhausting games. He also demands to spend the first night—the notorious *jus primae noctis*—with every young bride in his domain. The citizens of Uruk are upset by Gilgamesh's domineering ways and appeal to the gods for help. The gods respond by creating Enkidu, a "natural man" who lives among the beasts of the fields.

Word soon gets back to Gilgamesh that a wild man has entered his kingdom. He enlists the help of Shamhat, a leading harlot at one of the all-women temples. Shamhat goes out into the fields and seduces Enkidu. He succumbs and they make love for six straight days. Seeing this happen, the beasts of the field realize Enkidu is not one of them and they shun him. So he is forced to live among men.

Enkidu abides for a while among shepherds. One day, he sees a man pass by and asks where he is going:

The man said to Enkidu, "I am on my way
To a wedding banquet. I have piled the table
With exquisite food for the ceremony.
The priest will bless the young couple, the guests
Will rejoice, the bridegroom will step aside,
And the virgin will wait in the marriage bed
For Gilgamesh, king of great-walled Uruk.
It is he who mates first with the lawful wife.
After he is done, the bridegroom follows.
This is the order that the gods have decreed.
From the moment the king's birth cord was cut,
Every girl's hymen has belonged to him."
As he listened, Enkidu's face went pale
With anger.

Enkidu is so offended by the custom of *jus primae noctis* that he rushes to the wedding and confronts Gilgamesh. They square off in a titanic battle, but after testing each other's strength to the limit, they suddenly fall back in admiration of each other and decide to become friends. Gilgamesh accepts Enkidu as his brother-in-arms and takes him to his mother Ninsun, the goddess, who adopts Enkidu as her son.

Now that they have become brothers, Gilgamesh and Enkidu embark on several heroic quests together. Ishtar, the principal goddess of Mesopotamia, has let loose the Bull of Heaven because she is angry Gilgamesh has spurned her advances. Gilgamesh and Enkidu slay the Bull but the gods decide that Enkidu must die as a result. The king is left devastated.

Suddenly aware of his own mortality, Gilgamesh journeys to the edge of the world to seek out Utnapishtim, the sole survivor of the Great Flood and an obvious forerunner of the Biblical Noah, whom the gods have granted immortality. Gilgamesh enters the Land of the Dead and is rewarded by hearing Utnapishtim tell him the long tale of how he survived the Flood. But he is also told by the keeper of an inn on the border of the Land of the Dead that he cannot have immortality himself but must enjoy life as it has been given to him.

Gilgamesh, where are you roaming?
You will never find the eternal life
that you seek. When the gods created mankind,
they also created death, and they held back
eternal life for themselves alone.
Humans are born, they live, then they die,
this is the order that the gods have decreed.
But until the end comes, enjoy your life,
spend it in happiness, not despair.
Savor your food, make each of your days
a delight, bathe and anoint yourself,
wear bright clothes that are sparkling clean,
let music and dancing fill your house,
love the child who holds you by the hand,
and give your wife pleasure in your embrace.
That is the best way for a man to live.

Gilgamesh does learn of a plant from the bottom of the ocean that will give him eternal youth. With much effort he secures it. But on the way home a snake steals it from him so that the snake is given the power to renew itself by shedding its skin while Gilgamesh is left with his own mortality. He returns to his city, chastened, but realizes that in building the walls of Uruk he has done good work:

This is the
wall of Uruk, which no city on earth can equal.
See how its ramparts gleam like copper in the sun.
...[F]ollow its course
around the city, inspect its mighty foundations,
examine its brickwork, how masterfully it is built,
observe the land it encloses: the palm trees, the gardens,
the orchards, the glorious palaces and temples,
the shops and marketplaces, the houses, the public squares.

It will long outlive him.

The *Epic of Gilgamesh* seems to measure the exact moment when cities were getting big enough to be called "civilizations" and when growing wealth was raising the old temptation for high-status men to gather as many women as possible. Ahead lies a future in which emperors and sultans would collect whole harems and palaces full of concubines. But the *Epic of Gilgamesh* represents a point when, in the popular literature at least, Ancient Mesopotamian civilization did *not* turn in this direction.

Enkidu represents a "natural man," almost certainly the unconscious memory of hunter-and-gatherer society, when men lived simply and equally and monogamy was the universal standard. Modern scholars are trying to reinterpret the relationship between Gilgamesh and Enkidu as homosexual, but that it obviously not the case. Their friendship is a reestablishment of male brotherhood that has been the core of our line of evolution since we were chimpanzees.

For the first time in history, however, we see a civilization wrestling with the *biological* urge of successful men to take as many wives as possible. In the *Epic of Gilgamesh*, the issue is resolved emphatically in favor of monogamy. Nor would it be the last time that the poets would come down on the side of the more equitable and peaceful outcome. But the tides of history have often swung the other way. And as we shall see, the fates of civilizations have depended on it.

CHAPTER 10

EGYPTIAN AND HEBREW BEGINNINGS

I n the majority of pre-Classical civilizations, monogamy was the de facto standard for most of society while men at the very top took multiple wives. Egyptian civilization followed this pattern. The Egyptians were also a very insular people—they never ventured out into the Mediterranean—and this was reflected at the top, where considerations of dynastic succession and keeping wealth in the family meant a pharaoh's first wife was usually his sister. Later he might marry his daughter. By the time of the Middle Kingdom (2055 to 1650 BC) inheritance was passed entirely through the female line and a man became pharaoh only by marrying into the royal family.

Such machinations became the source of endless conspiracy and intrigue. Ankhesenamun, for example, the third daughter of the Pharaoh Akhenaten, was first married to her father, possibly producing one daughter, before Akhenaten died. She then married her younger half-brother, Tutankhamen ("servant of the god"), who comes down to us as

"King Tut." He died mysteriously a few years later at the age of eighteen. Some archaeologists now suspect that Ay, the grand vizier and Tutankhamen's advisor, may have murdered him.

Ankhesenamun became heir to the throne at age twenty-one. Whoever married her would become the next pharaoh. In one of the most extraordinary finds in archaeological history, a letter has turned up in the Hittite city of Hattusa (now in modern Turkey) addressed to Suppiluliuma I from an anonymous Egyptian Queen. She tells Suppiluliuma, then perhaps the most powerful king in the Mediterranean, "My husband has died and I have no son. They say about you that you have many sons. You might give me one of your sons to become my husband. I would not wish to take one of my subjects as a husband.... I am afraid." Suppiluliuma hesitated but eventually sent one of his sons to Egypt. Unfortunately, he was intercepted at the border and murdered. Shortly after, Ankhesenamun is believed to have wed Ay, who declared himself pharaoh. Ay already had a senior wife, who became his official consort. Shortly after that, Ankhesenamun disappears from the pages of history.

Brother-sister marriages continued in the Egyptian royal family down through Cleopatra, who married her younger brother. Some lesser families followed this practice as well. Brother-sister marriages were not entirely abolished until the Egyptians adopted Christianity.

Monogamous marriage, however, seems to have been the norm throughout the general run of the population. Ample marriage records survive and the indication is that girls generally married around age twelve and boys at age fifteen. (The average life expectancy was forty.) Marriages were usually arranged by parents, although the bride and groom might have had some say in the matter, and there are stories of love matches and romantic entanglements. There was no brideprice and no formal marriage ceremony administered by religious or civil authorities. Instead, couples signed a kind of pre-nuptial agreement in which they specified what property belonged to them in entering the marriage. Women had the right to own and inherit property. Children went with the mother in case of divorce but divorce was not common. There is no evidence of female infanticide.

In fact women had such high status in Egypt that Herodotus was not favorably impressed. He wrote:

> The Egyptians appear to have reversed the ordinary practices of mankind. Women attend markets and are employed in trade, while men stay at home and do the weaving! Men in Egypt carry loads on their head, women on their shoulder. Women pass water standing up, men sitting down. To ease themselves, they go indoors, but eat outside on the streets, on the theory that what is unseemly, but necessary, should be done in private, and what is not unseemly should be done openly.

Unlike many other cultures, Egyptian literature is not filled with stories of young couples defying their parents or overcoming great odds to achieve a love match. Love poetry does not appear in literature until late in Egyptian history and when it does arrive it has a very familiar ring:

> I was taken as a wife to the house of Naneferkaptah [and Pharaoh] sent me a present of silver and gold.... [My husband] slept with me that night and found me [pleasing. He slept with me] again and again, and we loved each other.

When we come to the Hebrew tradition, which has certainly had more effect on later Western history than the Egyptian, we find the record is not as clean as we might expect. In fact, living originally in the desert and later settling into small kingdoms at the eastern end of the Mediterranean, the early Israelites practiced the kind of polygamy common to most nomadic tribes.

The list of Old Testament Patriarchs who had more than one wife is long. The first is Lamech, the son of Methuselah and the father of Noah, who had two wives, Adah and Zillah. When it appears that Abraham will not be able to conceive with his wife Sarah, he has a son, Ishmael, by her Egyptian servant Hager, with Sarah's permission. Then Sarah has a son Isaac in her old age and, as often happens in polygamous situations, the two sons and their mothers become rivals. Ishmael is exiled to Egypt, where he becomes father of his own nation, from which all Muslims claim descent. In later years, Abraham also took another wife, Keturah, and several concubines.

An even more memorable instance of sororate polygamy is Abraham's grandson Jacob, who is told by his kinsman Laban that he must work for seven years to earn his beautiful daughter Rachel. But when the seven years are over is told he must first accept her older sister Leah. So he serves Laban another seven years to have the daughter he really wants. I once heard a Protestant minister explain this story by saying that every spouse has their good and bad side and "If you want to have Rachel, you've got to take Leah." It was a nice attempt at allegory, but the Biblical story is undoubtedly more literal.

Jacob actually took two more wives after Rachel and Leah and after that the list only grows longer. Moses took an Ethiopian woman for his second wife after marrying Zipporha. When his brother and sister, Aaron and Miriam, objected, they are punished, Miriam with leprosy. Then there is that endlessly embarrassing passage in the Book of Numbers in which Moses leads the Israelites into battle against neighboring Midianites:

> And Moses spake unto the people, saying, Arm some of your-
> selves unto the war, and let them go against the Midianites,
> and avenge the Lord of Midian....
>
> And they warred against the Midianites, as the Lord com-
> manded Moses; and they slew all the males.
>
> And they slew the kings of Midia....
>
> And the children of Israel took all the women of Midian
> captives, and their little ones, and took the spoil of all their
> cattle, and all their flocks, and all their goods.
>
> And Moses was wroth with the officers of the host, with
> the captains over thousands, and captains over hundreds,
> which came from the battle.

And Moses said unto them, Have ye saved all the women alive....

Now therefore kill every male among the little ones, and kill every woman that hath known man by lying with him.

But all the women children, that have not known a man by lying with him, keep alive for yourselves. (Numbers 31, verses 1-18.)

The pattern of killing men and children but keeping the nubile females is utterly typical of a polygamous tribe seeking more wives.

Polygamy does not become associated with guilt until the story of David and Bathsheba. David, King of Israel, already has seven wives when he is smitten by Bathsheba, the wife of the Hittite general Uriah, who is fighting alongside the Israelites at the siege of Rabbath. David seduces Bathsheba and gets her pregnant. He then summons Uriah to Jerusalem in the hope that he will sleep with Bathsheba and not become suspicious of her pregnancy. But Uriah does not want to abandon his fellow soldiers and remains at the battlefront. Alarmed that his infidelity will be discovered, David instructs Uriah's commander to abandon him on the field and make sure he is killed. Once the valiant Uriah is dead, David marries Bathsheba, who becomes the favorite of his eight wives.

But David's duplicity is challenged by the Prophet Nathan, who condemns him in public for "despising the word of God" and "doing evil in his sight"—proving that the Hebrews were often served better by their prophets than their kings. Nathan threatens him with three punishments: 1) his house will be condemned to endless violence; 2) the prophet will "take your wives and give them to one who is close to you," and 3) "the son born to you [and Bathsheba] will die." David repents publically but the son of his favorite wife still dies.

David's son Absalom rebels against him and David's armies defeat him and kill him in battle. His eldest surviving son Adonijah eventually declares he wants to inherit the throne, but Bathsheba and the Prophet Nathan persuade David to seat Bathsheba's son Solomon instead. According to the Bible, King Solomon had seven hundred wives, although this is probably an exaggeration. But as in ancient Egypt and Imperial

China, the men at the top took multiple wives while the rest of the population generally settled for monogamy.

So we are left with the question of how Christianity, the offshoot of Judaism, became the most powerful force for implementing monogamy in Western history. The answer comes from the words of Jesus Christ, who, like the long line of Prophets who preceded him, was uncompromising in condemning the excesses of rulers.

> Some Pharisees came and tested him by asking, "Is it lawful for a man to divorce his wife?"
>
> "What did Moses command you?" he replied.
>
> They said, "Moses permitted a man to write a certificate of divorce and send her away."
>
> "It was because your hearts were hard that Moses wrote you this law," Jesus replied. "But at the beginning of creation God 'made them male and female. Therefore shall a man leave his father and mother and be united to his wife, and the two will become one flesh.' So they are no longer two, but one flesh. Therefore what God has joined together, let no one put asunder."
>
> When they were in the house again, the disciples asked Jesus about this. He answered, "Anyone who divorces his wife and marries another woman commits adultery against her. And if she divorces her husband and marries another man, she commits adultery."

This is obviously a harsh regimen but one the Catholic Church has adhered to throughout its history. What is most significant is Jesus' rejection of Mosaic Law on the basis that monogamy was the *original* form of human marriage. Like the mythical Enkidu, Jesus was attempting to return to origins. The passage he quotes—which has become the definition of marriage in the Western tradition—is of course from the Book of Genesis.

Western Civilization came to monogamy through both the Christian and the Greco-Roman tradition. And so it is to the Greeks that we will turn next.

CHAPTER 11

THE ILIAD AND THE ODYSSEY

I n Book VI of *The Odyssey*, after ten years at sea, Odysseus is ship-wrecked and washes ashore on his native Ithaca. He is exhausted and falls asleep by a stream. Next morning a party of young maidens, led by princess Nausikaa, the daughter of Alkinoos, comes to the stream to wash their clothing. When one of them throws a ball into the water and chases it, Odysseus comes stumbling out of the bushes looking like a wild animal.

> Streaked with brine, and swollen, he terrified them,
> so that they fled, this way and that. Only
> Alkínoös' daughter stood her ground, being given
> a bold heart by Athena, and steady knees.

Odysseus, instead of begging for help, engages her in conversation:

Mistress: please: are you divine, or mortal....
If you are one of earth's inhabitants,
how blest your father, and your gentle mother,
blest all your kin. I know what happiness
must send the warm tears to their eyes, each time
they see their wondrous child go to the dancing!
But one man's destiny is more than blest—
he who prevails, and takes you as his bride. . .
And may the gods accomplish your desire:
a home, a husband, and harmonious
converse with him—the best thing in the world
being a strong house held in serenity
where man and wife agree. Woe to their enemies,
joy to their friends! But all that they know best.

Upon this brief passage is all of Western Civilization built.

Let's look at a few of the particulars.

First, Odysseus is an older man who is trying to return to his wife. He is not interested in pursuing a younger woman but compliments Nausikaa by saying that the young man who marries her will be lucky indeed. In a polygamous society, this conversation would likely take a very different turn, because no man is ever too old or married too many times to take another young bride. This is why in a polygamous society you will always find old men marrying teenage girls and younger.

Second, Odysseus appreciates the joys of fatherhood and recognizes how proud the parents must be to see their daughter growing to maturity. In a monogamous society, the incest taboo generally extends not only to daughters but to all young women old enough to be a man's daughter. This separation of generations is a product of the monogamous nuclear family and is what makes childhood, as we understand it, possible.

Third, and equally important, is the existence of *spirited young women*. Polygamy is not just advantageous to powerful old men. It also tempts young women to bypass the pains of starting out life with an awkward young man and instead attach themselves to older, higher-status males. We will come across this time and again in Western history—high-status aristocrats trying to make concubines and morganatic wives out of lower-status women and the women, often peasant girls, standing up to them and refusing to comply. If there is one individual who is the lynchpin of a monogamous society, it is the Virtuous Woman.

Finally, there is Odysseus's hymn to monogamy, of the joys of hearth and home.

> A joy to their friends, a warning to their enemies,
> But only they know the true meaning of it.

Has any poet ever said it better?

It did not start out this way. In *The Iliad*, which comes at the beginning of Classical Greek society, we confront a very different world—one that is in some ways indistinguishable from the warrior cultures of the mountain pastures of New Guinea or Napoleon Chagnon's Yanomamö warriors. Two tribes fight over a woman, many warriors are killed, others take revenge. It did not end that way, either, as by the end of the fifth century B.C. Greek dramatists had seen fit to explore almost everything that could go *wrong* with the nuclear family. Should a father sacrifice his daughter to appease the gods? Was a son ever justified in killing his mother? But let us start at the beginning with the mysterious poet called Homer whose epics the Greeks took as their bible and which we consider the first great works of Western literature.

Helen of Troy, the most beautiful woman in the world, "the face that launched a thousand ships," has been seduced. She was in what was presumably an arranged marriage with a much older man, the king Menelaus. When she runs away with Paris, a handsome young Trojan warrior, the Greeks sail for Troy to recapture her. There is never any suggestion that Helen has gone *unwillingly*. It is entirely a matter of patriarchal honor. Helen has been captured by a rival tribe and must be returned.

But there are complications. Agamemnon, brother of Menelaus and leader of the Greek forces, and Achilles, the Greeks' greatest warrior, are in a dispute over concubines. Achilles has taken one from a captured city and she has become his favorite. Agamemnon has exercised his royal privilege and confiscated her. Hence the "wrath of Achilles" and his refusal to fight for the Greeks until the situation is rectified.

These are the problems of a polygamous society. When the leaders and principal warriors can take as many women as they want, then men will inevitably end up fighting over women. *The Iliad* takes place on a very bleak landscape. There is no peace, no salvation, no perceivable end to the contest. Men fight and die. Their greatest accomplishment is to be remembered with honor. Paradoxically, the domestic scenes are all on the *other* side. (The Greeks were always very good at seeing things from the other person's perspective. *The Persians*, Aeschylus's great drama about the Battle of Salamis, is told from the enemy's point of view.) In what is probably the most moving passage of *The Iliad*, Hector says farewell to his wife on the ramparts of Troy, knowing that he is doomed to die in battle against Achilles. Andromache, his wife, begs him not to go. Achilles has already killed all seven of her brothers and Hector is all the family she has left. She tells him a father and husband's place is in the home.

> Oh, my wild one, your bravery will be
> your own undoing! No pity for our child,
> poor little one, or me in my sad lot—
> soon to be deprived of you! soon, soon
> Akhaians as one man will set upon you
> and cut you down!

To which he replies:

> Lady, these many things beset my mind
> no less than yours. But I should die of shame
> before our Trojan men and noblewomen
> if like a coward I avoided battle,
> nor am I moved to. Long ago I learned
> how to be brave, how to go forward always
> and to contend for honor, Father's and mine.

Then in one of the most memorable scenes in literature, Hector tries to say goodbye to his infant son but the boy is frightened by his warrior's helmet:

> As he said this, Hektor held out his arms
> to take his baby. But the child squirmed round
> on the nurse's bosom and began to wail,
> terrified by his father's great war helm— . . .
> His father began laughing, and his mother
> laughed as well. Then from his handsome head
> Hektor lifted off his helmet and bent
> to place it, bright with sunlight, on the ground.
> When he had kissed his child and swung him high
> to dandle him, he said [a] prayer [to Zeus].

And so Hector goes to his death, and Andromache is forced to watch his body dragged around the city seven times by a vengeful Achilles. *The Iliad* ends with the funeral of Hector and nothing else resolved. The famous story of the Trojan Horse does not occur until *The Odyssey*.

With *The Odyssey* we enter an entirely different landscape. The epic poem portrays the birth of monogamous society. Odysseus is not the bravest or the most powerful of the Greek warriors, but he is the "man of the many stratagems" who uses his tongue and brain to escape dangers. He is also something new in world literature—a man whose love for his wife transcends everything else. His whole odyssey is an effort to return to his home and family.

And his wife Penelope is something new as well, faithful to him beyond all else. She is besieged by suitors demanding she marry one of them. She cunningly says she will—as soon as she finishes weaving a shroud for her lost husband. But every night she sneaks out and undoes the work she has done the day before.

The Odyssey is a hymn to monogamy. At one point Odysseus is detained by the goddess Calypso, who has an affair with him. She offers him *eternal life* if he will stay with her but he turns her down. He would rather return to his wife and son.

> The goddess welcomed me lovingly, tended me, offered me immortality and eternal youth; yet she never won the heart within me.

The virtues of monogamy—the fidelity of husband and wife, the resisting of temptation—saturate the text. Even Helen, in an often neglected passage of *The Odyssey*, regrets that she ever left Menelaus but apologizes for "such a wanton was I." When Odysseus finally returns to his home disguised as a beggar, he finds Eurycleia, the aged servant of his father Laertes. Only she recognizes him, from a scar on his leg:

> She was the daughter of Ops, son of Peisenor,
> and Laertes bought her on a time with his wealth,
> while as yet she was in her first youth, and gave for her the
>   worth of twenty oxen. And he honoured her even as he
>   honoured his dear wife in the halls,
> but he never lay with her,
> for he shunned the wrath of his lady.

When Zeus looks for a sign to warn Penelope's suitors of their transgressions, he sends an appropriate symbol, a pair of mated eagles, to wreak havoc on them:

> Wing-tip to wing-tip quivering taut, companions
> till high above the assembly of many voices
> they wheeled, their dense wings beating, and in havoc
> dropped on the heads of the crowd—a deathly omen—
> wielding their talons, tearing cheeks and throats;
> then veered away on the right hand through the city.

The poem ends with the suitors routed and Odysseus returned to his hearth and home.

It has long been argued that *The Iliad* and *The Odyssey* were written by different authors. Some put the works centuries apart. Scholars have done language analysis, counting words and phrases, trying to prove that the two books are unrelated. One scholar even proposed that *The Iliad* and *The Odyssey* represent different *levels of consciousness*. Whereas in *The Iliad* characters actually think they are being addressed by the gods, *The Odyssey* represents the "birth of the bicameral mind" where the gods faded in the background and people realized they control their own actions.

I would like to offer another possibility. I would suggest that there was a real Homer and that *The Iliad* was handed down to him through oral tradition, which he reworked and formalized. *The Odyssey*, however, was his own composition. The stories are obviously different and representative of different eras of Greek history. It was neither the first nor the last time that a poet or prophet has come down firmly on the side of the monogamous social contract.

CHAPTER 12

GREECE AND THE BIRTH OF MONOGAMOUS SOCIETY

The Athenians were the first known urban society in which an alpha male was *not* allowed to take more than one wife, and was shamed if he divorced. They were also the world's first democratic society.

Is there a connection? I believe there is, although perhaps not in the way we might first imagine. It might not be the case that once a society establishes *sexual* democracy it goes on to extend political rights and become democratic. Rather it may be that once the people are given a voice through democracy, they *impose* monogamy on their rulers. Remember, it is low-status men who resist polygamy at the top while high-status men favor it. But let us see how it worked out in Athenian history.

First it is important to note how unique Athens was, even in comparison to other Greek cities. Athens spent most of its history in conflict with neighboring Sparta, where the nuclear family gave way to a kind of warrior-matriarchy. When Spartan babies were born they were bathed in wine under the theory that any congenital weakness would send them into convulsions. If they failed the test, they were put to death. Even if they passed, the father was required to bring the child before a council of elders to be examined for any deformities or weaknesses. If any were discovered, the child was left on Mount Teygetos to die.

In their early years, children were raised by the mother with very little contact with their father, who was confined to the military compound. At age seven, boys began thirteen years of "Spartan" training that emphasized constant physical activity and hardship. The regimen for girls was only slightly less rigorous. At age twenty the young men and women were allowed to marry but almost certainly on an arranged basis, since they were rarely in each other's company. The ritual was for the bride to shave her head and don men's clothing so she could join her husband for one night in the barracks. After that the couple lived separately, with the husband joining her only as a temporary reprieve from his military duties. Not until age thirty was the couple allowed to live together.

Interestingly, this regimen left women in charge of most of the business of society—much as African women run most of the affairs of daily life. Spartan women were known for their grit and independence and had much more freedom than Athenian women, who were generally regarded as intellectual inferiors. Still, in this brutally regimented society, there was no concentration of wives at the top of the social hierarchy. Every Spartan warrior was guaranteed a wife and so the loyalty of the lowest-ranking males was retained.

In Athens, women were largely confined to the home and not allowed to participate in the Agora, the public square, where men congregated to argue politics and serve on juries. Still, women had their domain. Xantippe, Socrates' wife, was a notorious scold whose name has come down to us as the symbol of a querulous spouse (although we haven't heard her side of it yet—Socrates could be pretty obstreperous himself). With women out of the picture, the pursuit of philosophy veered off into sexual relations between adult men. Although no one likes to talk about it, this "corrupting of the young" was one of the main reasons Socrates was put on trial and executed. Madame de Stael, the great eighteenth century French literary critic, argued that the failure to educate women was the great weakness of Greek society. Had women been given greater opportunity, the connection between intellectual pursuits and homo-eroticism might not have been so firmly established.

Not that women were completely excluded. As has often happened, houses of prostitution—often operating as "temples"—became a refuge where women could educate themselves and achieve a certain amount of professional independence. In 445 B.C. Pericles, the elected leader of Athens, divorced his wife and alienated his children by taking up with Aspasia, a highly intelligent courtesan thought to have been running one of the city's most notorious brothels. Aspasia appears in Plato's Dialogues and is generally portrayed as an intellectual equal of the great philosophers. The couple's home became the city's foremost salon, and Aspasia is even rumored to have helped write Pericles' great funeral oration reproduced by Thucydides in the *History of the Peloponnesian War*. Even so, the city's leader was unable to renege on his marriage vows without arousing public hostility. Many people blamed his consortship with Aspasia for Athens' deteriorating fortunes during the Peloponnesian War. This is the mark of a society where monogamy has become the norm.

You might expect, then, that Athenian dramatists would celebrate love, romance, and marital fidelity in the manner of *The Odyssey*. On the contrary, Athenian drama focuses on the tensions and conflicts inherent in the nuclear family—the rules set in place and the awful consequences of violating them.

The most famous, of course, is Sophocles' *Oedipus Rex*, which centuries later became the cornerstone of Sigmund Freud's psychoanalysis. A prophet tells Laius, king of Thebes, that the child just born to his wife Jocasta will grow up to kill him. Laius orders Jocasta to murder the child. She cannot bear to follow his orders however, and gives the infant to a servant to abandon on a mountain. The child is found by a shepherd, and is presented to the childless king and queen of Corinth.

Eventually told he is not the king and queen's real son, the young Oedipus consults an oracle, who tells him he will one day kill his father and marry his mother. Horrified, he flees Corinth but meets Laius on the road, argues with him and kills him. He arrives in Thebes and marries the widowed Jocasta to become king. At the outset of the play, Thebes is suffering a terrible plague, and Oedipus is trying to learn the cause of it. When he discovers his crime—and the resultant curse on the city—he blinds himself and goes into exile. (Critics have often scoffed at the idea that a young man would marry a woman the age of his mother but we should remember that dynastic marriages often involved couples of widely divergent ages. Across the Mediterranean was a civilization in which brother married sister and father married daughter in order to maintain the royal line.)

The play was first presented in 429 B.C., the third year of the Peloponnesian War. Pericles had moved the entire Athenian population within the city's walls and a plague had broken out, killing large numbers of people. Sophocles, a general in the Athenian army, might have intended the play as an indirect indictment of Pericles' own miscalculations and matrimonial misdeeds.

Another violation of the incest taboo is told in Euripides' *Hippolytus*. The young Hippolytus, the illegitimate son of Theseus, the first king of Athens, is exiled at birth. He meets his father again, however, when Theseus himself is sent into exile for a year for killing another king. Theseus brings with him his new young wife Phaedra, who falls in love with her stepson. In an earlier version, now lost, Phaedra is openly seductive of Hippolytus and the affair is consummated. But audiences were extremely offended, as was the chorus (which represents popular opinion in Greek tragedies). In the surviving version, Hippolytus is horrified by Phaedra's confession of love. She commits suicide, leaving behind a letter saying that Hippolytus has raped her. Theseus is enraged and again exiles his son, but as Hippolytus is leaving the city he is severely injured by a runaway chariot. The goddess Artemis intervenes and tells Theseus of Hippolytus's innocence but Theseus is not reconciled. Hippolytus forgives his father, however, and dies.

What is notable here is the enormous passion suddenly unleashed by the emergence of the nuclear family as the model for society. We are witnessing—there can be no other words for it—the inaugural "battle of the sexes" now fought with particular passion by people being enfolded into closely tightened relationships.

Take the story of Medea, the barbarian princess who meets Jason and his Argonauts as they venture into the Black Sea in search of the Golden Fleece. Medea falls in love with Jason and betrays her own father in order to help him gain his prize. She returns to Greece with him, having borne him two children. There, however, Jason decides he must make a dynastic marriage with Glauce, the daughter of the neighboring king Creon. He proposes to divorce Medea but keep her as a mistress, which infuriates her. Using barbarian magic, she kills Glauce, Creon, and her own two children as revenge against Jason. In a polygamous society, this situation is easily resolved. She simply becomes the senior wife in a polygamous marriage. With the new monogamy, however, it sets off the most bloody and horrifying consequences.

But no Greek battle of the sexes matches the *Oresteia* of Aeschylus, which tells of Agamemnon's slaying of his daughter Iphigenia at the outset of the Trojan War. Stymied by poor winds, Agamemnon has consulted the Delphic oracle and is told he must offer his daughter in sacrifice in order to set sail. When he returns ten years later, his wife Clytemnestra still has not forgiven him. She has taken a lover, Aegisthus, and is plotting revenge. Cassandra, a captive Trojan prophetess, foretells Agamemnon's death but, as fated, no one believes her. Clytemnestra and Aegisthus kill Agamemnon and Cassandra, thus ending *Agamemnon*, the first play of the trilogy.

In the second play, *The Libation Bearers*, Orestes, Agamemnon and Clytemnestra's son, returns to avenge his father. Accompanied by his friend Pylades, he reunites with his younger sister Electra at Agamemnon's grave and together they plot against their father's murderers. The three sneak into the palace dressed as wayfarers and kill Aegisthus. Clytemnestra recognizes Orestes and pleads with him not to kill his own mother but he is persuaded by Pylades to slay her. Yet that doesn't end the cycle of violence. After leaving the palace, Orestes is besieged by the Erinyes or Furies, goddesses of vengeance, who promise to torment him the rest of his life.

In the third play, *The Eumenides*, Orestes, driven by the Erinyes, runs to the goddess Athena for deliverance. She summons a jury of eleven Athenians to hear the case. Apollo represents Orestes while the Erinyes speak for the dead Clytemnestra. Instead of arguing for Orestes' guilt or innocence, however, Apollo launches into a long speech expounding the theory of procreation that would hold through the Middle Ages—that the womb is simply a shelter that nurtures an embryo delivered by the male—the reverse of the theorgy that women are impregnated "by the wind."

> That word mother—
> we give it to the one who bears the child.
> However, she's no parent, just a nurse
> to that new life embedded in her.
> The parent is the one who plants the seed,
> the father. Like a stranger for a stranger,
> she preserves the growing life, unless
> god injures it. And I can offer proof
> for what I say—a man can have a child
> without a mother. Here's our witness,
> here—Athena, child of Olympian Zeus. [Apollo points
>   to Athena]
> No dark womb nursed her—no goddess bears
> a child with ancestry like hers. Athena,
> since I know so many other things.
> I'll make your city and your people great.

Athena was, of course, the female goddess born directly from the head of Zeus. And so Apollo carries the day. The jury splits 6 to 5 against Orestes but Athena casts the last vote to create a tie, which she has announced will mean his acquittal. In compensation, she renames the Erinyes the "Eumenides," meaning "the kind ones," and promises they will be patron goddesses of Athens, which will one day be a great city. It was a temporary victory for men that would eventually be reversed by science.

Sons slaying fathers and mothers, stepmothers seducing stepsons, scorned wives murdering their own children—how the Athenians resolved these issues may be less important than that they were wrestling with them at all. *The Greeks were the first complex society in history to impose monogamy on its members, top to bottom.* Not surprisingly, because the family is now a more tightly knit unit, the internal tensions become more powerful.

There is, of course, another side to Greek literature that deals with the lighter side of romance and the family—the pastoral poetry of the "simple swain and his shepherdess" and couples that find happiness in humble circumstances. Daphnis and Chloe, which dates from the second century A.D., tells the story of a boy and girl both abandoned at birth and raised by shepherds who grow up to fall in love. Still they go through all kinds of adventures, seductions, abductions, and kidnappings by pirates before finally being reunited with their birth parents, marrying, and living happily ever after. Greek pastorals tell us that love and marriage work best when lovers are freed from concerns of lineages, estates, and dynasties and left free to make their own choice. Then there is the memorable story in Ovid's *Metamorphoses* of Baucis and Philemon, an elderly couple who are the only people in the town to open their door to Zeus and Hermes when they come disguised as beggars. When asked to name a reward, the couple's only request is that they be allowed to die together. Their wish is granted and they are transformed into two trees, an oak and a linden, intertwined with each other.

No survey of Greek attitudes toward marriage would be complete, however, without taking note of Plato's *Republic* and its plan for abolishing the family and turning over its responsibilities to the state. Plato toyed with eugenics—only the best should be allowed to breed—and outlined a system where children would be requisitioned by the state at birth with parents not even allowed to know which were their own offspring. As Ferdinand Mount wrote in *The Subversive Family*, "In the interest of general political concord Plato aims to destroy the particular private attachments and affections which obtain within the family in order that the love so selfishly concentrated should be spread throughout the community." It was a tactic that would be pursued by totalitarian regimes on several occasions during the twentieth century.

Overall, though, what the Greek tragedies tell us is that powerful passions lie within the tightly knit monogamous family. For the first time since the last hunter-and-gatherers, the egalitarianism of the original human society has been restored. Replicated within a more complex and urbanized society, however, the dynamics of monogamy are like the dance of particles at the center of the atom. As long as a balance is maintained, the family functions smoothly in a productive manner. If this equilibrium is disrupted, however, the release of its forces can be devastating.

The story would be told over and over in Western history. The Greek triumph was to be the first to chart it out for us.

CHAPTER 13

THE RAPE OF LUCRETIA AND THE FOUNDING OF ROME

R oman history begins with the rape of the Sabine women, a story that played an iconic role in Roman mythology and became a favorite subject of European art.

Romulus, the founder of Rome, governs a populous of predominantly young men who have migrated to the new city. Around them live the Sabines, a more settled people with a healthy female population. The Romans ask the Sabines for permission to marry some of their women but the Sabines decline. So Romulus hatches a plot. He proclaims a festival of Neptune and invites Rome's neighbors. In the midst of the feast, the Roman men seize the Sabine women.

The "rape," however, is not a sexual assault. Instead, according to both Livy and Plutarch, Romulus reasoned with the women, telling them that their fathers were being too possessive and should not deny the Romans "the right of intermarriage to their neighbors." If the Sabine women were agreeable, "They would live in honorable wedlock," own

Roman property, share Roman civil rights, "and—dearest of all to human nature—would be the mothers of free men." The women consented and the institution of Roman marriage was born.

In the city's earliest days, the Romans practiced *manus* marriage, of which there were two variations, *cum manu* (with hand) and *sine manu* (without hand). In the first, the woman became lawfully part of her husband's family. Technically, she was adopted and had the same legal rights to inheritance as their children. In the latter, she remained part of her father's family and became heir to his wealth but not her husband's. The husband had no permanent claim on her property—which included her dowry—but the children remained in his line. And it should be noted once again, the dowry is the signature of a monogamous society.

Yet even with monogamy established in custom, the age-old problem of high-status men asserting sexual claims on lower-status women remained. Then, in one incident celebrated throughout Roman history, the violation of the monogamous norm became the turning point in the abolition of the monarchy and the establishment of the Roman Republic.

"The Rape of Lucretia" played approximately the same role in the history of the Roman Republic as the battles of Lexington and Concord and the signing of the Declaration of Independence played in American history. Retold in Livy's *History* and Ovid's *Fasti*, it has been the subject of paintings and dramatizations throughout European history. Titian, Rembrandt, Dürer, Raphael, and Botticelli all painted representations. Shakespeare wrote his longest poem about it. Chaucer tells his own version of the story and Dante places Lucretia in the circle of virtuous pagans. The Rape of Lucretia became a central metaphor in Samuel Richardson's *Pamela*, another crucial tale of female virtue. In 1932 it played on Broadway, and in 1946 Benjamin Britten wrote an opera about it. Lucretia has been the icon of a monogamous society.

She was the wife of a provincial governor and daughter of a Roman prefect under the reign of the Etruscan king Tarquin. While besieging the city of Ardea, Tarquin sent his son Sextus Tarquinius to visit the province to raise troops. There he was courteously welcomed by Lucretia, whose husband was away with the army. That night, however, the young Tarquin slipped into her bedroom, urging her to leave her husband and become queen when he inherited the throne. When she refused, he held a sword to her throat, saying if she did not submit he would kill her and a slave and put them in bed together, telling everyone he had discovered them in adultery. She submits, not wanting his lie to disgrace the reputation of Roman women.

Lucretia was so humiliated by the transgression, however, that she begged her father to avenge her. He summoned a council of elders to plot revenge. Even as they debated, however, Lucretia unveiled a concealed dagger and plunged it into her heart, dying in her father's arms.

Lucretia's suicide led her husband and several other young noblemen to rebel against the Tarquins. The body of Lucretia, dressed in funeral array, was paraded throughout the city, rallying the people to arms. When the Tarquins returned, they found Rome barricaded against them. They withdrew into exile. The young rebels agreed to share power until turning it over to a new legislative council, the Senate. The Roman Republic was born.

It is almost exactly what Freud described as occurring at the beginning of human history. A rebellious brotherhood overthrows a licentious patriarch and distributes power (and women) among themselves. It shows that such scenarios need not be wholly imaginary. In fact the tensions created by the polygamous desires of men at the heights of power have been a flashpoint throughout Western history, as we will see again when we come to the French Revolution.

After the establishment of the Roman Republic, the plebeians established the Tribunes as a counterpart to the aristocratic Senate. In 452 B.C. the two factions agreed to appoint ten wise men—the Decemviri—to write the laws for the city. The Decemviri produced the Law of the Twelve Tables and on Table XI, concerning marriage, the first law read, "Marriages between plebeians and patricians are forbidden." This statute was adopted not out of patrician snobbery but at the behest of the plebeians, who feared upper-class men invading their ranks in search of concubines (a position with semi-legal status) and mistresses.

It didn't take long for things to come to a head. Appius Claudius, the most influential of the Decemviri, fell in love with a centurion's daughter, Virginia, a plebeian already betrothed to a former Tribune. When the

Decemviri's terms expired in 450 B.C., Appius had himself appointed to the succeeding council and worked to repeal the law so he could take Virginia as a concubine. The controversy soon engulfed the city and finally came to a tragic end when Virginia's father stabbed her to death in the Forum rather than allow her to become the mistress of a rich man. Plebeian riots ensued and the Decemviri council was abandoned. The tension about marriage across class lines remained.

"Matrimony," a Roman word, rooted in *mater* ("mother"), became a body of law that is still with us today. A knot became the symbol of Roman marriage, "belting and binding" the couple to each other. The knot could be untied only in bed. In the waning days of the Republic (in the first century B.C.), the old *manus* marriage, where the wife was attached to her natal family or husband, gave way to "free marriage," in which both parties entered the union on an equal basis. The dowry was open to negotiation and the wife was no longer under the legal control of either her father or her husband. Either husband or wife could initiate a divorce and only one party's consent was required. It might seem as if this would lead to a rampant breakup of marriages, but there was one important constraint that held families together. This was the rule that children remained with their father after divorce.

Although the Romans probably did not articulate it, the premise was purely biological. Having children is a more difficult process for women and must occur at an earlier age. For men, it is relatively easy to go out and start a new family with a younger woman. Therefore, paternal custody works to the *dis*advantage of *both* parents and *for* the institution of marriage. If divorce means a woman must leave her children, she will be much less inclined to abandon a marriage. And it is awkward for a father trying to start a second family if he must retain custody of his children from the first. For this reason—despite the legal ease of divorce—Roman families remained relatively stable.

The family that emerged from this was very much characterized by the term *pater familias*. The authority invested in fathers over their children was enormous. Even the Greeks were surprised at the degree to which a Roman father could determine the fate of his sons and daughters.

Originally the father had the right of life and death over every member of his family, although this was almost never exercised and was eventually limited by law. A father could veto any marriage of his children, although he did not have the power to force them to marry. Roman families often adopted, and if a father became particularly close to a young associate in business or politics, he would adopt him and make him heir to his fortune. By the time of the Late Roman Empire, it was routine for an emperor to adopt his political favorite as his son—and murder relatives that might obstruct his way to the throne. If children disappointed their father, he could always turn to adoption to find a better heir.

Upper-class men still made use of concubines, although it met with public disapproval. The most spectacular example is Julius Caesar, who had the reputation of being "every woman's husband and ever man's wife" and eventually became involved in a "second marriage" with perhaps the most famous woman in history, Cleopatra, queen of Egypt.

After his ascent to power in Rome, Caesar intervened in the Egyptian civil war. While there he fell under the spell of the Egyptian queen, over thirty years his junior, who won his heart. She accompanied him back to Rome, where he established her in a villa, but this scandalized the populace. Caesar, after all, already had a wife, Calpurnia, who was "above suspicion." The "foreign queen" was deeply resented (Cicero mentions this hatred in his letters) and when Caesar was assassinated in 44 B.C., Cleopatra and her entourage fled back to Egypt.

Now Marc Antony, Caesar's protégé, and Octavian, Caesar's nephew, became embroiled in a public rivalry. Antony visited Cleopatra in order to consolidate his eastern holdings and Cleopatra ensnared him in what is probably the most famous romance in history. She gave birth to twins, and Antony married her according to the Egyptian rite. This lost him favor in Rome, however, since he was already married to Octavian's sister, and Cleopatra became forever fixed in the Roman mind as a sinister seductress from an alien culture. Open conflict finally broke out between Octavian and Antony in 34 B.C., and Antony and Cleopatra were routed at the Battle of Actium. They fled back to Egypt, where, although none of the histories tell the same story, she and Antony both committed suicide. Octavian had himself declared Caesar Augustus and the era of the Roman Empire was born.

Octavian's rise to power as "Augustus Caesar" marked the revival of ancient Roman family values. In particular, Augustus was alarmed that upper-class Roman families were no longer having children. In the Lex Julia, adopted in 18 B.C., he imposed penalties on couples who did not have children and rewarded those who did. Unmarried persons were not allowed to receive inheritances or legacies and married couples without children could receive only one-half their inheritance. Couples or individuals without children were also taxed at a higher rate. Women who were divorced were required to remarry within six months and widows within a year.

Divorce laws were tightened slightly but in general divorce remained relatively easy, particularly as *manus* marriage faded and free marriage became the rule. Augustan law increased the penalties for adultery, though prostitution remained legal, in part to divert men who might otherwise sleep with other men's wives and break up families. A man was entitled to kill his wife or married daughter if he caught either in adultery, as long as he killed her lover as well. If he only killed one he was guilty of murder.

What concerned Augustus, of course—and what later events confirmed—was that the Roman Empire was rotting from within. The reluctance of people in the upper ranks to raise children, the libertine culture that was beginning to gain an upper hand, the loss of the yeoman ethic and the "old Republican values" all presaged the decline that was to come.

Yet it proved difficult if not impossible to stem the tide, and Augustus set a poor example. He was married three times, twice taking other men's wives, and was never able to produce a son, apparently because he had contracted gonorrhea in his youth. Leaving no heir, he opened the door for a long series of ever more troubling successions in which emperors eventually fought their way to the throne, usually with the help of the army.

Yet while emperors routinely had multiple wives and mistresses, no Roman emperor ever had a harem or was surrounded by eunuchs, as the Ottoman and Chinese emperors would eventually be. The Romans believed the nuclear family to be the foundation of their success even as they dissipated its strength through falling birth rates and a rising tide of sexual permissiveness.

As a result, the Roman system of family law, and the monogamous morality it established became the foundation of Western Civilization by other means. As Arnold Toynbee wrote in his great *Study of History*, the essence of every civilization survives in the religion that it passes on to future generations. It was Rome's religious legacy—Western Christianity—that now was to establish monogamy as the norm of Western society.

CHAPTER 14

CHRISTIANITY, *DROIT DU SEIGNEUR*, AND THE VIRTUOUS WOMAN

Christianity played *the* crucial role in making monogamy the norm in Western society. It did so as the state religion of the Roman Empire in a Greco-Roman world where polygamy was associated with barbarism. The Roman Catholic Church prohibited adultery and divorce and viewed monogamous marriage through the prism of Jesus' admonition that in marriage a husband and wife became indivisible, "one flesh." For 1,500 years, the Catholic Church proclaimed, essentially without rebuttal in Christian Europe, that indissoluble monogamous marriage was ordained by God.

Much has been made of whether the Bible truly codifies monogamy and whether polygamy was completely outlawed. There was much discussion in the early years of church history, some of which continues today. The Gnostics and a few other early Christian sects are reputed to have lapsed into polygamy. Even today, African missionaries are constantly troubled with the problem of whether to insist that their converts renounce polygamy or take them into the church and hope they will abandon it later.

One of the most influential passages in church history has been a casual aside in the First Epistle to Timothy about the qualifications of a bishop:

> A Bishop then must be blameless, *the husband of one wife*, vigilant, sober, of good behaviour, given to hospitality, apt to teach. (1 Timothy, 3:2, King James Version, emphasis added.)

Church scholars point to this passage as an endorsement of monogamy but others say it clearly suggests there were bishops and others who may have had more than one wife.

What was harder to overlook was the practice of polygamy in the Old Testament, which in some Jewish communities persisted until the second century A.D. Justin Martyr (c. 160 A.D.) rebuked the Jews for allowing the practice to continue: "Your imprudent and blind masters even until this time permit each man to have four or five wives. And if anyone sees a beautiful woman and desires to have her, they quote the doings of Jacob."

Jacob's example and that of other Old Testament figures was also a problem for sixteenth century Protestant reformers, with their belief in the Bible alone, stripped of the teachings of the Catholic Church. Martin Luther, for instance, wrote in a private correspondence:

> I confess that I cannot forbid a person to marry several wives, for it does not contradict the Scripture. If a man wishes to marry more than one wife he should be asked whether he is satisfied in his conscience that he may do so in accordance with the word of God. In such a case the civil authority has nothing to do in the matter.

John Milton, the voice of English Puritanism, was also unable to find any Scriptural prohibition against polygamy but kept his musings to himself. In *De Doctrina Christiana*, published after his death, Milton wrote:

In the definition which I have given, I have not said, in compliance with the common opinion, *of one man with one woman*, lest I should by implication charge the holy patriarchs and pillars of our faith, Abraham, and the others who had more than one wife at the same time, with habitual fornication and adultery.... Either therefore polygamy is a true marriage, or all children born in that state are spurious; which would include the whole race of Jacob, the twelve holy tribes chosen by God. But...such an assertion would be absurd in the extreme....

It appears to me sufficiently established by the above arguments that polygamy is allowed by the law of God.

Anyone who seeks a firm rejection of polygamy in the Bible is probably doomed to frustration. As the saying goes, the Devil can quote scripture as well. In any case, scriptural prohibitions are not always followed anyway. As Mark Twain points out in *Roughing It*, the *Book of Mormon* specifically prohibited polygamy but that did not prevent Joseph Smith and the other founders of the Church of Jesus Christ of Latter-Day Saints from adopting it.

The real reason monogamy prevailed in Western Civilization was not because of the examples of the Bible, but because the Catholic Church had a crucial ally in a new icon of Western Civilization—the Virtuous Woman. We see her in Penelope in *The Odyssey* and in Lucretia in Rome. We meet her continuously in the Church with its veneration of the Virgin Mary, the lives of the saints, and the deeming of monogamous marriage as a sacred institution.

For our purposes, the Virtuous Woman has a specific definition. She is a woman content with marriage to a male of similar status to herself, who rejects the opportunity to mate in an adulterous affair or in a polygamous relationship with a higher-status male.

The biggest challenge to the Virtuous Woman, before the French Revolution, was the tradition, myth, or rumor (depending on which historians and anthropologists you believe) that the lord of the manor was entitled to spend the first night with any newlywed bride in his domain. You will recall this goes back as far as *Gilgamesh*, the first great epic in world literature.

Throughout the Middle Ages the *jus primae noctis* was commonly depicted in paintings, stories, and poems. While not definitive proof of its existence (dragons, after all, figured prominently in medieval art), it is evidence of a widespread *belief* that the *droit du seigneur* was practiced by at least some noblemen. Who, after all, is to say what happened in the bedrooms of every manor house in Medieval Europe? Whether the scholars are right in arguing that it never actually existed, they are certainly wrong in suggesting that this specter of high-born men violating the rules of egalitarian monogamy did not haunt the medieval imagination.

Another story scholars like to tell is that "romantic love" is a medieval invention, created by the troubadour poets of the twelfth century. That sounds clever, but the idea that men and women never experienced romantic love until troubadour poets pined for ladies locked up behind castle walls is contradicted by the love poetry of the Bible, the stories of Daphnis and Chloe, Pyramus and Thisbe, and all the other romantic couples of classical mythology. Horace wrote a book advising young men and women on how to court each other. If we don't have definitive proof of the *droit du seigneur*, we surely have definitive proof that human love existed long before the Middle Ages.

What differentiated the troubadours is that they were negotiating a world of *arranged marriages* where a young woman could be betrothed to a loveless marriage with a much older man. The troubadours, often as not, were of the same age as the lady. Their declarations of love had an abstract and "platonic" quality because the social circumstances meant their entreaties were likely to be denied. This made for beautiful poetry and might even attract other, more accessible young women, but the troubadours did not invent romantic love. They only sang of it better than anyone else had ever done.

With the flowering of the Renaissance, one of the first places we encounter the new concept of egalitarian love resting upon a woman who is as trustworthy as she is beautiful is in *Peribanez and the Commander of Ocana*, perhaps the most famous play of Lope de Vega (1562–1635), the great dramatist of Spain's Golden Age.

The play opens with a handsome peasant couple, Peribanez and Casilda, marrying in front of their village. Don Fadrique, the resident commander, is captivated by Casilda and vows to seduce her. Dressed in a cloak, he visits her anonymously with a message that Don Fadrique is in love with her. She spurns the offer, telling the stranger she loves Peribanez. When the king calls up an army to fight the Moors, however, Don Fadrique assembles a company of peasants and makes Peribanez their commander, intending to seduce Casilda while her husband is away. (Shades of Lucretia and David and Bathsheba.) Peribanez performs heroically but gets wind of Don Fadrique's intentions and returns to confront him. They fight a duel and Peribanez slays him. He is about to be condemned for murder when the king hears the story and intervenes to pardon him. The story ends happily.

What is notable about this tale is the spirited nature of the peasant girls—saucy, self-confident, and perfectly willing to stand up to their social superiors. When Don Fadrique visits Casilda in disguise, she tells him:

> Even if the Commander did love me with all his soul, in defiance of all codes of honor and virtue, I love Peribanez in his old brown cape more than the Commander of Ocana in his cloak embroidered with gold. I would rather see Pedro in his white shirt riding toward me on his gray mare, with frost in his beard, his crossbow over his shoulder, a brace of partridge or a couple of rabbits hanging from his saddle, and the old dog running beside him, than see the Commander of Ocana in silks and diamonds.

De Vega was himself the son of an embroiderer and it is not surprising to find him here defending the loyalty and integrity of people of humble origin. But the important thing is that people of such humble origin in Catholic Spain had the law on their side. They could always appeal to religion and the matrimonial bond.

Many of de Vega's plays (he wrote over 1,500 of them) have similar themes. In *Fuenteovejuna*, based on a real incident from the previous century, an almost identical situation occurs. Fernan Gomez de Guzman, the commander of the town of Fuenteovejuna, falls in love with a peasant girl and tries to seduce her. This time the entire town rebels and the commander finds himself fighting a civil war. Ferdinand and Isabella, the king and queen of Spain, are drawn into the conflict and side with the peasants in defense of monogamy and the Virtuous Woman. The play ends with the commander given rough justice—killed, by a mob.

To be sure, not all plays of the Renaissance era end with this reaffirmation of conventional monogamy. One of the favorite themes of Italian Renaissance comedy is the cuckolded husband who is fooled by the wily rival. In Niccolò Machiavelli's *The Mandrake*, for example, the wily young suitor establishes himself in the buffoonish husband's household where he is able to carry on a permanent liaison with the householder's frustrated wife. But the comedy works only because the audience accepts monogamous marriage as the norm. Such comedies might express the frustrations of monogamy, but they do not deny its paramount role in society. Shakespeare's comedies, in this respect, are the gold standards of the Western tradition with couples generally pairing off at the end so that "All's Well That Ends Well."

With the rise of prosperity in Europe and the growth of commercial society, we might expect to see these old class conflicts afflicting matrimony beginning to fade. Instead, we find with the end of feudalism and the rise of a middle class, the old issue of women's virtue, mistresses, and concubines becoming more acute, both in the theater and the new form of literature, the novel. This conflict between aristocratic privilege and the rising bourgeois morality was to reach a crisis at the outset of the French Revolution.

CHAPTER 15

THE FRENCH
REVOLUTION
AND THE END OF
ARISTOCRACY

A rising in the seventeenth and eighteenth centuries was a burgeoning middle class, made up of shopkeepers, small trades-
men, entrepreneurs, and small property owners. As this middle
class gained in wealth and political power, conflict with the old landed
aristocracy became inevitable. In England, this was played out in the
seventeenth century in the English Civil War between the Cavaliers, made
up of the old courtier aristocracy, and the Roundheads, whose Puritan
values were rapidly creating a new kind of prosperity. Although the
Puritans won the contest, the constitutional monarchy was restored, with
diminished powers, in the Glorious Revolution of 1688. In France, the
royal power lasted another century but when it finally came down, its
fall was mighty.

What is interesting for our purposes is that this growing tension
between the old aristocracy and the rising middle class was expressed—
in literature at least—in the still thorny issue of whether aristocratic men

should have access to women of the lower classes. Samuel Richardson's *Pamela, or Virtue Rewarded* (1740), was the first serialized novel that came to engross the whole of England. Pierre Beaumarchais' *The Marriage of Figaro* was banned from the stage in 1781 by Louis XVI, but when it finally appeared three years later it caused a sensation that reverberated all across Europe. Georges Danton, an early leader of the French Revolution, said "*Figaro* killed off the nobility." Napoleon remarked that *Figaro* was "the Revolution in action."

In Samuel Richardson's *Pamela*, the title character is a fifteen-year-old servant girl living in the household of a widowed aristocrat and her spoiled son, Mr. B. After his mother dies, Mr. B. tries to seduce Pamela, who has nothing to rely on except her good upbringing and the counsel of an elderly maidservant. After months of unsuccessful importuning, Mr. B. abducts Pamela and locks her away in an isolated estate. He discovers her letters to her parents, however, and begins to feel sorry for her. He tells Pamela he would be willing to marry her except for the great gulf of class that lies between them. He proposes that she become his well-kept mistress, but once again Pamela rejects him. Finally, he offers to marry her, but she suspects his motives and asks to return to her mother. He lets her go. On the journey home, however, Pamela realizes Mr. B.'s offer is serious and that she is falling in love with him. She returns to Mr. B. and they are finally united in marriage.

The story is told through a series of letters to her mother and in the process Richardson invented the "epistolary novel." For perhaps the first time in history, the thoughts of ordinary people appeared on paper, revealing an inner complexity. The novel became a form of moral education that had enormous impact on people's lives. For English readers, it seemed as if the whole fate of their yeoman society rested on one young girl's shoulders—and in fact it did. If aristocrat men could have their way with servant girls whenever they wished, it would disrupt marriage at both ends of the scale, cutting into the chances of lower-class men while turning upper-class marriage into the gaggle of mistresses and concubines so common in other societies. Whole villages listened to the story aloud. As one historian recounts:

The blacksmith of the village had got hold of Richardson's novel of *Pamela, or Virtue Rewarded*, and used to read it aloud in the long summer evenings, seated on his anvil, and never failed to have a large and attentive audience.... At length, when the happy turn of fortune arrived, which brings the hero and heroine together, and sets them living long and happily...the congregation were so delighted as to raise a great shout, and procuring the church keys, actually set the parish bells ringing.

The Pamelas were to become the lynchpin of monogamous Western culture. It was their virtue that ensured that a male suitor could not have sex without making a commitment to marriage and fatherhood. This was no easy task, as can be seen in the work of Henry Fielding, a rakish young satirist from an aristocratic background who was appalled by the popular success and bourgeois sentiment of *Pamela*. In response, he penned a lengthy satire, *Shamela*, in which it is revealed that, far from being a chaste servant girl, Pamela was actually a wanton young woman trying to entrap her master, Squire Booby, into marriage. Fielding was a Tory and his cynicism was much more popular among the upper classes—and remains so in the English departments of American colleges today.

———

Across the English Channel, Figaro's creator, Pierre Beaumarchais, was a provincial watchmaker's son who rose to prominence as an inventor and jack-of-all-trades. He was an early supporter of the American Revolution. Trying his hand as a playwright, he authored *The Barber of Seville*, a straightforward, boy-meets-girl story first performed in 1775. The barber is Figaro, a scampering, unsuccessful playwright who embodied the "new man" in French society—a middle-class entrepreneur born without title or inheritance who survives on his wits, very much like Beaumarchais himself.

Figaro is actually a minor character who facilitates the courtship between Count Almavira and Rosina, a beautiful young aristocrat whose parents have died and left her in the hands of Dr. Bartholo, a pedantic conniver. One day the Count catches sight of Rosina and immediately falls in love. Not wanting to overwhelm her with his wealth and station, he decides to court her while disguised as a penniless troubadour. Standing beneath her window, he encounters Figaro, his former servant, who tells him that Dr. Bartholo intends to marry Rosina even though he is old enough to be her grandfather.

As a barber, Figaro has permission to enter Dr. Bartholo's house and helps the Count gain access to Rosina's chamber. She is entranced with the daring Count without realizing his high position. When his title and fortune are revealed, that only seals the bargain. Dr. Bartholo is thwarted and the play ends happily, with Figaro winning plaudits for his wily schemes.

In *The Marriage of Figaro*, things suddenly take a revolutionary turn. The Count is now middle-aged and settled down with Rosina. Figaro is his chief valet and about to marry Suzanne, Countess Rosina's spirited young servant. The Count has given his blessing and even provided Suzanne with a dowry. However, he is starting to experience that midlife crisis where men lose interest in their first wives and start pursuing younger women. He has quietly confided to Suzanne that he would like to enjoy his *jus primae noctis*. In fact, he tells her, the marriage might not take place unless his wish is granted.

The drama begins with Figaro and Suzanne settling into their quarters between the Count and Countess's bedrooms when Suzanne suddenly announces she dislikes this arrangement.

> FIGARO: But you can't just take against the most convenient room in the whole castle. It's between the two apartments. If her Ladyship doesn't feel well in the night, she'll ring from that side and, tipperty-flip, you're there in two ticks. If his Lordship wants something, all he has to do is ring on this side and, hoppity-skip, I'm there in two shakes.

SUZANNE: Exactly! But when he rings in the morning and sends you off on some long wild-goose chase, tipperty-flip, he'll be here in two ticks, and then, hoppity-skip, in two shakes...

FIGARO: What exactly do you mean by that?

SUZANNE: I want you to listen quietly to what I'm going to say.

FIGARO: Good God, what are you getting at?

SUZANNE: This, my sweet, Count Almavira is tired of chasing all the pretty women in the locality. Now he's got something closer to home in mind. Not his wife—it's yours he has his eye on, are you with me? And he thinks that putting us in this room won't exactly hinder his plans.... He means to use the dowry to persuade me to give him a few moments in private for exercising the old droit de seigneur he thinks he's entitled to. You know what a disgusting business that was.

FIGARO: I do indeed. And if his Lordship hadn't renounced his nauseating right when he got married, I'd never have considered holding our wedding anywhere near his estate.

SUZANNE: Well, if he really gave it up he now wishes he hadn't. And it's with your bride that he's going to reinstate it. Today.

Figaro departs to try to come up with a scheme to foil the Count's plan without offending him. Now the Count corners Suzanne in her new bedroom.

COUNT: You've heard that the king has appointed me as his ambassador to London. I'm taking Figaro with me. It's a very good opportunity I'm offering him. And since it's a wife's duty to follow her husband...

SUZANNE: If I could only speak my mind!

COUNT, *pulls her a little closer*: Go ahead, speak, my dear. Speaking freely is a right you have acquired over me for life, so you might as well make a start now.

SUZANNE, *fearfully*: It's not a right I want. I don't want anything to do with it. Just leave me alone, please!

COUNT: But first say what you were going to say.

SUZANNE, *angry*: I don't remember what it was.

COUNT: About a wife's duty.

SUZANNE: Very well. When your Lordship stole your wife away from under [Bartholo's] nose and married her for love and on her account abolished a certain horrible custom...

COUNT, *laughing*: The one the girls all hated! But Suzette, it is a charming old custom! Come and talk to me in the garden later, when it's getting dark, and I'll make it worth your while—it's only a tiny favor...

Faced with this threat, Figaro finally hits upon a strategy. He will call together the peasants and household servants and hold a public celebration of the Count's renunciation of the *droit du seigneur*.

FIGARO: My Lord, your loyal vassals, in appreciation of your having abolished a certain unseemly custom which, for love of her Ladyship . . .

COUNT: Yes, yes, the custom has ceased to exist. What are you trying to say?

FIGARO, *deviously*: That it is high time for goodness of such a considerate master received some form of public acknowledgement. I myself am today a beneficiary of that goodness, and it is my wish to be the first to celebrate it at my wedding.

COUNT, *even more discomfited*: No need for that, old friend. Banning a degrading custom is enough in itself to indicate the high regard I have for decency. Any full-flooded Spaniard is entitled to try to win a lady's love by paying his court to her. But demanding the first and sweetest use of her as though it were some servile due is uncivilized, barbarous behavior, not a right which any true-born Castilian nobleman would ever wish to claim...

FIGARO: All together, friends!

ALL: Long live his Lordship!...

COUNTESS, *entering*: I add my voice to theirs, my Lord. This ceremony will always have a special place in my heart, because it began in the tender love you once felt for me.

And so the fourth party in this sexual quadrille enters the scene—the high-status woman who is being undercut by her lower-status rival. The Countess quickly takes Suzanne into her confidence, not blaming her but confessing to a world-weary acknowledgment of vulnerability.

COUNTESS: You mean, Suzanne, that he seriously intended to seduce you?

SUZANNE: Oh no! His Lordship wouldn't go to all that bother for a servant. He tried to buy me...

COUNTESS: He doesn't love me anymore.... I loved him too much. I've bored him with my affection, wearied him with my love. Those are the only wrongs I have done him. But I won't allow your honesty in telling me this to harm your future. You shall marry Figaro.

Figaro, Suzanne, and the Countess then hatch a plot to make the Count believe the Countess has struck up a flirtation with Cherubin, a teenage boy whose innocent looks have been winning the hearts of older women. The Count falls for it and when the deception is revealed, he confronts his wife.

COUNT: Rosina!

COUNTESS: I have ceased to be the Rosina you once pursued so passionately! I am poor Countess Almavira, the sad, deserted wife you do not love anymore.

COUNT, *beseechingly*: For pity's sake!

COUNTESS: Pity? You showed me no pity.

COUNT: But there was the note…it made my blood boil…It was that hare-brained Figaro who told me he'd got it from some yokel…I'll see he pays for the whole lot of them!

COUNTESS: You want to be forgiven yourself but you won't forgive others. Just like a man! If I ever felt I could forgive you because you were misled by the note, I'd insist that everyone involved was forgiven, too!

COUNT: And so they shall, with all my heart, Countess. But how can I atone for making such a shameful mistake?

COUNTESS, *rising*: We should both be ashamed…

COUNT: We men think we're rather good at politics but really we're only children who play at it. You're the one, Madame, the king should send as his ambassador to London! Have all women put themselves through an advanced course of self-control to be as good at it as you are?

COUNTESS: Men leave us no alternative.

And so things are resolved, but not before Figaro delivers a fiery speech that was to become the hallmark of the Revolution:

No, my lord Count, you won't have her…you won't have her. Just because you're a great nobleman, you think you're a great genius! Nobility, riches, a title, high positions, that all makes a man so proud! What have you done for such fortune? You went to the trouble of being born, and nothing else. Otherwise, a rather ordinary man; while I, good grief, lost in the obscure crowd, I had to use more skill and planning just to survive than has been put into governing all of Spain for the last hundred years.

When Louis XVI finally lifted the ban on *The Marriage of Figaro* in 1784, the response was so overwhelming that three people were crushed to death on the opening night. The play electrified Paris and quickly spread to other countries, where Figaro's confrontation of aristocratic privilege became a watchword for republican revolutionaries everywhere. Beaumarchais was no Robespierre, of course, and his happy resolution was quickly overtaken by the horrors of the Reign of Terror. But it was the beginning of the end for the old aristocracy. The egalitarian principles of the Revolution finally triumphed.

So does it seem outlandish to claim that a single drama portraying the overthrow of the aristocratic *droit du seigneur* should play such a crucial role in the history of Western society? Well, consider this. In 1826, a group of Republican sympathizers started a weekly satirical newsletter that took its motto from Figaro's famous soliloquy: "*Sans la liberté de blâmer, il n'est point d'éloge flatteur*"—"Without the freedom to criticize, there is no true praise." The publication quickly became the voice of France's rising middle class. In 1854 it went daily and by 1866 was France's leading newspaper. Throughout the nineteenth and twentieth centuries, it had the largest circulation of any French newspaper, being surpassed only in the last few years by *Aujourd'hui en France*.

Today the paper is considered "conservative" and even "right-wing," but it has never wavered in upholding the middle-class values that produced the unprecedented prosperity and social stability of Western society.

The name of the publication is *Le Figaro*.

CHAPTER 16

THE VICTORIAN ERA AND THE TRIUMPH OF MARRIAGE

Monogamous marriage, supported by middle-class morality, became the cornerstone of unprecedented prosperity and social stability in the nineteenth century. There were no major wars between the end of the Napoleonic Era in 1815 and the outbreak of the First World War in 1914. During that time much of Europe—and particularly Great Britain—flourished in a way that had never been deemed possible.

For the first time in history, it became plausible for the broad sweep of the population to have rising expectations. Granted, much of the century was spent lamenting the failure of these aspirations—the poverty of factory workers, the plight of orphans, the degradation of young girls forced into prostitution. But the ideal remained. The world was no longer divided into a nobility that had inherited wealth and privilege and a peasantry that had no hopes of rising. Middle-class values, and the sense of respectability that came with them, were within everyone's reach. The central component of middle-class respectability was a secure marriage and family life.

Monogamous marriage was protected by law and custom. In Catholic countries, marriages had to be sanctioned by the church and divorce was nearly impossible. In Protestant countries, divorce was more common but still regarded as a mark of shame. Paternal custody plus the barriers of proving fault and paying alimony made it a dispiriting ordeal.

The woman who gave her name to this era was Queen Victoria of England. Born in 1819, while King George III of American Revolutionary War fame was still on the throne, she led an isolated childhood. As the only child of the monarch's deceased youngest son, she had little place at court and almost no prospect of succession. Her mother, Princess Victoria of Saxe, was scandalized by the dens of iniquity and warrens of courtesans and illegitimate heirs that the royal courts of Europe had become and kept her only daughter far removed.

George III was succeeded by his eldest son George IV in 1820, but he died without an heir in 1830. His younger brother, William IV, also childless, took the throne, leaving eleven-year-old Victoria next in line. William swore to his niece he would live until she reached maturity and was old enough to rule without a regent. He just made it, dying in 1837, so that a month after her eighteenth birthday Victoria became queen. She would rule for sixty-four years, surpassing George II as the longest-reigning monarch in British history, and living to be the oldest monarch, until surpassed only recently by Queen Elizabeth II.

During her adolescence, Victoria had been introduced to several potential husbands and eventually found favor with her cousin Albert, who stood in line for half the Hanoverian kingdom. In 1839, Albert visited from Germany and Victoria proposed to him. They were married six months later. The household soon set the standard for bourgeois conventionality. Within a year Victoria had given birth to the first of nine children. Most of them eventually married into other European royal families and Victoria became known as the "grandmother of Europe."

Unlike previous monarchs, Victoria and Prince Albert publicly experienced all the usual tribulations of marriage, including one huge row over whether to keep Victoria's childhood governess, whom Albert despised. (He won.) Then in 1861 their storybook marriage came to an end. A rumor of an affair between their eldest son and an Irish actress sent Albert rushing to Cambridge University to confront him. Albert died several months later, having contracted typhoid fever. Victoria always blamed "the sordid affair" for Albert's premature death. She wore black mourning clothes for the remaining forty years of her life.

With the self-sufficient family unit now the economic core of society, Great Britain and much of Europe, not to mention the United States, were able to reach levels of prosperity never before achieved in history. Much of this, of course, came through the Industrial Revolution—the steam engine, the railroad, electricity, all the advances that suddenly cascaded out of scientific discoveries. But these technologies were available in other countries and did not produce the same results. Only Britain, the United States, and Western Europe were set up to take advantage through a system of independent families joined in cooperative effort with governments not overburdened with the task of providing basic necessities. It was from the perspective of this system of self-sufficiency that people in next-century America would look back on their childhoods and say, "We didn't know we were poor." The emotional satisfactions of growing up in an intact family and having enough to eat were sufficient.

None of this was won easily, however, and the argument over whether it was even possible constituted one of the grand social issues of the age. At the outset of the nineteenth century, Thomas Malthus had written his famous *On Population*, which posited that the mass of humanity was doomed to eternal poverty through overpopulation. The subject of birth control was broached occasionally but quickly ran up against church opposition and practical limits. So the main strategy for controlling population growth became the regulation of marriage. Governments, church authorities, parents, and the entire adult citizenry combined to enforce the principle that childbirth should occur only within marriage and that marriage should not take place until the couple was capable of supporting themselves. In Austria, couples had to receive state permission before marrying. Most militaries discouraged officers from marrying until they reached the rank of captain. Waiting for a prospective husband to acquire enough money to support a wife and family became a standard theme of popular culture. There is a famous 1850s painting, "The Long Engagement," depicting a poor country parson and his fiancée longing for each other and creeping into middle age while waiting to accumulate enough savings to get married. It was an age when women prized their virginity and men expected to deflower their new brides on their wedding night. This strict morality was not just enforced by social convention but embedded in people's minds. In Thomas Hardy's *Tess of the D'Urbervilles*, a young husband discovers that his wife previously had a child by another man and is so devastated that he leaves the marriage.

To be sure, society's standards were occasionally violated. Yet as Gertrude Himmelfarb notes in her great study of Victorian values, *The De-Moralization of Society*:

> From 7 percent in mid-century, the illegitimacy ratio declined to 4 percent by the end of the century. Premarital pregnancy was far more common, as high as 40–50 percent in some parishes early in the century, although far lower later. While such pregnancies are suggestive of sexual laxity, the large differential between the illegitimacy and premarital pregnancy figures testify to the power of the moral code: the obligation to marry once a child was conceived. It is also consistent with Victorian "family values," since that child, and all subsequent ones, were brought up in a stable family.

This ethic of personal and familial responsibility paid off handsomely in rising prosperity. The population of England doubled between 1840 and 1900 yet living standards rose dramatically—something that had seemed impossible a hundred years before. Mortality rates fell and it was the first century without a major health epidemic. The Malthusian trap had been avoided by a combination of strict sexual morality and family formation. As Himmelfarb observes, even as advances in science began to shake the religious underpinnings of this moral code, faith in the family remained firm:

> Indeed, [the Victorians] affirmed moral principles all the more strongly as the religious basis of those principles seemed to be disintegrating. There were dire predictions, after the publication of Charles Darwin's *Origin of Species* in 1859, that the theory of evolution, and the progress of science in general, would undermine not only religion but morality as well. What happened instead was that morality became, in a sense, a surrogate for religion. For many Victorians, the loss of religious faith inspired a renewed and heightened moral zeal.

As belief in a literal interpretation of the Bible and as faith in the church as an institution with all the answers waned, the shelter of "home and hearth" took its place. As Benjamin Disraeli wrote:

> England is a domestic country. Here the home is revered and the hearth is sacred. The nation is represented by a family— the Royal Family; and if that family is educated with a sense of responsibility and a sentiment of public duty, it is difficult to exaggerate the salutary influence they may exercise over a nation.

It was the alpha couple supreme.

What is most interesting is that capitalism and the family values that wrought this prosperity were to a certain degree in conflict. Nineteenth century capitalism treated all family members as equals and was willing to employ six-year-old children in mines and factories in place of grown men. As early as 1835, Scottish reformer Andrew Ure wrote:

> [T]he constant aim and tendency of every improvement in machine [is] to supersede human labor altogether or to diminish its cost, by substituting the industry of women and

children for that of men.... The effect of substituting a self-acting mule (i.e., a machine) for the common mule (i.e., a man) is to discharge the great part of men spinners and to retain adolescents and children.

Upon visiting the home of an unemployed tradesman in the Midlands half a century later, Friedrich Engels wrote in *The Condition of the Working Classes in England*:

> Jack was sitting before the hearth fire, darning his working wife's sock. A tear lay in his eye. "No," the wretched man said in a thick Yorkshire accent, "there is plenty of Wark for Wemen and Bairns in this quarter but very Little for men— thou may as well go try to finde a hondred pounds, as go to find wark abouts heare—but I hed not ment neather thee nor eneyone els to have seen me manding t'wife's stockings, for it's a poar job."
>
> "I do not [k]now what is to become of us," he whimpered, "for she as been t'man now for a long time, and me t'woman— it is hard wark." When he had married, Jack said, he held a fine job and the couple "gat on very well—we got a firnished Home.... I could wark for us boath. But now t'world is turned upside down. Mary has to turn out to wark and I have to stop at home to mind Bairns—and to Wash and Clean—Bake and mend." At that point, Jack lost control and wept violently declaring over and again his wish that he had never been born.

To unregulated capitalism, men, women, and children were interchangeable. Each could be hired in place of the other. Moreover, by expanding the work force, all could be paid lower wages. In the simplified, mass production of a factory, untrained women could do jobs formerly done by skilled craftsmen. In a mine, children could squeeze into small shafts inaccessible to adults. Children could also be apprenticed as chimneysweeps. Under this regime, children could become a principal source of income, even as they put their parents out of work. The grueling logic of this system became a great threat to the family.

The response was a series of reforms that attempted to limit the role of women and children in the workplace. The English Factory Acts of 1802 limited children to twelve working hours a day. In 1810, reformer Robert Owen began a crusade for an eight-hour day under the slogan, "Eight hours of work, eight hours of recreation, eight hours of rest." It would be a long, long time before that was achieved, but women and children in Britain were granted a ten-hour day in 1847 and all French laborers won a twelve-hour rule after the Revolution of 1848. Across the Atlantic, Ohio adopted the first law limiting women and children's hours in 1852. The first minimum wage laws, adopted by Massachusetts in 1912, applied only to women and children. The U.S. Supreme Court consistently overturned these statutes, arguing that women and children should be free to contract their labor like anybody else. Not until 1938 did Congress finally write a minimum wage law that won the approval of the Supreme Court.

All this came to a crescendo in the Family Wage Movement of the early twentieth century, led by a coalition of the Catholic Church, the labor unions, the social welfare movement, and even some Socialist political parties. The core principle was that the head of a household should be able to make a "living wage" that would support his family without his wife and children having to work. As John A. Ryan, a leading American Catholic reformer, wrote in *A Living Wage*, published in 1906: "The welfare of the whole family, and that of society likewise, renders it imperative that the wife and mother should not engage in any labor except in the household."

Marvelously, the "Family Wage" achieved three major reforms at one stroke: 1) it raised men's wages by limiting the size of the workforce; 2) it strengthened families by freeing women to concentrate on child-rearing; and 3) it *equalized incomes across society*. If employment were a free-for-all, then the family that could throw wives and children into the workforce would do best. But if each family could be limited to *one breadwinner*, then a much more equal distribution could be achieved.

Although never actually formalized by statute, the Family Wage system became an informal contract in European and American society through the first half of the twentieth century. The general principle was that married women should not work. Unmarried "career girls" were a staple of the workforce, although they were usually restricted to "women's jobs" where they would not compete with married men. It was acceptable that widows and divorced mothers raising children could hold "breadwinner jobs" but the idea of a husband and wife both working (and leaving the children unattended) was regarded as socially baneful.

Victorian morality remained the touchstone of family life, both in England and the United States until the mid-twentieth century. After that, a series of "reforms" undermined most if not all of the legal structure that supported the family. The process began early in the twentieth century with the gradual shift to maternal custody, which—as outlined previously—makes divorce much easier for both men and women. From there the dismemberment of the Family Wage, the loss of censure against illegitimacy, the rise of single motherhood, and the overall retreat from marriage and family all followed. Whether all these personal liberations will create a happier population or whether we are just demolishing the foundation on which our society is built remains to be seen.

But it is worth pausing a moment to take note of the achievements of our forebears, often accomplished at great personal sacrifice. Victorian Morality was no easy regimen and even the most august were not exempt from its pains.

After Albert's death, Queen Victoria became exceedingly fond of her Scottish manservant, John Brown, seven years her junior. Members of the royal family grew to resent Brown's influence and rumors of an affair became so common that the queen was surreptitiously referred to as "Mrs. Brown." (A movie of that title was made in 1997.) Brown died in 1883. Then, after celebrating her Golden Jubilee in 1887, the queen once again became very attached to one of her Muslim Indian waiters, Abdul

Karim, who became such a confidant that it was rumored he was influencing her against the Hindu majority in India.

When Victoria finally died in 1901, every crowned head of Europe attended her funeral. (The pageant forms the opening chapter of Barbara Tuchman's great portrait of nineteenth century Europe, *The Proud Tower*.) After forty years of mourning, the queen left instructions that she once again be dressed for burial in her white wedding gown. At her side was placed one of Albert's dressing gowns with a plaster cast of his hand locked in hers. Concealed in her left hand, however, and hidden from family members, was another memento—a picture of John Brown and a lock of his hair.

CHAPTER 17

MORMONISM: A NINETEENTH CENTURY DISSENT FROM MONOGAMY

W henever I suggest to people that there might be a connection between polygamy and contemporary terrorism, they inevitably respond, "What about the Mormons? They practice polygamy, don't they? They're not out bombing people."

Anyone who thinks there was no association between violence and the religion of Joseph Smith and Brigham Young knows nothing about the history of Mormonism in the United States.

━━━━━

Joseph Smith, the founder of Mormonism, was an ambitious young man born in upstate New York's "Burnt-Over District," a region famous for its religious enthusiasms. In 1823, at the age of eighteen, he became involved in "treasure hunting," a practice that involved putting "seer stones" in a stovepipe hat and using their reflections to help direct him to buried treasures. Smith was in the process of being charged with fraud by one of his clients when he announced that he had been visited by an angel named Moroni. Moroni had revealed to him the location of a set of Golden Plates buried by one of the Lost Tribes of Israel that had made it to the New World. Smith claimed he was not allowed to move the plates until he found someone similarly gifted with prophecy. While awaiting his trial at a boarding house, he found that person in a young woman named Emma Hale. They eloped.

Smith moved the plates to his home and, with the help of a prosperous neighbor, Martin Harris, began transcribing them. Smith sat behind a curtain dictating the contents of the plates to Harris without ever letting him see them, though Harris and Oliver Cowdery, another transcriber, claimed to have seen the plates in an angelic vision and became with Smith the original "Three Witnesses." Parts of the *Book of Mormon* later proved to be lifted wholesale from the Old Testament but parts were original. As Mark Twain would later write:

> The author labored to give his words and phrases the quaint, old-fashioned sound of our King James's translation of the Scriptures; and the result is a mongrel—half modern glibness and half ancient simplicity and gravity.... Whenever he found his speech growing too modern—which was about every sentence of two—he ladled in a few such Scriptural phrases as "exceedingly sore," "and it came to pass," etc., and made things satisfactory again. "And it came to pass" was his pet. If he had left that out, his Bible would have been only a pamphlet.

Harris eventually became dubious of the existence of the actual plates, but by that time Smith was out seeking converts. One of his prophecies was that a New Jerusalem would be founded somewhere in the Midwest. In 1830, Smith dispatched Cowdery to Missouri to find the location. On the way to Missouri, Cowdery passed through Kirtland, Ohio, and discovered another breakaway congregation called the Disciples of Christ. They were practicing Christian Communism under the direction of a charismatic leader named Sidney Rigdon. Cowdery converted Rigdon and his congregation to Mormonism and encouraged Smith to come to Kirtland. As word spread of a new religion, hundreds of chiliasts and millenialists began descending on Kirtland to join. They named their congregation the Church of the Latter Day Saints. In 1837 they built a temple that still stands today.

Smith moved a young follower named Fanny Alger into his house, treating her as a second wife until the faithful Emma eventually kicked her out. Sensing that Smith might make plural marriage part of his revelations, Cowdery became disillusioned and fell away. Along with founding a religion, Smith started a bank. It failed within a month and he was soon under indictment for bank fraud. On the night of January 12, 1838, he and Rigdon hightailed it out of Kirtland and headed for Missouri.

Some of their disciples followed and work began on another temple. Cowdery pursued them with a lawsuit, the Mormons dissented among themselves, and residents in surrounding communities became alarmed about the fanaticism of the newcomers. Anti-Mormon militias began to form. On the Fourth of July, 1838, Rigdon gave an address promising a pro-Mormon "war of extermination" against the "Gentiles." A series of raids and counter-raids followed, kicking off the Missouri Mormon War. After a Mormon militia attacked a Missouri State Militia at the Battle of Crooked River, Governor Lilburn Boggs issued an executive order vowing that Mormons should be "exterminated or driven from the state."

The Mormons surrendered on November 1, 1838, and Smith and Rigdon were imprisoned. While they awaited trial for treason, a new disciple named Brigham Young rose to power. Young decided to lead the congregation of fourteen thousand Saints out of Missouri and into Illinois in search of a new home. A few months later, Smith bribed one of his jailers and escaped, joining them. The refugees set up camp on the banks of the Mississippi and Young appealed to the federal government for reparations as a persecuted minority.

Smith's millennial prophecies, meanwhile, converted John C. Bennett, the quartermaster general of Illinois. Bennett helped charter a new city, "Nauvoo" (Hebrew for "beautiful"). Nauvoo was allowed to raise its own militia and soon Smith was leading the largest armed battalion in the state.

In April 1841, Smith married Louisa Beaman as his first "plural wife" and began developing the doctrine of "sealing" marriages, providing women with a pathway to heaven. In Smith's *Doctrine and Covenants*, he declared: "In as much as this church of Christ has been reproached with the crime of fornications, and polygamy: we declare that we believe, that one man should have one wife; and one woman, but one husband, except in the case of death, when either is at liberty to marry again." The declaration is still cited by Mormons today as proof that their forebears opposed polygamy.

Behind the scenes, however, multiple marriages were becoming commonplace. Bennett, the state quartermaster, was one of the first to take advantage and in 1844 Smith and his brother expelled him. "If any man write to you, or preaches to you [of polygamy]," wrote Smith in 1844, "set him down as an imposter." Yet within a year Smith had received another "revelation" counseling his wife Emma to accept the new doctrine of "sealing." Smith continued to enter "sealing marriages" and within three years had accumulated an additional thirty women, one-third of whom were teenagers, including two fourteen-year-old girls. Emma vigorously objected but Smith cited divine revelation to prove his case.

In 1842, a would-be assassin shot and badly wounded former Missouri governor Lilburn Boggs. A former Mormon was identified as the assailant. This prompted the new governor once again to seek Smith's extradition to Missouri but the Nauvoo city council passed an ordinance saying no citizen could be extradited without approval of its municipal court, which defended Smith. Meanwhile, Bennett, the state quartermaster who had now quit the group, wrote a lurid exposé of Smith's multiple marriages. Public outrage in Illinois was rising. In response, Smith petitioned the federal government to make Nauvoo an independent territory or, alternatively, to grant the Mormons a western territory where he could establish a "theodemocracy." In 1844 he ran a third party campaign for the presidency.

On June 27, 1844, Smith and his brother Hyrum were jailed for treason. An armed mob broke into the prison and killed them both. Five men were tried for the murder but all were acquitted. Smith was buried in Nauvoo and although he had accumulated anywhere between thirty-three and forty-eight additional wives, none of them ever gave him a descendant except for his original wife Emma, who bore him nine children, four of whom lived to adulthood. When the faithful Emma died years later, she vowed that Smith had never practiced polygamy.

With Smith gone, Brigham Young became the undisputed leader. Born in Vermont and married at nineteen, he had read the *Book of Mormon* on its publication in 1830 and become an immediate convert. When his wife died in 1832, Young decamped to Kirtland, joined the congregation there, and followed the exodus to Missouri and Illinois. In 1835, he was appointed to the Quorum of the Twelve Apostles, one of the governing bodies of the church. Upon Smith's death, Young gave a speech in which he argued that leadership should pass to the Quorum instead of to Rigdon, who had always been presumed to be Smith's heir. Members of the congregation were amazed at how much Young resembled Smith and leadership passed into his hands.

Brigham Young had his first encounter with polygamy while trying to make converts among the followers of Jacob Cochran, a New Hampshire prophet of the early 1800s who had invented a practice called "spiritual wifery" and was eventually jailed for polygamy. While visiting the Cochranites in 1835, Young, at this time a widower, married one of the followers. When Smith later revealed his doctrine of multiple marriages, Young was initially appalled. "It was the first time in my life that I desired the grave," he later wrote. He recovered his composure, however, and by the end of his life had accumulated fifty-five wives, sixteen of whom gave him fifty-six children, forty-six of whom reached adulthood.

After Smith's death, anti-Mormon hostility in Illinois became so great that Young launched a new exodus in 1846 into "Winter Quarters" in Nebraska and then into what was at the time northern Mexico. Francis Parkman encountered these Mormons on the Oregon Trail:

There was something very striking in the half-military, half-patriarchal appearance of these armed 20 fanatics, thus on their way with their wives and children to found, it might be imagined, a Mormon empire in California.... As we came up the Mormons left their work and...began earnestly to discuss points of theology, complain of the ill-usage they had received from the "Gentiles," and sound a lamentation over the loss of their great temple of Nauvoo. After remaining with them an hour we rode back to our camp, happy that the settlements had been delivered from the presence of such blind and desperate fanatics.

On July 24, 1837, almost a year after departing Nauvoo, the Mormons made their famous arrival at the Salt Lake Basin, far outside the borders of the United States. In Utah it is still celebrated as "Pioneer Day." When the territory was annexed to the United States as a result of the Mexican War, however, Young once again found himself in the belly of the beast. He immediately petitioned President James Buchanan to create a new state called "Deseret" and appoint him governor. Instead, the Compromise of 1850 established the Utah Territory, but Young was appointed governor. As head of both the government and the church, he was, as Mark Twain put it, "the only absolute monarch in America."

Young obstructed federal officials and in due time President Buchanan dispatched a non-Mormon governor, accompanied by 2,500 federal troops, to regain control of the territory. The Mormons turned out their own militia and ambushed them. The two sides fought to a standoff over the winter of 1857–1858, with Young's militia stealing the U.S. Army's cattle and burning supply wagons in what eventually became known as the Utah War. Young made plans to burn Salt Lake City and move his followers south to Mexico but relented at the last minute and agreed to step down as governor. He eventually received a pardon from Buchanan but continued preaching fiery sermons against the United States, raising the sense of embattlement among the population.

Polygamy among the Mormons created other pressures, including an inexhaustible demand for more women, and small parties of Mormons trekked into other settlements to gather up prospective wives. This caused further tension among the disciples. At one point, Heber C. Kimball, who already had forty-three wives, advised Mormon missionaries:

> You are sent out as shepherds to gather the sheep together; and remember that they are not your sheep; they belong to Him that sends you. Then do not make a choice of any of those sheep; do not make selections before they are brought home and put into the fold. The brother missionaries have been in the habit of picking out the prettiest women for themselves before they get here, and bringing only the ugly ones for us; hereafter you have to bring them all here before taking any of them, and let us all have a fair shake.

In April 1857 on a visit to Arkansas, an apostle named Parley Pratt lured one Eleanor McLean away from her husband Hector who, enraged, killed Pratt. Five months later, when a wagon train known as the Baker-Fancher Party ventured through Salt Lake City—now a regular stopping place on the way to California—rumors circulated that Hector McLean was among them. Seeking revenge, a Mormon militia group disguised as Paiute Indians attacked the Baker-Fancher Party at Mountain Meadow, two hundred miles south of Salt Lake City. The homesteaders circled their wagons, piled up earthen fortifications, and prepared to repel the attack.

Worried that the settlers would soon recognize them as white men, a group of Mormons led by John D. Lee approached the wagon train waving a white flag and offered to help. They said they knew the Paiutes and could keep them at bay. Lee told the Baker-Fancher group that if they left behind their arms and cattle, he would lead them to a town thirty-six miles away where they could restock. The party of about 150 agreed. Women and children went first and the men followed in single file, each with an armed Mormon walking alongside. After they had gone about a mile, at a signal, the Mormons turned and shot each man. Two managed to escape but were eventually hunted down and killed.

Fearing that the women and children would be future witnesses against them, the Mormons shot them as well. Only seventeen infants deemed too young to remember the incident were spared. They were farmed out to Mormon families. When the Mormons asked the real Paiutes to help cover up the deed, the Indians were appalled, refusing to be bribed with the party's stock and cattle. They told the Mormons they were taught not to steal. The victims were left to be eaten by wolves. Their bones were later discovered along a two-mile stretch by U.S. Army investigators.

The Mountain Meadow Massacre caused a national sensation. It proved difficult to prosecute, however, because Utah residents resisted the investigation. Federal Judge John Cradlebaugh convened a grand jury in Provo in 1859 but the jurors refused to return an indictment. Judge Cradlebaugh publicly accused Brigham Young of having sanctioned the murders but was never able to offer proof. With the start of the American Civil War the investigation fell into abeyance, but John D. Lee was finally tried and executed for his part in the massacre in 1874.

During the Civil War, polygamy and slavery were known as the "twin barbarisms" and stamping out the practice in Utah was often put on a par with subduing slavery in the South. In 1862, President Abraham Lincoln signed the Morrill Anti-Bigamy Act outlawing polygamy in the territories. In the end, however, Lincoln decided not to enforce the law for fear that Brigham Young would enter the Civil War on the side of the South. Young, in the event, remained neutral.

In the midst of the war, a former Confederate soldier named Samuel Clemens joined his brother, who had been appointed secretary of the Nevada Territory, on a trip west, a journey Clemens would later recount in *Roughing It* under the pen name "Mark Twain." In Salt Lake City he marveled at the power of Brigham Young, "an absolute monarch—a monarch who defied our President—a monarch who received without emotion the news that the august Congress of the United States had enacted a solemn law against polygamy, and then went forth calmly and married twenty-five or thirty more wives."

Describing his first visit to a Mormon household, Twain wrote:

[W]e changed horses, and took supper with a Mormon "Destroying Angel." "Destroying Angels," as I understand it, are Latter-Day Saints who are set apart by the Church to conduct permanent disappearances of obnoxious citizens. I had heard a great deal about these Mormon Destroying Angels and the dark and bloody deeds they had done, and when I entered this one's house I had my shudder all ready. But alas for all our romances, he was nothing but a loud, profane, offensive, old blackguard!... There were other blackguards present...[a]nd there was one person that looked like a gentleman—Herber C. Kimball's son, tall and well made, and thirty years old, perhaps. A lot of slatternly women flitted hither and thither in a hurry, with coffee-pots, plates of bread, and other appurtenances to supper and these were said to be the wives of the Angel—or some of them, at least. And of course they were; for if they had been hired "help" they would not have let an angel from above storm and swear at them as he did.... This was our first experience with the western "peculiar institution," and it was not very prepossessing.

After the war, Congress made Utah's admission to the Union contingent upon abolishing polygamy. Young refused to cooperate. George Reynolds, a secretary to Young, put himself forth as a test case and was indicted and convicted of bigamy by the Utah courts, which were turning in favor of the United States. Reynolds appealed all the way to the U.S. Supreme Court on the grounds of religious freedom, but in 1878 the Court issued its famous verdict—saying that while the Constitution protected religious *belief*, it did not condone all religious *practices*.

Even as the case was being argued, Fanny Stenhouse, a Mormon apostate, published a book entitled *Tell It All: A Woman's Life in Polygamy*, with an introduction by Harriet Beecher Stowe, author of *Uncle Tom's Cabin*. Stenhouse wrote:

It would be quite impossible, with any regard to propriety, to relate all the horrible results of this disgraceful system.... Marriages have been contracted between the nearest relatives;

and old men tottering on the brink of the grave have been
united to little girls scarcely in their teens; while unnatural
alliances of every description, which in any other community
would be regarded with disgust and abhorrence, are here
entered into in the name of God.

In Washington, the crusade against plural marriage became a major issue.
The 1882 Edmunds Act made polygamy a felony and denied the right to
hold office, serve on a jury, or vote to anyone who expressed a *belief* in
polygamy. The 1887 Edmunds-Tucker Act dissolved the Mormon church
as a corporation and allowed the seizure of its property by federal mar-
shals.

In September 1890, Wilford Woodruff, now president of the Church
of Latter Day Saints, traveled to San Francisco to try to muster moral
and financial support among the city's sizable Mormon population. He
found the tide turning against him. That night in his hotel, "wrestling all
night with an angel," he wrote a 510-word statement in which he vowed
the church would abandon plural marriages. On October 6, the statement
was presented to the General Conference of Latter Day Saints and
approved. The church officially disavowed polygamy, clearing the way
for Utah's entry into the United States. Members of the Church still regard
the 1890 document as divine revelation.

In that moment the Mormons were set upon the road to becoming
the straitlaced, moral, Boy-Scout and family-oriented, economically successful and entrepreneurial, God-fearing, monogamous community they
are today, a community that produces presidential candidates who say
"Gosh!" and "Gee whiz!" But this is a world apart from the original
Mormonism of the nineteenth century—and this has been wholly to the
Mormons' credit.

"Had Max Weber lived a century later, he might have made sweeping
generalisations about the 'Mormon work ethic,'" concluded a profile in
The Economist. A recent study found that Salt Lake City has the highest

rates of upward mobility of any metropolitan area in the United States. The American dream is still alive in the provinces of Utah.

All this is the outcome of the Mormons' late nineteenth century conversion to monogamy. When Mitt Romney debated the seven other Republican presidential candidates in the 2012 primaries, it was often remarked that he was the only man on the stage who had had only one wife.

———

It would be fitting if the story ended there. Unfortunately, it does not. Not all Mormons accepted Wilford Woodruff's revelation. There were several break-away sects, the largest of which settled in Colorado City, a desolate area on the Arizona-Utah border, where they eventually established the Fundamentalist Church of Jesus Christ of Latter Day Saints (FLDS for short), and occasionally spawned offshoot communities elsewhere in the West.

State and municipal authorities have, for the most part, left them alone and very little is known about them, except for a steady trickle of wives and daughters who flee to the outside world and write memoirs. There is a whole genre of such books: *Stolen Innocence* by Elissa Wall, *Escape* by Carolyn Jessop, *Favorite Wife: Escape from Polygamy* by Susan Ray Schmidt, *Shattered Dreams: My Life as a Polygamist's Wife* by Irene Spencer.

But these women are in the minority. By 2000, an estimated 10,000 to 15,000 FLDS members were living in the Colorado City area. As Scott Anderson wrote in an insightful article in *National Geographic* in February 2010:

> [O]ne of the most curious aspects of the polygamous faith [is] the central role of women in defending it. This is not new. In Brigham Young's day a charity rushed to Utah to establish a safe house for polygamous women seeking to escape this "white slavery"; that house sat virtually empty. Today FLDS women in the Hildale-Colorado City area have ample opportunity to

"escape"—they have cell phones, they drive cars, there are no armed guards keeping them in—yet they don't.

Nevertheless, trouble came in 2002 when forty-six-year-old Warren Jeffs succeeded his late father as leader of the FLDS in Colorado City. He issued a directive, "Hands off my father's wives" and within a week married several dozen of them, excluding only his own mother. He then claimed prophetic powers to begin "reassigning" wives to other men. In January 2004, Jeffs expelled twenty men from the community, including the mayor of Colorado City, assigning their wives to other disciples. He also continued to enter "celestial marriages" with younger women, including girls as young as twelve. By some counts he had soon accumulated more than seventy wives.

Things began to fall apart in July 2004 when his nephew, Brent Jeffs, filed a lawsuit charging that Jeffs had sodomized him in the 1980s. Two other nephews soon made similar charges and one committed suicide. In June 2005, Jeffs was indicted for sexual assault and misconduct for arranging the marriage of a fourteen-year-old girl, Elissa Wall, who later wrote *Stolen Innocence*. He fled the state and was put on the FBI's Ten Most Wanted list.

Meanwhile, homeless teenage boys started turning up on the streets of Las Vegas and Los Angeles. They had been expelled from Jeffs's community for such infractions as wearing a short-sleeved shirt, watching a PG-13 movie, having a girlfriend, or talking to a teenage girl. At Jeffs's command, families would take their accused teenage sons—some as young as thirteen—and abandon them by the side of the road, telling them not to return. Within a few months an estimated three hundred of these "Lost Boys" were found living in homeless shelters or wandering the streets of western cities. Their families refused contact with them—even turning away Mother's Day presents—and some of the boys attempted suicide. Dan Fischer, a Salt Lake City dentist and FLDS apostate who has worked to place boys in foster homes, calls the sect "the Taliban of America." In 2010, filmmakers Tyler Measom and Jennilyn Merten made a documentary of the boys' plight, *Sons of Perdition*, which won festival awards.

On August 28, 2006, a Nevada State Trooper pulled over the driver of a Cadillac for not displaying its license plates. In the car were Jeffs, his brother, and one of his wives. Jeffs was extradited to Utah, where he was tried and convicted in September 2007 on two counts of being an accomplice to a rape and sentenced to ten years to life. The Utah Supreme Court overturned the conviction on a technicality and, rather than try him again, Arizona and Utah extradited him to Texas, where he was tried on two counts of aggravated sexual assault on underage girls. Jeffs dismissed his lawyers and gave long speeches to the jury claiming divine inspiration and justifying celestial marriages as the only route to heaven. At the penalty phase, prosecutors played a tape found in his possession where he instructed five twelve-year-old girls to submit to his sexual advances. He also taped himself having sex with a fifteen-year-old in the church's baptismal font. In his diary, Jeffs left copious records of his activities but at one point seems to have had regrets. "If the world knew what I was doing here," he wrote, "they'd hang me from the highest tree."

The jury sentenced Jeffs to consecutive life sentences. The mainstream Mormon church, home of the Mormon Tabernacle Choir, now abjures all connection with these sects.

———

In the nineteenth century, Brigham Young was often called "the Mohammed of America." And indeed there are obvious parallels: the charismatic leadership, claims of divine revelation, multiple wives, child brides, internal conflicts, and violent relations with neighbors. It is the link between polygamy and violence that we will turn to next as we confront the vast reaches of the Muslim world.

PART IV

THE
Non-western
WORLD

CHAPTER 18

NOMADIC WARRIORS
AND ISLAM

I n his famous book *The Clash of Civilizations*, political scientist Samuel Huntington pointed out the obvious—Islam has bloody borders. Of course, all civilizations have violent elements and have been involved in wars of conquest. But the most violent civilizations are those of polygamous nomadic warriors, and Islam, not coincidentally, sprang up among nomadic Arabs.

Islam, as a civilization, has proven itself incapable of living at peace with itself or with others, from the perpetual conflicts of the Arab world to the Muslim Moros of the Philippines. Huntington provided the data to back up his observation but reading history, or the newspapers, or Muslim writers themselves offers an equally powerful testament. As Ibn Khaldun, the famous Islamic philosopher wrote, "In the Muslim community, the holy war is a religious duty, because of the universalism of the [Muslim] mission and [the obligation to] convert everybody to Islam either by persuasion or by force.... The other religious groups did not have a universal mission, and the holy war was not a religious duty for them, save only for purposes of defense.... [Islam is] under obligation to gain power over other nations."

It is not only that Muslims have been at war with each other and against the "infidels" since the day Mohammed died. It is that historically, warrior civilizations of nomads have found sympathetic chords in Islam. The Turks were not forcibly converted to the religion of the Prophet but adopted it after conquering most of the Middle East. Genghis Khan embraced Islam as did Tamerlane the Great, who completed the Mogul conquest of India.

Relevant to our discussion is that among the nomadic warrior tribes of Mongolia and the Central Asian steppes—who terrorized the Eurasian landmass all the way from China to Rome—polygamy and concubinage were routine. Genghis Khan said the great joy of conquest was to take the wives and daughters of conquered people for himself. He took many.

Nomadic warrior culture is designed for conquest. "Raids are our agriculture" is an old Arab proverb and it applies to any and all nomads living on the edge of civilization. Conquest is how nomadic societies not only gain wealth but women as well. Genetic studies imply that roughly 16 million people—approximately the entire population of Kazakhstan—can claim descent from Genghis Khan and his male relatives.

———

The first Asian nomadic warriors to burst into European history were not Muslims but Attila the Hun, who provided a preview of what was to come. The Huns are believed to have originated in China. By around 350 A.D. they were on the borders of Eastern Europe, and in their ferocity and cruelty and taste for war, drove the Ostrogoths and Visigoths, themselves regarded as barbaric tribes by the Romans, farther west, prompting the barbarian invasions of the Roman Empire, with the Visigoths sacking Rome in 410 A.D. The Huns established a domain that extended from Armenia to the Danube with its capital on the Hungarian Plain. From there they extracted tribute from the Gothic tribes and the eastern Roman Empire. When they became impatient with

Constantinople, they invaded the Eastern Empire and laid waste the Balkan peninsula as far south as Greece. They were eventually stopped at the gates of Constantinople where the Emperor Theodosius had constructed a double wall. When Theodosius sent out an army, however, it was defeated and eventually the city had to pay double the annual tribute in gold.

The greatest of the Hun leaders was Attila, who invaded Gaul in 451 and Italy in 452 in an attempt to claim Honoria, a Roman princess, as one of his many wives. Attila and his army laid waste to most of northern France and sacked most of northern Italy, including Venice. When he reached the Po River and was about to sack Rome, however, he was met by Pope Leo I, who dissuaded him from an attack. Attila later said he saw an angel hovering over the pope's shoulder. Chastened, he retreated to Hungary, where he died a year later in 453. One story says he died in a drunken stupor celebrating his marriage to yet another conquest, the beautiful young Ildico, but another says he was stabbed in a rage by Gudrun, a jealous older wife.

If Attila was too early in history to become a Muslim, Genghis Khan was not. He was born on the plains of Mongolia sometime around 1162, well after the warrior tribes of Arabia had created a Muslim empire that would extend from Spain to India. By 1218, Genghis Khan had subdued the tribes of Mongolia, established a foothold in China, and reached the borders of Muslim Persia, which he put to the sword. Capturing city after city, the Mongols slaughtered most of the inhabitants. The Persian historian Juvayni writes that at Urgench, a trading city, fifty thousand Mongol soldiers were each given the task of beheading twenty-four men, bringing the total to over a million. The only people spared were skilled artisans, sent back to Mongolia, and young women, divided among the soldiers as booty.

Mongol forces entered Bulgaria in 1240 with a cavalry front one hundred miles wide. This was followed by forays into Armenia and southern Russia. These were not illiterate barbarians. When the Mongols entered Russia they had scholars in their train preparing to translate the Russian Orthodox Bible into Mongolian. Then the Great Khan turned his attention back to China and Tibet. There he died, according to some accounts, when a Tanguy princess he had just married castrated him with a knife she had hidden in her clothing, then committed suicide in the Yellow River. Another legend, however, says the castration only put him in a trance and one day Genghis Khan will return again to lead the Mongolian people. The death toll of his conquests is generally put at about 40 million.

While he collected wives and concubines by the hundreds and his offspring numbered in the thousands, the Great Khan always tried to ensure that Jochi, the son of his childhood sweetheart Borte, became his heir, even though there was some doubt about his paternity since he was born nine months after Borte had been kidnapped by a rival tribe. After the sons of the great Khan rampaged through the Middle East and into Europe in the thirteenth century, Jochi's progeny eventually established a new khanate, the Golden Horde, which ruled Central Asia until the fifteenth century. In 1258, a grandson of Genghis Khan invaded Mesopotamia and ransacked Baghdad. From there it was on to Egypt, and invasions of Poland, Germany, Austria, and Russia. Kublai Khan, another grandson of Genghis, established the Yuan Dynasty, the first non-Chinese emperors to rule all of China. He also invaded Vietnam and Korea, turning them into vassal states, and attempted an invasion of Japan.

In *Back of History*, the historian William White Howells wrote that "first invaders conquer a civilization, then they marry it." Kublai Khan found it politically expedient to adopt Buddhism and Confucianism in China, but much of the rest of the post-Genghis Khan Mongol empire, which included Tartars, Turks, Kazaks, Uzbeks, Tajiks, Azerbaijanis, Chechens, Kyrgyz, and Afghans, adopted Islam. The religion of Mohammed provided a ready rationale for polygamy and armed conquest.

That was certainly the case with the Mongol Muslim, descended from a grandchild of Genghis Khan, known in Western history as "Tamerlane the Great." Coming 150 years after Genghis, Tamerlane's dream was to revive the Mongol Empire. By 1369 he had established his capital at Samarkand from whence he moved north across the Caspian into Russia and conquered Persia. When the city of Isfahan rebelled, Tamerlane slaughtered all seventy thousand inhabitants and built a pyramid of their skulls. In 1398, he burst into India, arguing that the Muslim Sultanate ruling from Delhi was too tolerant of its Hindu subjects. In the slaughter that followed, Tamerlane's army, which received no pay, rewarded itself with wives, slaves, and booty.

Returning to the Middle East, Tamerlane's armies conquered Damascus. He showed no compunction at slaying fellow Muslims. He, after all, carried the reforming torch of "true Islam." In 1401, he invaded Baghdad and ordered every soldier to bring him two severed heads. The Ottoman Sultan, Bayezid I who was about to besiege Vienna turned instead to fight Tamerlane. Their armies clashed and Tamerlane won—earning the gratitude of Renaissance Europe. Christopher Marlow's admiring two-part play, *Tamerlane the Great*, is essentially a thank-you note to the conqueror for saving Vienna.

Tamerlane then returned to Samarkand and was planning to invade China to bring down the Ming Dynasty, which had overthrown the Mongols in 1368, when he caught cold during the winter campaign of 1405 and died at the age of sixty-eight. The death toll of his conquests is usually estimated at 17 million. If this all seems like ancient history, it shouldn't. Tamerlan Tsarnaev, the young Chechnyan immigrant who killed three people and wounded over 260 others at the Boston Marathon in 2013, was named after Tamerlane the Great.

The violence of Islam isn't limited to historical Mongols and Tamerlanes. The Prophet Mohammed himself led troops in battle, promising seventy-two virgins to all those who died for him. After his death, the religion he founded divided into armed camps, Shia and Sunni, that battle unto this day. But that's not even half of it. Islamic history is one long story of splinter groups going off into the desert and deciding, like Tamerlane, that what was being practiced back at the Sultan's palace is not "true Islam." Then they come crashing back into the capital, overthrow the regime, and set up another one just like it. Despite its profession as a "religion of peace," Islam is a creed that has been forever at war with itself.

The founder of Islam, the prophet Mohammed, was the last of the "Lawgivers," a group who appeared around the sixth and fifth centuries B.C.—including Zarathustra, Solon of Athens, Socrates, the Buddha, Confucius, and Lao-Tzu—all of whom established religions, laws, and civilizations that transcended tribal and ethnic bonds. Jesus of Nazareth was a relative latecomer to this cultural flowering, but offered perhaps the most radically egalitarian vision of all. As Paul, the great apostle to the Gentiles put it, "There is neither Jew nor Greek, there is neither slave nor free man, there is neither male nor female; for you are all one in Christ Jesus."

Mohammed was in some ways an egalitarian too. In the seventh century AD, he was a merchant living in Mecca, married, at age twenty-five, to a woman ten years his senior who was herself a successful merchant. They lived prosperously and had four children, although their sons died in infancy.

When he was forty, Mohammed received visions of the Angel Gabriel and retreated to a cave where the angel dictated scriptures to him that would become the Koran. Gabriel told him all men are brothers belonging to one big clan, the brotherhood of believers who worship the one true god, Allah. Mohammed was the last true prophet, surpassing Moses, Jesus, and the earlier Hebrew prophets.

In 622, Mohammed and his followers fled the hostile clans of Mecca for Medina, two hundred miles to the north, and wrote the Constitution of Medina, an attempt to unite the tribes on the basis of religion instead of blood ties. The "Ummah" would be the community of all Muslims. Jews and Christians, as "People of the Book," would be tolerated as long as they paid a special tax to Islamic authorities.

Mohammed, however, also wielded a sword. He led raids on Meccan caravans and eight years after he had fled, returned with an army of ten thousand, whereupon Mecca opened its gates to him. Mohammed's converts destroyed the old pagan idols and established an Islamic state under Sharia, the laws set out in the Koran.

Through the Koran and the Hadith (thousands of pages of commentary by people who knew Mohammed), Islam regulates the daily life of the believer as few religions have ever done. Among these rules are rules governing polygamy. Mohammed sanctioned the practice, but tried to limit it by prescribing that a man could take only four wives and had to support all equally. He did not, however, abide by this rule himself. All told, Mohammed had an estimated thirteen wives, with perhaps eleven at one time. His inner circle also took numerous wives.

What happens in a society, like Islamic society, where men at the top can accumulate multiple wives and men at the bottom are left with nothing? Well, holy war, jihad, was part of Islam from the beginning. After conquering the Middle East and North Africa, Muslim armies pushed into sub-Saharan Africa and the Caucasus in search of slaves. In the West, slavery was about work. When Western merchants shipped slaves to the New World, male slaves outnumbered females two to one. In Islamic countries, female slaves outnumbered male slaves by the same ratio. These "slaves" were in fact extra wives and concubines. Only one attempt was ever made to set up plantation slavery, in Baghdad in the ninth century, and this led to the Zanj Rebellion. After that, male slaves were recruited only for the army or to be made into eunuchs.

Despite the supply of women from conquered provinces, there was always a shortage, and the most common reaction of lower-caste Islamic men deprived of women became the desert retreat where dissident sects plotted the overthrow of the regime. Of these perhaps the most extraordinary was the "Assassins," a Shia sect founded in Egypt in the eleventh century that became the scourge of rulers all over the Islamic world. The Assassins established themselves in the Castle of Alamut, a mountain redoubt in northern Persia that is still difficult to reach today. There they set up an early version of al Qaeda, training young recruits to plant "sleeper cells" around the Middle East and insinuate themselves into the circles of the prominent officials they wanted to assassinate. Passing through the region two centuries later, in 1273, Marco Polo wrote:

> The Old Man kept at his court such boys of twelve years old as seemed to him destined to become courageous men. When the Old Man sent them into the garden in groups of four, ten or twenty, he gave them hashish to drink. They slept for three

days, then they were carried sleeping into the garden where he had them awakened.

When these young men woke, and found themselves in the garden with all these marvelous things, they truly believed themselves to be in paradise. And these damsels were always with them in songs and great entertainments; they received everything they asked for, so that they would never have left that garden of their own will.

And when the Old Man wished to kill someone, he would take him and say: "Go and do this thing. I do this because I want to make you return to paradise." And the assassins go and perform the deed willingly.

So began the familiar Islamic pattern: young men with very little hope of rising in society are offered enlistment in a dissident sect that sanctifies violence, promises revolution, and offers martyrs a prize of seventy-two virgins. This is how polygamous societies end up at war with their neighbors. A shortage of women means a volatile male population. Lower-status males are either turned into eunuchs or formed into slave armies (the Mamluks of Egyptian history) or molded into assassins and terrorists and sent off to holy war. Seventy-two virgins await in heaven—a reward it should be noted, that does not have any particular appeal to the female half of the population.

Like Mohammed, the invading Turks, who founded the Ottoman Empire in the thirteenth century, ignored the Koranic limitation of four wives and collected palaces full of concubines. Indeed, the emblem of Ottoman rule for the European imagination was always the sultan and his harem. In order to avoid dynastic wars among the numerous potential heirs, the Sultan chose a successor, then locked all the others in a special prison on the fifth floor of the Topkapi Palace where, when the heir reached maturity, they were all strangled.

The practice of collecting harems extended to court officials and the aristocracy. The harem was also the home of that other great characteristic figure of polygamous society, the eunuch. One of the peculiar paradoxes of a ruler surrounding himself with hundreds of women is that the harem always became a hive of political gossip and intrigue and eventually a center of power. Mostly this was mothers trying to promote their sons to the fore. We will see this with the Chinese emperor as well. In the Ottoman Empire, most harem eunuchs were slave boys from Nubia or Abyssinia who were castrated at age eight. Only 10 percent of the boys survived the procedure but those who did were sold for a very high price in the Turkish market. Prospective court eunuchs were not the only ones who were castrated. There were also the Janissaries—Christian slave soldiers—who often accepted castration in order to rise in government service. In Ottoman society, a poor family might sell a young son into the Janissaries, just as a young girl might find her best security in a sheik's harem.

The Ottomans, of course, were not the only Islamic power practicing and promoting polygamy and its attendant customs. The Wahhabi Movement, born at the time of George Washington, rallied Sunni tribesmen of the Arabian desert to the banner that, once again, the Islam being practiced in Mecca was not the "true Islam." They crashed into the Holy City, smashing works of art, and destroying some of Islam's most sacred shrines, including Mohammed's tomb. Then they established the version of Islam that still dominates life in Saudi Arabia. The Saudis have spent millions of their oil wealth in spreading Wahhabism throughout the Muslim world via madrasas—schools that teach young boys the version of Islam that we see in al Qaeda, the Muslim Brotherhood, and the Taliban.

While the Wahhabis are strict Islamists, they are, like so many Muslims before them, liberals when it comes to the number of wives a Muslim man may take. Mohammed bin Laden, one of Arabia's most successful businessmen and father of Osama, had fifty-four children by twenty-two wives.

In such societies, the frustrations of lower-caste Arab-Muslim men fester. Since conquest is no longer really an option, only martyrdom remains. If they cannot practice polygamy in this life, they trust that they will enjoy the fruits of the afterlife with seventy-two virgins.

"But," it is often objected, "many Islamist terrorists we've read about were already married and even had children. What could be motivating them?" This is to judge Muslim men by Western standards. In monogamous, Western society, marriage for a man means settling down, supporting a wife and children, and taking part in family life. But in polygamous societies wives are a sign of wealth. Having only one wife can be a sign of inferiority. There is no Nash Equilibrium in Islamic or any other polygamous society. The demand for women always exceeds the supply and no one ever has enough.

For men of modest means, women can seem almost unattainable. In a 2004 *New York Times Magazine* article, a graduate student in his twenties described what it was like growing up in Saudi Arabia. He said that he had never been alone in the company of a young woman. He and his friends refer to women as "BMOs—black moving objects," gliding past in full burkas. Brideprices are steep and men cannot think of getting married until they are well established in a profession. All marriages are arranged and it is not uncommon for the bride and groom to meet at their wedding. Those without money are out of luck. During the last few years of the Hosni Mubarak administration, the Egyptian government became so worried about couples having to put off marriage that it began subsidizing bride-wealth payments and sponsored mass marriages. In reporting on the early days of the Arab Spring, the *New York Times* found "the long wait for marriage" to be the second most pressing grievance in Egyptian society, behind only general poverty.

Yet because of the shortage of women, young girls have value and families refuse to lower the price of their assets. For this reason, an enormous number of marriages are contracted between cousins so that wealth is kept in the family. The only other avenue, of course, is bringing younger and younger women into the marriage pool. Muslim countries are the world champions of child marriage. In Yemen, 52 percent of girls are married before age eighteen and 14 percent before age fifteen. Some are betrothed as young as eight. In 2008, a ten-year-old Yemenite girl named Nujood Ali made headlines when she threw herself upon the mercy of a court, asking to be released from a three-month-old marriage to her thirty-two-year-old cousin who had repeatedly beaten her since their wedding. *Glamour* made her Woman of the Year in 2008 and sparked an effort to outlaw child marriages. *New York Times* columnist Nicholas

Kristof exuded, "Little girls like Nujood may prove more effective than missiles at defeating terrorists." Unfortunately, it probably won't be that easy. As long as polygamy prevails, the demand for young women will always exceed the supply, and extend to young girls.

Polygamous households, with their unrelated wives and half-siblings, create strained relationships and unavoidable rivalries. Arab fathers tend to be distant and uninvolved with their offspring. That job is left to their mothers. Osama bin Laden hardly knew his father and was engaged in numerous disputes with his extended family. Arab culture turns these endemic tensions and hostilities outward. As the Arab proverb has it: "My brother and me against my cousin, my cousin and me against my tribe, my tribe and me against the world."

Is there anyone in the Islamic world who lives differently? There is. The Druze are a Shia sect dating from the eleventh century. They are thought to have been influenced by Gnosticism, Pythagoreanism, and Neoplatonism, but are so secretive about their beliefs that they refuse to reveal them to outsiders. The Druze have often been condemned as heretics and had fatwahs issued against them. Still, they have managed to survive, often serving as a military caste and earning a reputation as fierce fighters in the service of various rulers, including the Mamluks. Today there are about a million Druze scattered across the Eastern Mediterranean basin in Syria, Lebanon, Jordan, and Israel. Aside from their tradition of military service, they generally live at peace with their neighbors and do not become engaged in sectarian fighting. They have integrated particularly well in Israel, where they predominate in many villages of the Golan Heights and sit as members of Parliament. Is there anything unique about the Druze? Yes, they are the only Islamic sect that practices monogamy.

Aside from the Druze, if there is an alternative strain in Islamic culture, it comes from the poets, especially as expressed in the greatest classic of Arab literature, *The Tales of Arabian Nights* (also known as *A Thousand and One Nights*).

The Tales of Arabian Nights tells the story of an ultimate kind of polygamy, a man who murders his wives after spending one night with them. Shahryar is a king of ancient India married to a wife whom he thinks of as loyal and faithful. When his brother comes to visit him, the brother tells him he has just caught his own wife in the arms of a black slave and killed them both. Shahryar assures his brother that his own wife is faithful, but when they set a trap to test her, they find her and her serving maids cavorting with black slaves. Convinced that all women are unfaithful, the king murders his own wife and instructs his vizier to bring him a new virgin every night. He sleeps with her and then has her executed the next morning.

His rampage continues until the vizier can find no more virgins, as anyone with a daughter has fled the city. With the vizier's own life now in danger, his daughter Scheherazade volunteers to be the next victim. When the night is almost over, however, she begins to tell the king a story. As the night wanes, she tells him she will not be able to finish and he will have to wait until the following night to hear what happens. The king agrees and postpones her execution. The same thing happens the following night and the night after that, and on and on it goes. Scheherazade enraptures the king until, after a thousand and one nights, he agrees to marry her. They live, as the saying goes, happily ever after.

A Thousand and One Nights reverses the process of courtship to fit the mode of polygamy. Instead of withholding sex until the man agrees to marry her—as monogamy worked until recently, at least—Scheherazade uses her wiles to keep the king fascinated until he decides he doesn't want to marry anyone else. The moral of the story is clear. One woman is sufficient for one man. The poet who devised *The Tales of Arabian Nights* understood this. Not only can a man and a woman find fulfillment in each other, but their civilization depends on it.

The Tales of Arabian Nights has always been vastly more popular and influential in the West than it has been in the Islamic world. But its lesson is timeless. Let us hope our Muslim brethren will one day take it to heart.

CHAPTER 19

MARRIAGE IN INDIA

I n 1927, an American journalist named Katherine Mayo created an international scandal with a book called *Mother India*, setting off a fierce debate between Indians chafing for their independence and the British still trying to maintain colonial rule. One of the participants was Mahatma Gandhi.

Mayo, who was a bit of a bluestocking, wrote shockingly of the sexual habits of India. The subcontinent, she said, was a land of frustrated men. Deprived of sexual satisfaction, they resorted to masturbation, homosexuality, and a raft of other vices, the most prominent of which was child marriage. Having spent time in Indian hospitals gathering material, Mayo reported a steady stream of child brides injured and mutilated by being forced into sexual activity when they were barely out of infancy:

1.   Aged 9. Day after marriage. Left femur dislocated, pelvis crushed out of shape. Flesh hanging in shreds.

2. Aged 10. Unable to stand, bleeding profusely, flesh much lacerated.

3. Aged 9. So completely ravished as to be almost beyond surgical repair. Her husband had two other living wives and spoke very fine English.

4. Aged about 7. Living with husband. Died in great agony after three days.

5. Aged about 10. Crawled to hospital on her hands and knees. Has never been able to stand erect since her marriage.

Mayo chronicled the horror of ten- and eleven-year-olds trying to give birth.

> [The midwife] kneads the patient with her fists; stands her against the wall and butts her with her head; props her upright on the bare ground, seizes her hands and shoves against her thighs with gruesome bare feet, until, so the doctors state, the patient's flesh is often torn to ribbons by the [midwife's] toenails. Or, she lays the woman flat and walks up and down her body, like one treading grapes.... As a result of their infant marriage and premature sexual use and infection, a heavy percentage of the women of India are either too small-boned or too internally misshapen and diseased to give normal birth to a child, but require surgical aid. It may safely be said that all these cases die by slow torture, unless they receive the care of a British or American woman doctor, or an Indian woman, British trained.

What boiled her blood more than anything else—and of many others as well—was the practice of *sati*, the burning alive of a widow, particularly as applied to child brides who had not even reached puberty when their elderly husbands died.

> Be she a child of three, who knows nothing of the marriage that bound her, or be she a wife in fact, having lived with her

husband, her case is the same. By his death she is revealed as
a creature of innate guilt and evil portent [who must die as
well].

Mayo's book set off a firestorm. Critics charged she was crusading
against Indian independence, portraying the population as degenerate
and oversexed, incapable of self-rule. Gandhi dismissed *Mother India* as
"a report of a drain inspector sent out with the one purpose of opening
and examining the drains of the country to be reported upon." Mayo
did believe that the sexual appetites of Indian males were a problem, and
that Indians were incapable of responsible political autonomy, but she
was right on her particular facts that child marriages were endemic in
India and thousands of young girls suffered horribly as a result.

One immediate legislative result of her book in India was the Child
Marriage Restraint Act of 1929. The statute outlawed marriages for young
men under twenty-one and girls under eighteen. The punishments were
mild, however—fifteen days in jail—and the law was barely enforceable.
It has since been amended many times, including the Prohibition of Child
Marriage Act of 2006, which gave children the option of later voiding their
marriages. India remains, however, a center of child marriage.

Mayo's book prompted the question of how child marriage got
started in India in the first place. Historians and anthropologists ransacked the voluminous record of Hindu literature and investigated the
marital customs of obscure indigenous tribes in search of an answer.
What they found became an anthropologist's treasure trove, as the diversity of India tossed up myriad local cultures with a wide variety of customs and traditions, including rare instances of polyandry, where a
single wife marries several husbands. The conclusion they finally reached,
however, was that unusual practices like child marriage and the long
condemned ritual of *sati* were not common until the Mogul invasions of
the twelfth and thirteenth centuries. Child marriage, in other words, was
a gift of Islam.

One might assume, then, that child marriage is the result of polygamy, which requires expanding the range of marriageable females. This
is true, but in India it bears an interesting variation.

Hindu culture divides society into castes. At the top are the Brahmins, a stratum of scholars and priests believed to have direct contact with the godhead, Brahma. Below them came the Kshatriyas (kings, warriors, law enforcers, administrators), the Vaishyas (agriculturists, cattle raisers, traders, bankers), the Shudras (artisans, craftsmen, service providers), and finally the Untouchables (who do filthy jobs like trash collection).

Hindu gods are often married and frankly sexual. There is very little asceticism in the Hindu religion. This entered instead with Buddhism, which arose in the fifth century B.C. Although Prince Gautama, the Buddha, was born and preached in India, his teachings had little impact in his homeland but spread to the rest of Asia—confirming Jesus' dictum that "a prophet is always without honor in his own country." Buddhism preaches denial of the senses and withdrawal from the world and is mainly aimed at setting rules for a self-denying priesthood. Hinduism reserves the practice of asceticism for the end of life, when the performance of duty (*dharma*), the accumulation of possessions (*artha*), and the satisfaction of desire (*kama*) have been completed and a person is seeking union with the godhead (*moksha*).

There is some scant evidence that child marriages may have existed in the Vedic period (1500 B.C. to 150 B.C.), but it is very marginal. Professor K. P. Yadav of the University of Lucknow notes:

> The Vedic mantras, such as the Rigveda mention that a girl could be married only when she was fully developed both physically and mentally and that she was to be fully developed physically before leaving her father's home. Men were advised to marry a girl with a fully developed body. One hymn mentions that a female should be married only "when she is not a child."

Indeed, the evidence suggests that, before the rise of arranged marriages, a woman could choose a husband:

> The most popular form of marriage was the Swayamvara where grooms assembled at the bride's house and . . . [she herself

selected her] husband. (Swayam = self, Vara = husband.) Instances of the Swayamvara ceremony are found in our national epics, the Ramayana and Mahabharata.

This custom seems to have eventually been buried beneath the practice of marriages arranged by the parents of the bride and groom. Arranged marriages were always accompanied by a large dowry, rather than a brideprice, a firm indication that monogamy was the rule. In India, it appears that child marriage become common later only as a *defense against* Islamic polygamy. The logic is simple. As Islam intruded with its essentially insatiable demands for women, even girls considered below a marriageable age were vulnerable. The Hindu population defended itself by marrying off its daughters, even at birth, so that they were already taken. As Sudheer Birodkar writes in "Dowry, Sati, and Child Marriage":

> During the reign of the Delhi Sultans...the worst sufferers were Hindu women. During these dark days were spawned customs like child-marriages ...
>
> The predatory Sarasenic feudal lords and prince-lings...were a source of constant threat. Hence parents would seek to get...their daughters...married off before they reached the marriage age. The custom of child marriages with the "bride" and "groom" still in their cradles was a culmination of this tendency. This way the danger to a growing girl's virginity was somewhat reduced.

The practice of *purdah*, the Asian version of veiling and secluding women, also entered India with the Mogul invasion. Despite later becoming associated with the entire country—"the veil of India"—it was and still is largely practiced by the Muslim minority. Its obvious purpose is to avoid premature sexual activity and to preserve the value of the bride-price for families with young daughters. Where Hindus have adopted "the veil," it is worn by *married* women, marking them off as no longer available.

Most fascinating and horrifying was the practice that would ultimately become the symbol of the "backwardness" and "indifference to
life" supposedly characteristic of Indian society—*sati*, the immolation of
widows on their husbands' funeral pyres.

Sati had a history in India before the Mogul invasions. Aristobulus
of Cassandreia, a Greek historian who accompanied Alexander the Great
into India, reported witnessing one. But the practice did not become
widespread until after the fourteenth century and then only among the
highest castes. Women who immolated themselves were highly honored.
Shrines were built for them and handprints in temples preserved the
memory of their sacrifice. The Mogul emperors were appalled by the
practice and did much to stamp it out, which earned them a reputation
for humanity among Western colonialists. The Portuguese and British
were also offended and passed numerous laws against it. Some Hindu
reformers picked up the banner and *sati* was eventually suppressed in the
early twentieth century, although there are still scattered reports of it
today.

How could such a barbaric practice come to be so honored in Hindu
culture? The answer lies in the story of the twelfth century Rani Padmini,
which has been immortalized in Indian legend. It was the subject of the
epic poem, *Padmavat*, by sixteenth century Sufi mystic Malik Muhammad Jayasi and was turned into an opera by French composer Albert
Roussel in 1923. In India the story is still recounted in comic books.

Rani Padmini was the queen of Chittor, a city in the northwest of
India, directly in the path of the Mogul invasion. Her husband, King
Ratnasen, was not only loyal and loving but an enlightened ruler and
patron of the arts. She had selected him as a husband in a *swayamvara*,
arranged by her father.

At their court was a magician named Raghav Chetan who practiced
evil sorcery. The king discovered his secret and had him expelled. The
wily magician insinuated himself into the neighboring court of the Sultan
of Delhi, who was always interested in expanding his stable of wives and
concubines. The magician told the sultan of Rani Padmini's extraordinary
beauty.

Posing as a friendly neighbor, the sultan asked King Ratnasen if he could meet his beautiful wife. The good-natured king consented but Rani Padmini was suspicious and refused. Trying to accommodate his powerful neighbor, the king made an arrangement where the sultan could come to his castle and view his wife in a mirror. The sultan arrived with a retinue of soldiers—who took careful inventory of the castle's defenses. When he viewed the beautiful Rani Padmini in the mirror, he became even more inflamed and vowed to have her.

While being escorted to his camp, the sultan seized and imprisoned King Ratnasen and demanded that Rani Padmini be delivered to him. The next day 150 covered palanquins, the sedan chairs used to carry important women, left the fortified castle and arrived before the sultan's camp. It was a trick: 150 armed men jumped out of them, and rescued the king.

Now the sultan and the king were in open war. The sultan laid siege to the castle and King Ratnasen realized he couldn't hold out. He declared he would open the castle doors so his soldiers could fight one last battle against the much stronger enemy, dying with honor. Rani Padmini assembled all the women of the city and said they would die rather than submit to the victors. They built a huge funeral pyre and one by one the women followed the queen to their deaths. Their sacrifice coined a new term—"jawhar"—describing a mass suicide by women in the face of dishonor.

What we have here is the Hindu version of the Rape of Lucretia. A monogamous culture is defending itself against the demands of unconstrained high-status men. *Sati* became the ultimate expression of monogamy, a statement that a high-status woman would die beside her husband rather than be the second or third wife or concubine of a polygamist. Remember it is *high-status* women who are the natural defenders of monogamy and a *Virtuous Woman* who chooses to stand beside her husband rather than submit to a more powerful man. Women who committed *sati* were universally regarded as high-status and virtuous. As cruel and inhumane as it may have seemed, *sati* represented a heroic reaffirmation of monogamy.

These three Hindu customs—child marriage that would be consummated when the children were adults, *purdah* for married women, and *sati*—were a defense against the incursion of a polygamous society. For the most part, they worked, and while India remains a vast cauldron of languages and cultures, it is a relatively stable and successful democracy. The same cannot be said for Pakistan, where the legacy of the Mogul Empire remains in full force today.

Before we leave India, it is worth mentioning that one of the great myopic delusions of the American debate over the future of the family is that the family is somehow a Western institution. To state the obvious, the civilizations of India and China are far older than the civilizations of ancient Greece or Rome—and the family is a much stronger institution in the East than in the West.

One significant difference is that in the East, more important than the nuclear family of husband, wife, and child is the "joint family"—a larger unit of several nuclear families living under the same roof. The traditional ideal is a household of grandparents and even great-grandparents, plus brothers, cousins, and in-laws. These joint families are extremely patriarchal, with a distinguished grandfather or council of elders making all the important decisions.

The importance of this larger family unit is reflected in the custom that most marriages in India are still arranged. Professor K. P. Yadav expresses the traditional Indian view:

> Even as one is born into a particular family without the exercise of any personal choice, so is one given a spouse without any personal preference involved. Arranging a marriage is a critical responsibility for parents and other relatives of both bride and groom. Marriage alliances entail some redistribution of wealth as well as building and restructuring social realignments, and of course results in the biological reproduction of families.

The marriage of a young bride is a highly celebrated event. Dressed in elaborate wedding regalia, she says goodbye to her kith and kin, perhaps forever, leaving her natal home to marry a young man she may never have met. Traditionally, these brides become virtual servants of their new household, completely under the control of the older generation until they reach an age when they are able to command respect and authority themselves.

In the 1950s, David and Vera Mace, Christian evangelists who had set up a marriage counseling service in the United States, decided to extend their efforts to India. On their first visit, they ended up discussing the matter of arranged marriages with a group of Indian girls. "Wouldn't you like to be free to choose your own marriage partners?" they asked, and got the following response:

> "Oh no!" several voices replied in chorus.... "It makes getting married a sort of competition in which the girls are fighting each other for the boys. And it encourages a girl to pretend she's better than she really is. She can't relax and be herself. She has to make a good impression to get a boy, and then she has to go on making a good impression to get him to marry her."
>
> "In our system, you see," [another girl] explained, "we girls don't have to worry at all. We know we'll get married. When we are old enough, our parents will find a suitable boy, and everything will be arranged. We don't have to go into competition with each other."
>
> "Besides," said a third girl, "how would we be able to judge the character of a boy we met and got friendly with? We are young and inexperienced. Our parents are older and wiser, and they aren't as easily deceived as we would be. I'd far rather have my parents choose for me. It's so important that the man I marry should be the right one. I could so easily make a mistake if I had to find him for myself."

The Maces eventually had to concede:

This lively discussion gave us a good deal to think about. It was our first visit to the East. In our innocence, we had simply assumed that, because we in the West are so far advanced in technology and research, in medical and social services, in educational facilities and standards of living, we must naturally also have superior attitudes to love, marriage and family relationships. We knew that arranged marriages had once been the rule in some of our Western lands, but that they had been given up in favor of free individual choice. It had seemed too obviously that this was a manifestation of human progress that we had simply taken for granted. We did not for one moment consider that there was anything to be said for the other side.

The Maces recovered their composure enough to write an excellent book, *Marriage: East and West*, published in 1960. They did not give up entirely on the Western ideals of freedom, choice, and romantic marriage, but they were highly respectful of the stability and benefits that the system of arranged marriages offers the people of India.

Arranged marriages, with their focus on responsibility and duty, can lead to frustrations. As the Maces remind us, "Marriage in India is between *families*, not individuals." Even so, the literature of India, China, and Japan is filled with stories about young couples who fell in love and defied their parents, often with tragic consequences. In eighteenth century Japan, suicides by young couples who wanted to marry but were denied by their parents were so common that for a while such stories were banned upon the stage for fear of creating an epidemic. A common theme in Indian movies and novels today is the successful immigrant who becomes romantically involved with someone from his new country, but is betrothed in an arranged marriage back home, or alternately, an immigrant who can't find a spouse in his new country and dreams of an arranged marriage in India.

Yet these extended families can prove extremely useful when it comes to immigrating to new countries. Much of the remarkable success of Indian, Chinese, and Korean immigrants in the United States has come through networks of small businesses built around family ties. There is a block on East 22nd Street in Manhattan with more than a dozen successful Indian restaurants, all owned by members of one extended family. If there is a gas station between New York and Poughkeepsie that hasn't yet been bought by Indians, I haven't been able to find it. Indians have become far and away one of the most successful immigrant groups to the United States, and the strength of their families has been a large part of that.

CHAPTER 20

MARRIAGE IN CHINA

During the Tang Dynasty, which stretched from 618 to 907 A.D., the Chinese emperor's harem was so well organized that there was meticulous bookkeeping to keep track of each woman's menstrual cycle so the eunuchs could calculate the optimal time for having the emperor make her pregnant. The date of each concubine's coupling was stamped on her arm in indelible ink so that her offspring's place in line for inheritance would be known. More than one emperor is known to have complained that the most tedious and unpleasant part of his job was servicing the many women in his harem.

On the issue of monogamy versus polygamy, China presents a real paradox. Throughout China's history, its affluent and powerful men have taken second and third wives and concubines, even whole harems when it comes to the emperor. China did not ban polygamy until the twentieth century and it is still practiced, especially by businessmen who keep wives or mistresses tucked away in different cities. Yet China never developed the aggressive ideology of conquest that we associate with Muslim culture. The "Middle Kingdom" has tended to ignore or dismiss the rest of the world. It appears that the aggressive impulses generated by polygamy were in large part tamed by the Confucian ethic of filial piety—of duty to parents and ancestors—that kept the Chinese forever looking homeward. Confucian "family values" helped make polygamy less disruptive to Chinese society.

No one man has ever shaped the culture of a country more than Confucius (551–479 B.C.) shaped the culture of China. Of the same era as the other "Lawgivers," he did not claim divinity or to be in touch with the divine. He was only a scholar. "I spent my life until 40 studying," he said. "Then I was ready." Confucius roamed China trying to persuade local authorities to appoint him to positions of power but never had much success. Eventually he became a teacher, collecting almost a whole generation of followers. After his death, his pupils compiled his lectures and sayings into a book, *The Analects*, which became to Chinese civilization what the Koran is to Islam and the Bible to Judaism and Christianity. As with Mohammad, there was also a Hadith—a set of commentaries and conversations remembered and compiled by scholars and colleagues.

Confucius said there were five basic relationships that stood at the core of society:

1. Ruler and ruled
2. Father and son
3. Husband and wife
4. Elder brother and younger brother
5. Friend and friend

Friendship was based on equality, but the others are relationships of subordination. Rulers, fathers, and husbands were obliged to use their authority wisely and fairly, but they had dominion over their various spheres.

In such a society everyone has a distinct place. In terms of the family, the ideal, albeit hard to achieve, was the "Five-Generation Family," with five generations under one roof. Inheritance was traced through the male line. The birth of a boy was greeted as a triumph while a girl was a disappointment at best and often a candidate for infanticide. A wife had not fulfilled her obligations to her husband until she had delivered him a son. Children belonged to the husband's family and an unhappy wife had no claim on them. Chinese women often chose suicide over divorce.

In such patriarchal families, the authority of the elders was never challenged. An old Chinese adage says, "No parents are ever wrong." But that was only the beginning. The authority of Chinese parents did not really begin until they died. Then they were memorialized in family shrines that were the spiritual center of the household. The dead were asked to intervene in affairs, and success and misfortune were often attributed to their influence.

These family ties were then expanded into "lineages," which are traced over generations and centuries and become clannish units that bind people together. In China, of course, the first name is the family name and there are whole villages in which everyone has the same surname. These tightly knit communities become highly exclusive and are often in conflict with neighboring lineages—although they do not go to war over women since monogamy is the general rule. The Chinese are often as likely to identify themselves with their lineage as with their immediate family. A Chinese immigrant friend of my son had his lineage, going back to the fourth century, tattooed all over his body. Confucius's lineage, the Kong family, is in its eighty-third generation of direct father-to-son heritage with the latest male heir born in 2006. It is the oldest recorded pedigree in the world.

In addition to establishing filial piety, Confucianism led to the creation of a civil service bureaucracy that administered the nation's affairs for 1,500 years. Members of the civil service, who won their jobs through competitive examinations, became an intellectual aristocracy, the "mandarins," who represented the authority of the emperor in every town and village. In a vast rural society such as China's, government examinations were one of the few ways in which ordinary people could ascend the social ladder. Once a year candidates assembled at special exam headquarters to begin the three-day ordeal. Crowds of ten thousand applicants were not uncommon. Soldiers strip-searched candidates for implements of cheating and the candidates were then locked in cubicles barely three feet wide. Their cells were furnished with three boards—one to be used as a desk, one as a seat, and one on which to sleep. If the rain leaked in and smudged their script, they were ruined. Suicides were common.

From among fifteen thousand candidates, perhaps 120 would be chosen for government positions—an acceptance rate of less than 1 percent, one sixth that of Harvard's. But those happy few were granted enormous rewards and privileges. They were immediately appointed to a government position that promised gradual ascension through the ranks, extensive administrative power, and lifetime tenure. Whereas in other societies, people of great intelligence have often been shunted aside into celibate priesthoods or a marginal life as penurious scholars, China's men of intelligence became the nation's gentry. They married, prospered, and built large families—which may be one reason the Chinese now have the world's highest collective IQ.

The mandarin bureaucrats were very conservative, and opposed to merchants and the military. When entrepreneurs built the first Chinese railroad, the bureaucracy sent out workmen to tear it up again. Perhaps the most famous bureaucratic intervention occurred after the fifteenth century voyages of Zheng He, the Chinese admiral, navigator, and explorer. From 1405 to 1433, Admiral Zheng projected Chinese power across Asia, commanding an expeditionary force of more than a hundred ships that crossed the Indian Ocean to the Strait of Hormuz and East Africa, bringing back giraffes and other exotic animals to the court of the Ming emperor. While Columbus sailed ships that were so small you could drag your hand in the water, Admiral Zheng's vessels were the size of football fields. At one point he had twenty-eight thousand men under his command.

Yet the mandarinate did not like the military and mercantile implications of these voyages and when Admiral Zheng's patron emperor died they immediately put an end to them. The admiral's ships were burned and the records of his achievement were suppressed. Today Admiral Zheng is hardly remembered in China, but his feats are celebrated among the millions of overseas Chinese emigrants who have populated Southeast Asia. His largest monument is in the Stadthuys

Museum in Malacca Town, Malaysia, where the Chinese are 23 percent of the population.

A culture that honors intellect and close family ties has enabled the Chinese to prosper as immigrants. The overseas Chinese who inhabit every Southeast Asian country by the millions have become the "Jews of the Orient," a prosperous commercial minority that usually faces hostility from indigenous populations. Most of the Vietnamese "Boat People" who were expelled by the Communist government after the end of the Vietnam War were in fact a Chinese minority. Singapore, which split off from Malaysia in 1965, is 75 percent Chinese and has become a "mini-China" run on Confucian principles under the tight patriarchal grip of Premier Lee Kuan Yew. It now has the fourth highest per capita income in the world and one out of every six residents in the population of five million is a millionaire.

———————

So how is it that a civilization so attuned to family values tolerated polygamy? The record is very clear. From the earliest times, the Chinese emperor had a harem that included hundreds of concubines. Among the general run of the population, taking a second wife was a mark of rising status. Pearl Buck, who spent decades living in China as the daughter of missionaries, authored *The Good Earth*, which is a very accurate portrait of Chinese rural life. Wan Lo, the protagonist, marries a very homely peasant girl in his impoverished youth but as his farm grows and he prospers, he takes a second wife and relegates his first wife to a separate compound—even though she has given him several sons.

The priority given to male offspring and the covert practice of female infanticide inevitably led to male-female imbalances in the population; this, in turn, led to odd arrangements in a society that was overwhelmingly poor and monogamous. As Keith McMahon writes in *Polygamy and Sublime Passion*, a study of China's transition away from polygamy after the fall of the Qing Dynasty in 1912:

> [P]olygamous marriage…was only available to elite and wealthy men, who were a small minority of the total Qing

population. Monogamy was the practice of the vast majority of people, while the large surplus of single men...meant that marriage of any sort was unavailable to them. Studies of Qing China have revealed a "skewed sex ratio" between men and women by the mid-eighteenth century, which meant there was a shortage of women available as wives for poor rural men. One solution to this imbalance was polyandry, which [some] have argued was more widespread than polygyny. Although it was likewise a minority practice, polygamy occurred in many forms, its two main categories being that in which a husband and wife of poor means arranged for the wife to sleep with other men for income, thus engaging in a form of prostitution, and that in which a poor invalid husband or a poor husband with no sons contracted with a single outside man who moved into the household, shared the husband's wife and supplied the family with his labor, income, and offspring.... Polyandry was a strategy of survival driven by downward mobility and, though widely practiced and accepted, was never an exemplary model.

Although China never developed the religion or ideology of jihad and conquest of other cultures, it did share one prominent aspect of polygamy with Muslim culture and the Ottoman Empire—eunuchs. Although it is a practice that most Chinese would just as soon forget, eunuchs played an enormously important role through fifteen centuries of Chinese history, ending only in 1923, when the last of the imperial eunuchs were turned out on the world to fend for themselves. But to portray them only as miserable servants would be wrong. As in the Ottoman Empire, there was a simple formula: harems = eunuchs = bureaucratic power.

Sometime around the early Han Dynasty, two centuries after Confucius, the harem of the emperor had grown to several hundred women, and required, it was thought, male supervision, which could only be entrusted to eunuchs. As the home of dozens of imperial wives, all seeking to advance the lot of their sons, the harem became a center of power and intrigue. Entering the harem, which required castration, became, along with competitive examinations, another means of gaining a place in the government bureaucracy.

Historian Taisuke Mitamura, in his book on Chinese eunuchs, noted:

> A cultured man had only to pass the state examination in order to obtain high position. Some among the lower classes, lacking the means to high position through the examination system, chose another road to influence—eunuchism.
>
> The trend became stronger during the Ming Era [1368–1644 A.D.], leading one Emperor to conclude that anyone having himself castrated was only aiming at rank and wealth [and to] prohibit self-castration....

The Ming Era saw a return to Confucian values, after the long Mongol occupation of China, and self-castration was seen as a violation of filial piety and family values. Self-castrators were subject to capital punishment, and individuals, village heads, and even whole lineages could be punished if they concealed knowledge of such incidents. Still, this route to social mobility was now so ingrained that the prohibitions had little effect.

> The Huang Ming Shiih Lu, a compilation of facts by the government on voluntary castrations that occurred during the Chen Te era of mid-Ming,...describes the eunuchs as pulling the strings behind the Emperor and gaining privileges for themselves and their families, and then says the lower classes, upon seeing this, competed by having their children or grandchildren castrated out of a desire for wealth and rank. It reported that in one small village alone the number castrated reached the hundreds despite the strong prohibition.... Government officials even made allowances for voluntary castration, resorting to such subterfuges as claiming it was caused by a riding accident or a childhood disease.

The practice became so epidemic as to become a major social problem.

> [P]eople living near the capital who feared being drafted into
> the government's compulsory labor force or who dreamed of
> wealth and rank were continually imitating these eunuchs and
> having themselves or their descendants castrated, and
> thronged to the military headquarters where eunuchs were
> managed. From that time their number increased day by day
> and month by month into hundreds and thousands until they
> finally brought colossal harm to the country....
>
> During the Cheng Te era about 3,500 of these failures
> presented a joint petition to the government asking to be taken
> in. The government designated Nan Yuan, a vast park with
> orchards and ponds, in the suburbs of Peking, as a place for
> them to stay. The number of eunuchs admitted into the park
> increased by tens of thousands, and an enormous sum was
> expended on rations.
>
> The government finally sent them back to the provinces.
> But since the eunuchs had no place to go, they became home-
> less wanderers in the southern part of Hopei Province. Many
> became beggars or highway robbers. Local officials ignored
> them, with the result that they preyed upon the ordinary
> people.

The practice of self-castration continued right up until the Republican
Revolution of 1912. Even then, the last emperor was allowed to live in
the Imperial Palace with his entourage for another decade. Finally, on
November 5, 1924, the emperor and his entourage were asked to leave.
Dr. Tokio Hashikawa, a Japanese historian who witnessed this exodus,
wrote later:

> Shortly after noon on that day I saw a host of eunuchs with
> boxes and sacks containing their belongings slung either on
> their backs or on sticks carried by two men. They were coming

out of the Husan Wu Gate on the north side of the Tzu Chin Palace, crying pitifully in high-pitched, feminine voices.

The number of eunuchs expelled from the palace that day was estimated to be 470.

———

The greatest and most grotesque attack on the family in China came, of course, from the Communist regime of Mao Tse-tung. Like all radical intellectuals since Plato, Mao saw the family as a strong rival institution to his plans for a totalitarian state. The Communists "liberated" wives from their husbands, young people from their elders, peasants from land-owners, atomizing society until everyone was solely a creature of the state with personal and familial identity virtually obliterated. At the height of the Communists' farm collectivization, children were taken from their parents at birth and raised collectively. Parents were not even allowed to know which children were theirs. Yet the family survived. After the "Three Bitters Years" of famine from 1959 to 1962, in which millions died of starvation, collectivization slowly unwound and normal life returned.

The problem that China faces now is the One-Child Policy, instituted by Mao Tse-tung as his dying legacy in 1979. Given China's age-old emphasis on the male heir, the overwhelming response in the populace has been that this One Child should be a son. Estimates are that almost two million infant females are abandoned every year in China and the orphanages are stuffed with them. Almost two million Chinese girls have been adopted in the United States. Meanwhile, the policy has created several generations of "little emperors," only boys spoiled endlessly by their parents and lacking experience with siblings.

The result is a demographic time bomb. China now has the most skewed male-female ratio in the world, 120 marriageable males for every 100 females, a level reached only by polygamous countries like Saudi Arabia. The name the Chinese have attached to this surplus male popu-lation is "bare branches," meaning they will not marry and flower.

In their 2004 book, *Bare Branches: The Security Implications of Asia's Male Population*, demographers Valerie Hudson and Andrea den Boer warned that such surplus male populations are characterized by high levels of crime, addiction, and poverty, and that governments usually end up turning these pent-up aggressions outward against other countries.

> The Chinese government has attached enormous national pride and prestige on its ability to bring about Taiwan's eventual reunification with the mainland. Within twenty years, China may have close to 40 million bare branches to deploy in the event that tensions with Taiwan escalate into a military confrontation. The security logic of high sex-ratio cultures predisposes nations to see some utility in interstate conflict. In addition to stimulating a steadier allegiance from bare branches, who are especially motivated by issues involving national pride and martial prowess, conflict is often an effective mechanism by which government can send bare branches away from national population centers, possibly never to return.

What has kept the lid on these tensions is the millennial-old tradition of China as the Middle Kingdom, the stable, orderly society built around the Confucian values of loyalty to family, lineage, and the state. But such restraint may not last forever. We can only hope that those "bare branches" hanging out in drug dens and engaging in petty crime do not discover Islam.

PART V

MODERN QUESTIONS

CHAPTER 21

THE BLACK FAMILY AND THE EMERGENCE OF SINGLE MOTHERHOOD

I n 1965, Daniel Patrick Moynihan, an obscure Assistant Secretary of Labor in the Lyndon Johnson administration, published a memo warning of the "coming crisis" of single-parent families among African Americans. Moynihan had been raised by a single mother in the Hell's Kitchen neighborhood of Manhattan and was acutely aware of the disadvantages that came with having only one parent.

"The Negro Family: The Case for National Action" sounded an alarm. An unprecedented 25 percent of black children were being born out of wedlock! This had never occurred in any other culture. Moreover, the trend now seemed to be moving independent of poverty and employment. The figure that had caught Moynihan's eye was the comparison between black unemployment and the size of the welfare rolls. Since Aid to Families with Dependent Children (AFDC) became common in the 1940s, unemployment and welfare had always moved in tandem. When unemployment went up, welfare applications went up and vice versa.

This indicated that people were applying because they had lost jobs and times were hard. But as the country pushed toward full employment in the mid-1960s, a remarkable shift had occurred—the "Moynihan scissors," as it became known. Even as black unemployment approached unprecedentedly low levels, the welfare rolls were climbing. Something new was happening.

Moynihan identified it as a rise of illegitimacy and the breakdown in family formation. Although African American women were not getting pregnant at higher rates, they were no longer marrying the fathers of their children. Instead, they were going on the welfare rolls. Moynihan said this portended difficulties that went far beyond racial discrimination and civil rights, which were the principal concerns of the era. The breakdown of the family, Moynihan warned, would produce intergenerational poverty in which men would become an unmoored cohort freed from the traditional responsibilities of child support and protecting their families, while the children of these new households, following the role models around them, would produce another generation of unwed mothers. Borrowing a phrase from Kenneth Clark's *Dark Ghetto*, published in the same year, Moynihan said this would lead to a "tangle of pathologies," including delinquency, joblessness, school failure, crime, fatherlessness, and all that came to be characterized as "underclass" behavior.

What happened next is well known. Basically, all hell broke loose. President Johnson embraced the issue during one speech at Howard University and then fled for cover. African American leaders sounded a unanimous chorus declaiming that Moynihan was a racist and that the problems of African Americans lay in discrimination and the legacy of slavery and had nothing to do with marriage. Soon a battalion of academics went to work producing treatises proclaiming that there was nothing wrong with single-parent homes and that instead it was the "white" two-parent family that was a tangle of pathologies. Moynihan had mentioned that African family traditions were "matriarchal" and that this might have something to do with the situation. Some scholars denied this, but others said it was indeed true and celebrated it. Feminists got into the act, finding the whole concept of single motherhood "heroic" and saying it offered a noble alternative to the "patriarchal" family.

The debate raged off and on over the next three decades while—not incidentally—the problem continued to get worse. By the late 1970s illegitimacy among Africa Americans had risen to 50 percent and was pushing even higher in big city neighborhoods. At the beginning of his presidency, Jimmy Carter called for a White House conference to confront the problem. But infighting over who should sit on the commission kept it from assembling until 1980, at which point it became the White House Conference on *Families* with a single mother at its head.

Instead of addressing the problem of single motherhood, the problem became how to assist single mothers. School systems set up nurseries for the benefit of their new childbearing teenagers. Social welfare programs were expanded. Medicaid became an automatic addendum to AFDC, along with food stamps and sometimes even priority in public housing. Foundations sponsored programs on how to keep teenage mothers in school and even send them to college. Becoming a mother at fifteen almost became attractive. As Governor Mario Cuomo of New York said, "If we take a 16-year-old single mother, get her on welfare, give her food stamps, get her in her own apartment and have her back in school taking classes, what's the problem?"

What remained clear throughout the era, however, was that whatever was happening among African American families was *not* happening among whites. Illegitimacy rates among whites were nowhere near that of blacks, even when they were matched by income and other characteristics. This seemed to suggest that cultural factors were at work.

In his book *The Truly Disadvantaged*, published in 1987, William Julius Wilson, an African American scholar at the University of Chicago, tried to argue that the problem was the loss of factory jobs in urban neighborhoods. This had impoverished black men, who were no longer able to support their families. Black women went on welfare because they had nowhere else to turn. While this argument seemed superficially acceptable, it left several big questions unanswered. Why was the phenomenon limited to African Americans? Weren't other ethnic groups also affected by the loss of factory jobs? And why had family breakup only occurred after 1960? Hadn't things been *more* difficult for African Americans before the Civil Rights era or during the Great Depression? Weren't African Americans succeeding now in ways they hadn't before?

In 1986, Bill Moyers tackled the subject in an ambitious TV documentary entitled *The Vanishing Family: Crisis in Black America*. Assigned to little-watched TV times, the show nevertheless produced several memorable moments: 1) a room full of new mothers telling Moyers they had no interest in marrying the fathers of their infants; 2) a twenty-two-year-old lothario, in the delivery room watching his girlfriend give birth, bragging to Moyers about how many children he had fathered; and 3) an older black man in a pool hall complaining, "Those women are married to welfare. They're more married to the welfare than they are to the guy who's sleeping next to them at night." All this seemed to suggest that the subsidy for illegitimacy embedded in AFDC was having an impact. Defenders, however, refused to countenance the idea. "They have children because they want someone to love, not because they want to make money," was the common response. But wanting someone to love did not explain why illegitimacy was so much higher among African Americans than among whites, who presumably also wanted someone to love.

Another common response was that if welfare incentives to illegitimacy had a disproportionate impact on African Americans, the answer had to be found in the history of slavery. But if that were the case, why was it that the "crisis" of the black family didn't begin until the 1960s? Nor was the problem the disintegration of the black family as a whole, but a very specific phenomenon—teenage girls failing to marry when they became pregnant.

The argument that the African American family had not survived slavery was soon obliterated with the publication of Herbert Gutman's *The Black Family in Slavery and Freedom: 1750–1925*. Doing extensive research on slave customs, Gutman found that slaves had had their own marriage ceremonies and traditions completely unrelated to those of Southern whites—indicating they were indigenous and not learned from their masters. African Americans, for instance, did *not* approve of first cousin marriages, a practice extremely common among whites in the

South. They had wedding customs such as "jumping the broomstick" that had no American counterpart but were clearly brought from Africa.

Most significant, Gutman turned up careful records kept at two major plantations covering the period from 1776 to the outbreak of the Civil War, documenting the mother and father of each child. Both annals showed clearly that the vast majority of children were growing up in two-parent homes. Among one hundred families in the records at the two plantations, only eight constituted an unwed mother with her children.

Remarkably, Gutman's research also turned up a wave of marriages among blacks during and immediately after the Civil War. Anticipating emancipation, couples became worried that their "slave marriages" would not be recognized and they would be living in sin.

> [In] Goochland County, Virginia, ex-slaves registered 742 marriages in 1866. In 1860, the county had 1498 adult slave men and 1231 adult slave women. It is assumed that there were 1231 slave couples in 1860…The Freedman's Bureau registered slave marriages in 1866 and four county registers survive. [The] registers disclosed that mostly laborers and field hands registered slave marriages. The percentage of possible slave marriages was high in all four places: about three in ten among the Rockbridge [County] blacks, nearly half among the Nelson [County] blacks, three in five among the Goochland blacks and nearly two in three among the Louisa [County] blacks. The two counties with the fewest white residents and the most plantation slaves in 1860 had the highest percentage of possible registered slave marriages.

In North Carolina, couples were charged a fee of 25 cents to register their marriages. Gutman quotes the reminiscences of a Raleigh schoolteacher enlisted to the cause of registering marriages:

> One "grey-headed woman," who called at her schoolroom, "had six eggs in her basket; it was all she could spare…." She

wanted to "buy a ticket" because "all 'spectable folks is to be married, and we's 'spectable; me and my old man has lived together thirty-five years and had twelve children." Another woman, who brought a quart of strawberries to buy the "ticker," said "Me and my old man has lived more than twenty-five years together; I's proud the children's all had the same father."

Gutman found that into the first decades of the twentieth century, the vast majority of African American children raised in major cities lived in two-parent homes. Other data showed that while illegitimacy and marital breakup were more common among blacks than whites, the single-parent household was a recent invention, becoming predominant only after 1960.

So what had happened? The last major effort to answer this question was made by Nicholas Lemann, a New York journalist, who in 1991 published *The Promised Land: The Great Black Migration and How It Changed America.* Lemann traced the path Southern blacks had taken moving north to Chicago and other cities in the early twentieth century, lured by industrial jobs and the opportunity to escape from the Jim Crow South. It was indeed a huge migration and played an important part in shaping the character of many Midwestern cities. Hanging over the whole narrative, however, was the question of single motherhood—now approaching 75 percent of all African American births.

In order to trace the problem to its roots, Lemann visited Alabama and Mississippi where he interviewed African Americans who lived in cities and small towns. They assured him, in the most confidential tones, that "the rural" was in fact the seedbed of single motherhood. The practice had been common in the network of tenant farms and dirt-floor shacks that spread across the cotton-growing areas of the South, his informants assured him. From there he drew the obvious conclusion—these same rural people had carried it with them when they moved up North. Lemann never took the trouble to actually go out in "the rural" and see for himself, but he assured his readers that this was the answer to the mystery of black single motherhood. *The Promised Land* won the 1992 PEN/Martha Albrand Award for First Nonfiction and was nominated for the Pulitzer Prize.

And there the search for the origins of African American single motherhood more or less came to an end. After two previous vetoes, President Bill Clinton finally signed a welfare reform bill in 1996 and the debate faded into the past. While welfare dependency lessened, mainly through single mothers entering the work force, marriage rates did not improve and a staggering 80 percent of black children are still born out of wedlock.

The question then remains, what happened? Why did single motherhood suddenly explode after 1960? I think the answer can be discovered in those plantation records that played such a critical role in Gutman's thesis. Look carefully at the pattern Gutman discovered. He was perfectly right in saying that the vast majority of children ended up in two-parent families. But there is more to it than that. The most common pattern was for a woman to have one or two children by another man, often an "unknown father," and *then* settle down into a long-term relationship with a husband.

This is a pattern that can be traced to Africa. West Africa, remember, has the highest concentration of polygamy in the world. It is not the polygamy of Muslims, where women are sequestered and purchased by husbands at a hefty brideprice. Instead it is a polygamy where *women are extremely independent* and often far more economically productive than men. Most important, *it is not at all unusual for a woman to have children before she is married in Africa.* They are called "children of fortune" and generally considered as proof of fertility. It is common both in Africa and the Caribbean for a woman to have one or two children and have them cared for by her natal family before she is married. Only when the burdens of childrearing become too great on the grandparents does she set out to find a husband.

So what happened when this African mating pattern met Western culture? As Gutman details, any attempts among slaves to set up polygamous relationships were generally stamped out by slave owners on the basis of Christian morality. By the nineteenth century, African Americans had largely adopted Christian-based monogamy. But as Margaret Mead once wrote when describing Jamaican culture, it was a "brittle monogamy" with frequent divorces, multiple marriages, and early unwed pregnancies, as the plantation records clearly indicate. If you count them up, you will find that while 90 percent of the children on the two plantations ended up living in two-parent families, fully 40 percent of the births were fathered in early pregnancies involving other men.

I saw this pattern myself as a Welfare Rights volunteer worker in Clark County, Alabama, in the late 1960s. (It was my work in welfare rights that convinced me welfare wasn't such a great thing.) My job was to go around the county finding young unmarried mothers. It wasn't difficult. Almost every other household had a teenage mother living with her parents, with the grandparents often taking the lead role in childcare. This was considered normal. The African American teenagers among whom we worked refused to believe that one of our fellow volunteers—a twenty-three-year-old woman from Oregon—did not have a baby waiting for her at home.

Yet these girls eventually married. Most of the older women in the town had husbands. Granted, these men were often absent for long periods of time, and it was assumed that they were practicing a covert polygamy and had "outside children" and second wives in other towns. This was a common pattern in the South, memorialized in the Temptations' mournful 1970s threnody, "Papa Was a Rolling Stone," one of the most painfully evocations of American black life ever penned. But when all was said and done, even with relatively high illegitimacy rates, African American families did form around two-parent households until the 1960s. So what happened then?

With almost surgical precision, Aid to Families with Dependent Children began intervening at the precise moment when African American families usually formed—*after* a young woman had one or two illegitimate children and was ready to marry. Until the 1960s, most states recognized that Aid to Families with Dependent Children was designed for "widows and orphans." Before 1960, single mothers were not even allowed in New York City public housing. But as awards to unwed mothers eventually became automatic, especially under pressure from the "welfare rights movement," things changed. Now, instead of grand-parents telling a young mother to find herself a husband and move out, the young woman had another option. She could "marry the state" and collect a monthly check and other benefits, perhaps even a subsidized apartment. At that point, why surrender Medicaid and food stamps for the uncertain support of a man? As a Wisconsin mother of two illegiti-mate children by two different fathers once assured me, "You can't raise a child without that Medicaid card."

So to answer Mario Cuomo's question, "What's the problem?" the problem is that breaking down family formation seems to create inter-generational poverty and a lot of social chaos as well. Where do men go if they aren't lodged in families taking responsibility for raising children? They are out on the street, in pool halls, drug dens, and sooner or later in prison. A staggering 33 percent of African American men are now incarcerated at some point in their lives and a black man without a high school diploma is more likely to go to jail than to find a job. Workforce participation among unmarried men is at an all-time low. Unattached men have shorter lifespans and much higher rates of drug addiction and alcoholism, and more than that, they make life difficult and dangerous for everyone else living in their neighborhoods.

Yet the problem of absent fathers gets relatively little attention because it is usually redefined as "the feminization of poverty," and any attempt to impose monogamous standards is dismissed as reaction-ary or even part of an alleged "war on women" that would deny women their right to state benefits. The only real beneficiary here is the Democratic Party, which gains immensely since women who look to the state for deliverance from marriage vote overwhelmingly in their favor. African American women now vote 95 percent for Democratic candidates and have become a decisive bloc in many elections. Now that single motherhood is spreading to lower-class whites, we can expect the "marriage gap" to become an even greater social and polit-ical divide.

The most sobering lesson, however, may be this: although the two-parent family is a strong institution going all the way back in human evolution, it is not indestructible. With the proper economic incentives, it can be torn apart. And once it has been dismembered by the many adverse incentives offered by a contemporary welfare state, it may be very difficult to put back together again.

CHAPTER 22

WHAT IS HAPPENING TO THE FAMILY TODAY?

W e started off this book by celebrating how monogamous culture had triumphed in the 1950s—how men had been domesticated to a degree probably never before achieved in history and how there was "a girl for every boy and a boy for every girl." When the time came for critics to tell us what was wrong with this picture, it was necessary to import a word from another culture—"macho"—to express what was bad about men. In Spanish, "macho" describes a man who sleeps with every woman he meets and will kill any man who tries to seduce his sister. In English and American culture, the term had been "gentleman," derived from "gentle man." Certainly not all American men were gentle, but it was an ideal that had been long established and sometimes attained. You don't hear the term too much anymore.

Today the ideal of a "patriarchal" family and middle-class respectability is something almost everyone is rebelling *against*. Couples who are perfectly well suited for each other go ten years without tying the knot because they do not want to surrender to bourgeois values. Rebelling against "the establishment" is something that anyone can do, like getting a tattoo. In this new kind of conformity, everyone is rebelling against a 1950s establishment that hardly exists anymore.

So what happened? In the course of fifty years, how did marriage and a two-parent family go from being an ideal to which everyone could aspire to a fairytale to which only the most privileged can aspire? Why are 40 percent of children now born to single mothers? Why are only 40 percent of all children living with both their natural parents? Why are married couples less than half of all households and marriage rates at their lowest level in history? Why was Mitt Romney, an industrious, successful family man completely devoted to his wife and children regarded as some kind of space alien or at least a relic from another era when he ran for president in 2012?

The first thing to keep in mind—something we have learned throughout these pages—is that monogamy is, above all, a *cultural construct*. It is an *artificial* system that human societies impose upon themselves in order to create a more constructive social milieu. It does not satisfy everyone's individual desires. At its most demanding, it becomes a rigid moral code that stigmatizes all manner of deviation—homosexual inclinations, the temptation to dally with your neighbor's wife, pre-marital intercourse, having a child out of wedlock and so forth. There is nothing completely natural about monogamy, which is why it is always so easy to undermine.

Left to their natural state, almost all species end up practicing polygamy, since the strongest males will dominate the physically weaker males and females. The polygamous societies of Islam and tropical Africa and of pre-history are much more "natural" in that they give vent to a wider range of the deepest human impulses. They also end up promoting endless warfare among a population of intensely aggressive males. Monogamy is the end point of civilized behavior that recognizes, however unconsciously, that enforcing the rules creates advantages at the *societal* level. If we want a society that satisfies everyone's most individualistic desires, we will not stick with monogamy for very long.

Now granted, our evolutionary history has produced biological adaptations that make us more fit for monogamy. The reduction of male incisors was only the first. Married men experience lower levels of testosterone and a marked reduction of aggressive behavior. Even fruit flies raised in an artificially monogamous environment have been found to be less aggressive, while the females are in turn less defensive. Research has shown that monogamous men even suppress their awareness of attractive females when their wives become pregnant.

There is plenty of evidence that human beings are indeed happiest when living in stable, long-term marriages and—not incidentally—their children are much better off as well. But monogamy does ask people to make certain sacrifices. So let us begin by exploring what some of these sacrifices may be and how some people might eventually grow tired of making them.

Perhaps the most critical blow to the monogamous culture of the 1950s came with the demise of the "family wage," the system adopted informally in America and Western Europe at the start of the twentieth century. The goal of the family wage was to strengthen families and distribute income more evenly across society by limiting everyone to one wage-earner per family. In practice, this became a simple rule: unmarried, divorced, or widowed women could work but married women were expected to stay at home with their children. This was regarded by middle-class reformers as a triumph for lower-class women who would now be able to create a protected domain in the home just as their middle-class counterparts had already done.

Unfortunately, the family wage was a disadvantage to one specific group—highly educated, professionally ambitious women. They would spend four years at college gaining useful skills and then be forced to "retire" as housewives. One college graduate who found this particularly galling was Smith-educated Betty Friedan, who, when she married in 1947, was told by her employers that she must give up her job at a Peoria newspaper. Friedan was outraged but found work writing for women's magazines in New York and pursued her grievance, assembling a mountain of data and interviews, until they were finally published as *The Feminine Mystique* in 1963.

Returning to a Smith reunion, Friedan had been appalled by the undergraduates she found pursuing their "Mrs." degree. She thought women should be out studying physics and playing baseball. At the time, the average American woman married at age nineteen. Women, the vast majority of them single, constituted 30 percent of the workforce. To Friedan, this was a huge waste of brainpower. Women should be employed in professions instead of wasting their time at home.

Her manifesto had an earth-shattering impact. Today, women make up 47 percent of the workforce and most young college women would be offended at the suggestion that they are *not* preparing for careers. In 1950 women made up only 33 percent of undergraduates. Today they are a 57 percent majority. Women collect 60 percent of master's degrees and 52 percent of doctorates. They make up 47 percent of law students, earn 48 percent of medical degrees, and occupy 78 percent of the places in veterinary schools. Never in world history have women constituted such a large segment of the professional workforce.

But all this has come at a price, mostly concentrated at the lower end of the economic scale. As educated women entered the labor force, they displaced less-educated men. These men saw their job prospects diminished and so their wives in turn had to take jobs in order to supplement their husbands' salaries. During the recession years of the 1970s, the joke was that women were being forced into liberation because it now took two incomes to pay the bills. That is now a rule of thumb. But it was not the only result. As less-educated men's job prospects diminished, they also became less "marriageable," making family formation at the bottom end of the scale all the more difficult.

In 2013, the Pew Foundation released a study claiming that women were now the principal breadwinners in 40 percent of all households, an all-time high. This was celebrated as a triumph of women's progress. On closer inspection, however, the numbers proved much less salutary. In only 15 percent of married households did the wife make more than her husband. The explosion of female breadwinners was composed primarily of single mothers—56 percent divorced/spouse absent, 44 percent never married. The median income for these households was $23,000, while the median for the married couple households was $80,000. The real story of the past fifty years has been the increasing stratification of American society, with educated, two-income families at the top pulling away while family formation at the bottom has fallen apart.

The problem appears to be that what seems like only declamation in the upper-educated precincts of society translates into self-destructive behavior at the bottom. The Pew study found that divorce among middle-class people has actually stabilized since the 1980s and the number of divorced single mothers has not increased significantly. But the population of never-married mothers at the bottom has exploded. Among these, 40 percent are black and 24 percent are Hispanic. Half have only a high school diploma or less. Thus, while upper-educated women are often making the loudest case for the independence of women, it is among the poorest that the theory is being put into practice.

This is one aspect of the changes that began in the 1960s. A second and perhaps more significant has been the sexual revolution and resulting separation of sex from childbearing.

As we traced the gradual triumph of monogamy in Western Civilization we saw how its most important pillar was the Virtuous Woman. The Virtuous Woman was one of moderate means who resisted the importunities of a higher-status man to become his mistress or morganatic wife, and remained true to the man who would marry her. Along with this, of course, went the burden of persuading that man to marry her and remain true to his responsibilities of supporting her and her children. This is an enormous burden and one can understand how women might grow weary of it.

Being virtuous involved sexual chastity and before the advent of widely available contraception, pre-marital sex always carried the danger of unwanted pregnancy. I still remember my father advising me as a teenager—"It's a moment of pleasure, a lifetime of regret." Many a young couple ended up in a "shotgun wedding" to preserve their respectability. But unintended pregnancies, especially in the blue-collar strata of society, were also a key to family formation. A survey of working-class neighborhoods in Philadelphia in the early 1970s found that more than half of the marriages had occurred when the couple "made a mistake." The young lovers might date exclusively, sleep together, even move in with each other, but resisted marriage—both wanting to maintain their sense of independence. Then the woman would "accidentally" get pregnant and they would marry.

All this worked until the arrival of contraceptives, followed by legalized abortion. "The pill," introduced around 1960, freed young couples from the fear of pregnancy and opened up a whole new world of sexual experimentation. Gone were the worries about whether the woman would have her period at the end of the month. Abortion went even further. Now even if a young man *wanted* to marry the woman he had impregnated, she might not be willing. Alternately, it was no longer obligatory for the young man to marry his pregnant girlfriend because "she can always have an abortion." In short, within a very few years, the struts that had supported family formation, especially among the blue-collar classes, had been kicked out from under everyone.

Some at the time speculated that contraception might actually improve marriage. Reformers such as Bertrand Russell had long argued for "trial marriages" as a way of lowering divorce rates. Freed from the specter of forced unions, couples would now have more time to experiment and make the right choice. Unfortunately, it didn't work out that way. Saving sex for marriage had been a way of duplicating the bonding experience of other monogamous species. As late as the 1960s, essayist Ben DeMott could write about "the sublime release of sexual passion that comes during the first year of marriage." Today, however, in a world where college students regularly "hook up" with people they don't even like, all the novelty of sex has been thoroughly erased. If people are going to marry, it won't be for sex.

Coincident with this, and in many ways the outcome, was the discovery of untapped female sexuality, which became fodder for the burgeoning feminist movement. Feminists claimed that female sexuality lay far outside the bounds of conventional marriage. As Mary Jane Sherfey, an early pioneer in feminist theory, wrote in *The Nature and Evolution of Female Sexuality* (1966):

All relevant data from the 12,000 to 8000 B.C. period indicates that precivilized woman enjoyed full sexual freedom and was often totally incapable of controlling her sexual drive. Therefore, I propose that one of the reasons for the long delay between the earliest development of agriculture (c. 12,000 B.C.) and the rise of urban life and the beginning of recorded knowledge (c. 8000–5000 B.C.) was the ungovernable cyclic sexual drive of women. Not until their drives were gradually brought under control by rigidly enforced social codes could family life become the stabilizing and creative crucible from which modern civilized man could emerge.

Sherfey was once again engaging in the favorite feminist fantasy that paternity was unknown in prehistory and women ran free in sexual abandon before being immured by "patriarchy." (In the feminist lexicography, "patriarchy" refers to any family constellation that involves an adult male.) The main accomplishment of patriarchy, according to this theory, had been to suppress women's almost unlimited sexual appetite.

Yet none of this seemed to square very much with reality. For one thing, there is the biological principle of female coyness, which is not limited to humanity. In almost every species the female resists sexual intercourse because she has only so many eggs while the male, with far more numerous sperm, can be more indiscriminate. This means females must *suppress their sexuality* or have it suppressed for them by natural selection. There was a common scenario in colleges in the 1960s where a dashing lothario would rack up a string of conquests among the women on campus. Then suddenly he would run up against a woman who refused to sleep with him. So he would marry that one. Even today, advocates of "The Rules" advise young women that the best way to interest a man in a long-term commitment is to hold back on sex.

The liberation of sexuality from procreation, however, has revealed that women doubtless have greater capacity for sexual adventure than the Victorian Age would have imagined. In previous centuries, women who did not bridle their sexual appetite usually descended into lives of prostitution or a series of fruitless short-term relationships with men. They did not usually end up as wives and mothers. Now we have female high school teachers who seduce their students, neighborhood mothers who sleep with teenage boys, "groupies" who throw themselves at rock stars, and a whole variety of scenarios where women are the sexual aggressors. All this has made courtship a completely different affair, if not obliterating it completely.

But there is something else going on here as well. At the bottom of feminist rhetoric has always been the idea that women can do without men completely. "A woman without a man is like a fish without a bicycle," is the way Gloria Steinem elegantly expressed it. Once again, for high-status women with access to many resources—and possibly a high-status male as well—this may be just rhetoric. But for a young minority female facing the possibility of marrying only a footloose, irresponsible, jobless young man, the stability of a welfare grant is extraordinarily appealing. Moreover, having this financial backing allows her to pursue men who might otherwise not have been attainable. Instead of trying to lure a particularly attractive man into a long-term relationship, a one-night stand may be sufficient to "start a family."

And this opens up an entirely new world.

In 1979 Elizabeth Fisher, a women's studies professor at New York University versed in anthropology, offered a completely different view of human evolution. In a book titled *Women's Creation*, she postulated that the "alpha couple" that set us on the road to human evolution was not a male and female but *mother and child*. Fisher even maintained that the primary *sexual* relationship for human beings is between a mother and her infant, with "patriarchal" sexuality grafted on only later.

> Even a slight exposure to ethnographic literature points up the contrast with Western mother-child relations, where sexuality is culturally repressed. We can hardly imagine an American mother engaging in labial, clitoral, or penis stimulation of her infant without guilt or social condemnation, yet this is an accepted and expected pattern in many societies where mothering and sexuality are closely linked.
>
> As Western taboos have begun to loosen, more and more women acknowledge the eroticism of the mother-infant relationship. The sensation of nursing is another kind of orgasm.... In

our culture, where civilization and brain have begun to control physical and purely emotional responses and where the patriarchy has ruled these thousands of years, there is rejection and fear of maternal sexuality.... The male dominant family and political systems of the West, in combination with Christian theology, make a sharp distinction between motherhood and female sexuality. Maternity is culturally defined and differentiated from sexuality, so that women are asked to deny the evidence of their senses by repressing the sexual component of infant care.... It is to men's advantage to restrict women's sexual gratification to adult heterosexual intercourse, though women and children may pay the price of less rewarding relationships.

Projecting this scenario back to the beginnings of human evolution, Fisher once again discovered a world where women were the basic social unit with men only on the periphery.

The development of humanity centers around the first couple, mother and child. The children remain close to their mothers. Other males are brought in as her temporary or long-term mate, but daughters, sons, even grandchildren remain in close association with the mother figure over a period of years, stretching out into decades. The mother is the first teacher and out of her teaching came the communicative and socializing abilities which characterize human beings. [It is] the spark that set off the chain of events leading to the later development of our species.

What Fisher had done here is repeal monogamy. When monogamous species first pair off, you will recall, they bond through a sexual marathon that can last as long as thirty-six hours. This releases oxytocin and other hormones that bind them together in the same way the mother will later bond with her offspring.

Fisher has reversed the process—as anyone must in order to undo monogamy. In doing so, she has returned to the old pre-human, mammalian world in which the relationship between mother and child is primary and relations between males and females are ephemeral at best. This solipsistic view would not seem so significant if it did not bear such a strong resemblance to the world that is now emerging in American society—the "warrior-matriarchies" of black neighborhoods plus the small but growing numbers of educated women who want to "go it alone" in having children. Throughout history, most of mankind has regarded single motherhood as a personal misfortune if not a social disaster. But now there is a minority that celebrates it as a "new type of family," or even the reversion to an aboriginal mother-and-child society that in fact last existed when we were chimpanzees.

So let us ask a very uncomfortable question that most people are generally inclined to avoid: Although women have always been considered to be more devoted supporters of monogamy than men, is their support really that unconditional? Or to rephrase the question, while *most* women may prefer monogamy, is it possible there is a significant minority that sees it as a fundamental abridgement of their rights? And is that minority having a large and growing impact on what happens in American society?

CHAPTER 23

WHAT DO
WOMEN WANT?

I n 1986, a New Jersey woman named Mary Beth Whitehead caused a national sensation when she carried a baby under a surrogate contract for an affluent couple and then refused to give up the child, called "Baby M."

Whitehead was an attractive woman who had dropped out of high school and married a garbage man. After having two children by him, she had told him she did not want any more and insisted he have a vasectomy. Then she saw a newspaper ad placed by a well-to-do couple asking for a surrogate mother to bear the husband's child. (The wife had multiple sclerosis and feared she would not survive a pregnancy.) Whitehead volunteered and was artificially inseminated with the husband's sperm. She gave birth and turned the baby over to the couple but then showed up at their door twenty-four hours later demanding it back and threatening suicide. The frightened couple gave her the child but when Whitehead fled the state they filed legal proceedings. The New Jersey Supreme Court awarded Baby M to the couple "in the best interests of the child." White-head was granted visitation rights. Baby M grew up happy and severed all connections with Whitehead when she reached age twenty-one. Mean-while, Whitehead, having become famous, divorced her husband and married a wealthy stockbroker with whom she had another child.

The story is generally remembered as a landmark legal case in sur-rogate parenthood. But it is also something else. It is an example of a lower-status woman chafing at the bounds of monogamy.

In their path-breaking 2012 paper, "The Puzzle of Monogamous Marriage," Joseph Henrich, Robert Boyd, and Peter J. Richerson mar-veled at the "puzzle" that any society could establish monogamy when it is high-status men, who usually have the most influence in setting rules, whose interests are curtailed.

But there is another group that loses out under the rules of monog-amy. This is *low*-status women who are generally constricted in their choice of husbands to low-status men. Biology is a powerful thing and there is always an urge to move up the ladder, either in terms of greater financial support or "good genes." Mary Beth Whitehead had to take a somewhat circuitous route, because the rules of monogamous marriage were still relatively strict and clear. She would find the whole thing much easier today.

Anthropologist Sarah Blaffer Hrdy has postulated that the optimal female evolutionary strategy is to have as many offspring as possible with as *many different males as possible*. The most dominant male, of course, is always the favorite, but others may be nearly dominant or on their way to becoming dominant. Sexual reproduction originally won out over the self-fertilization of the annelid worm because it created the possibility of *variety*. So a female that mates with a number of different males is creat-ing her own variety, increasing the chances that her genes will achieve enough diversity to thrive in different circumstances or environments. Hrdy found confirmation of this in the discovery that, even within the chimp band, where females make sure to mate with every male, adult females often steal away and mate with the males of neighboring groups as well. Of course this incurs great risks. If she is caught, the males of her home troop will kill her offspring and perhaps her as well. But the risks are apparently worth it. "They are trying to widen the gene pool as much as possible," writes Hrdy.

What we have, then, is a picture of the Ur-Female, the naked evolutionary id that lies at the core of every woman. The Ur-Male is easy enough to identify. He is Genghis Khan, who conquered the world, burned every city he vanquished, slaughtered the men and children, and had his way with as many women as possible so that 0.5 percent of the *world's* population can claim descent from him.

So where do we encounter the Ur-Female in our society? She is the Welfare Mother, the woman who has a large brood of children by different men. Not all women who were on AFDC when it was finally abolished in 1996 fit this description. Forty-two percent had only one child and 30 percent had two. But the remainder—4 million single mothers—consisted of women with sizable broods, almost always by multiple fathers.

As it turns out, all that is required to unmask the Ur-Female in an advanced society is to remove the social norms that condemned illegitimacy and offer financial support to unwed mothers. The welfare system did this, easily overwhelming the fragile adjustment that African Americans had made to monogamy. Welfare also encouraged the footloose male who impregnated as many women as possible with no concern about who was going to provide for them. Even the sublimely tolerant Bill Moyers was unable to mask his contempt when confronted with a twenty-two-year-old bragging to him about how many children he had sired.

During the height of the crime wave in the 1980s and 1990s, a group of researchers gave a battery of psychological tests to young African American criminals and found—predictably—that they were very impulsive, with short time horizons, and almost no sense of social obligation. ("The police aren't fair," one young hood once complained to columnist Jimmy Breslin. "They arrest you for things you did two months ago.") But when the researchers gave the same test to young *females*, they found that *single mothers* had the exact same psychological profile. They were impulsive, had short time horizons, and very little sense of obligation to other people. Single motherhood, then, is a kind of female crime, a surrender to impulse over longer-term obligation. Yet however destructive these impulses may be, given enough financial support the young lothario and the single mother form a cultural pair that can rapidly overwhelm the norms and standards of monogamous society and even become the predominating type.

The problem might not be so great if it were not for another dissatisfied group—upper-educated women who cannot find any men to their liking. As Hanna Rosin writes in her provocative book, *The End of Men*:

> The whole country's future could look much as the present does for many lower-class African-Americans: the mothers pull themselves up, but the men don't follow. First-generation college-educated white women may join their black counterparts in a new kind of middle class, where marriage is increasingly rare.

Rosin's essay by the same name appeared in *The Atlantic Monthly*, which has become a kind of message board for highly educated women expressing their frustration with the bonds of monogamy. (One article entitled "Let's Call the Whole Thing Off" is subtitled, "The author is ending her marriage. Isn't it time you did the same?") In November 2011, *The Atlantic* published "All the Single Ladies," an immense, 11,000-word apologia by *Veranda* editor Kate Bolick justifying why she had ditched what she admitted was an "exceptional…intelligent, good-looking, loyal, kind," marriageable man at age twenty-eight in order to satisfy the whims of her feminist mother. Now she finds herself single and alone at age forty-two. However, Bolick finds solace in the world of welfare. She travels to Wilkinsburg, Pennsylvania, a largely African American community, where she meets a twice divorced single mother of four children, all by different fathers, one of whom, a fifteen-year-old, is now pregnant, as well as a niece and another black single mother, and remarks:

The affection between these four high-spirited women was light and infectious, and they spoke knowingly about the stigmas they're up against. "That's right," Denean laughed, "we're your standard bunch of single black moms!"

Then she comments:

> Today, with the precipitous economic and social decline of men of all races, it's easy to see why women of any race would feel frustrated by their romantic prospects. (Is it any wonder marriage rates have fallen?) Increasingly, this extends to the upper-middle class, too: early last year, a study by the Pew Research Center reported that professionally successful, college-educated women were confronted with a shrinking pool of like-minded marriage prospects.

Later she opines:

> I couldn't help thinking about the women in Wilkinsburg—an inadvertent all-female coalition—and how in spite of it all, they derived so much happiness from each other's company.... I am curious to know what could happen if these de facto female support systems of the sort I saw in Wilkinsburg were recognized as an adaptive response, even an evolutionary stage, that women could be proud to build and maintain.

At the terminus of this road lies the feminist dream of a world where childbearing is completely separated from the nuclear family. "We no longer need husbands to have children," Bolick exudes, "For those who want their own biological child, and haven't found the right man, now is a good time to be alive."

It would not be too much to say at this point that many American women have gotten swelled heads or that, replete with feminist dogma, they have simply decided that no men are good enough for them.

For these women, paternity can also be outsourced thanks to technology. Sperm banks, although nominally set up to deal with problems of infertility, have quickly become hubs of high-tech polygamy where women can choose the best genes from an anonymous donor without any emotional commitment. Sperm banks advertise choice for eye color, hair color, skin color, appearance, musical talent, intelligence, and other desirable qualities. One dubbed itself the Nobel Prize Sperm Bank, although only one prize-winner, racial supremacist William Shockley, contributed and the operators soon found women were much more interested in physical attractiveness than intelligence.

All this greatly underappreciates the evolutionary change wrought by the nuclear family. At the Yerkes National Primate Research Center at Emory University in Atlanta, researchers, on a whim, once tried an experiment of confining a mother and her offspring with an adult male in order to duplicate the nuclear family. "The male played very rough with them—batting them around and treating them much more physically than any female would ever do," the scientists said. "But the young chimps couldn't get enough of it. They kept coming back for more. In the end, those youngsters turned out to be the bravest, most self-confident chimps we ever raised here. It makes you realize there may be something very good about the way we raise our own children." This was back in 1974.

The statistics on the risks for children growing up without fathers are well documented. Children without fathers are more at risk for drug and alcohol abuse, dropping out of school, depression, delinquent behavior, crime, early sexual activity, and having illegitimate children in the next generation. They are more at risk for abuse, molestation, and incest. The chances of a child being murdered by a mother's boyfriend are 70 times greater than being killed by their natural father. This is the old principle of alpha male infanticide rearing its head—the reason we adopted monogamy in the first place.

In the absence of a father, feminists conjure up all kinds of visions of "alternative" and "extended" families that are supposed to compensate for not having a man in the house. Stephanie Coontz, a professor of history at Evergreen State College, writes endless books and articles, all with the same message, "The Good Old Days—They Were Terrible." The "good old days" are the 1950s, when monogamous culture was at its peak. Coontz wants to hearken back to the even better days of the 1920s and 1930s when people were poorer and multigenerational house-holds—with resident grandparents, aunts, and uncles—were more common. ("Have you ever lived with your in-laws?" one critic responded.)

Sarah Blaffer Hrdy has her own version of this, stemming from her thesis of "cooperative breeding":

> Compared to earlier phases in Western civilization children are better off today. But not compared to our Pleistocene ancestors.... [T]hose children who did survive back then were actually much better off in terms of the kind of nurturing environment that they experienced.

Then children were cared for by "grandmothers, great aunts and alloparents"—"alloparents" being a term she has invented to describe other adults who care for children. (It is unclear where Hrdy gets her information about parenting during the Pleistocene.) Fortunately, Hrdy does not practice what she preaches. She and her husband have raised three children on a successful California walnut farm.

The dean of collective parenting, of course, is Hillary Clinton, the former first lady whose famous bestseller *It Takes a Village*, says we should look to Africa for a model of society-wide parenting to supplement the nuclear family. Why anyone would look to tropical Africa, the home of polygamy and one of the most dysfunctional regions of the planet for an example, is a bit of a mystery. But by page thirty-seven the "village" has become the "government" and you can imagine what happens after that. Feminists have been pushing for the state to take over the role of the father almost since the feminist revival of the 1960s began. Barbara Ehrenreich has never stopped pushing for a welfare system to support middle-class single mothers. In her last book, Betty Friedan argued for a "federal subsidy for divorce" (she had divorced her husband in 1969). Sarah Blaffer Hrdy complains "politicians…are still out there talking about how they know children are healthier when they're reared with a mother who is married to their father."

Instead of acknowledging that what we are witnessing is the breakdown of the oldest human institution, feminists try to redefine the problem as the "feminization of poverty." This is a rhetorical trick to divert attention from the obvious fact that women have caused a great deal of the problem themselves by seeking alternatives to marriage. Single motherhood is now considered a progressive option that women openly embrace. Seventy-five percent of divorces are initiated by women, often for the most trivial of reasons. No-fault divorce and near-automatic maternal custody have made the process as painless as possible for both men and women. The "feminization of poverty" is simply a plea for a paternalistic state to take over the role of men.

Ironically, part of the problem is that educated elites don't practice what they preach. As Charles Murray has noted, most educated people keep their families together, defer childbirth until marriage, send their children to good colleges, and practice an ethic of ambition. It is the lower classes who are absorbing the message that marriage doesn't matter, that illegitimacy is no big deal, and that there is nothing wrong with being on the public dole.

In the middle of this, the strategy of the Democratic Party has become to peel off low-income women, the most vulnerable constituency, and turn them into a voting bloc entirely dependent on the government. This was epitomized by the Obama administration's egregious "Julia" campaign advertisement during the 2012 election, featuring the woman who received all her benefits from the government and never had to rely on a father or husband. The Democrats have already been wildly successful in recruiting African American women, who vote for them in banana-republic proportions. If they succeed in peeling off working-class women as well, they may have an unassailable national majority.

Central to this campaign is an imaginary "war on women," which has now become a staple in Democratic campaigns. Drawn straight from the feminist playbook, the "war on women" says that women are an oppressed class if they do not have: 1) unlimited access to free birth control; 2) unlimited access to abortion; 3) the right to complete wage parity with men, based on "credentials" rather than performance; and 4) the right to government support if all else fails. This is not an attempt to alleviate poverty or redistribute income across social classes. It is an attempt to set up a separate statist constituency that operates entirely separately from monogamous society.

Although barely acknowledged, this split has already become the main dividing line in the American electorate. A common theme in the reelection of Barack Obama in 2012 was that the votes of blacks and women put him over the top and that the Republican Party had simply become "too old and too white." "Too married" would be more appropriate. *Married* women voted by a margin of 7 percentage points for Romney and married *people* favored him by 14 points. It was the vote of single women—single mothers, divorced women, plus fire-breathing feminists convinced that society is making war on them—who supported Obama by a devastating 68-to-30 majority, putting him over the top. And of course the cohort of unmarried people is continually growing.

The major question facing future electorates is likely to be whether we will continue as a society built around the monogamous two-parent family or whether we will submit to a kind of "state polygamy" where women congregate around the major source of wealth—the government—while men slink off into their separate quarters to pursue a fading warrior culture—played out this time on video games.

The art of fatherhood does not come naturally but is a skill that must be passed on from generation to generation. It is being lost. And when it is lost, women may be the ones to suffer even more than men.

CHAPTER 24

WHAT MARRIAGE MEANS FOR CIVILIZATION

N ations' fates are not based on geography or east-west axes or natural resources or technology but on the human beings they generate. Monogamous families create socially conscious human beings ready to live in peaceful societies. They are the "little platoons" that Edmund Burke spoke of when he argued that society works best when people organize themselves in small, self-sufficient units instead of the across-the-board egalitarianism of the French Revolution.

So is there any chance of restoring the monogamous ideal to American society? The first thing I would suggest would be to recognize that our parents and forebears knew something. They were not hopeless prudes or sexually repressed puritans bound by senseless conventions and hopelessly outmoded proprieties. Instead, they were citizens of a monogamous society where both men and women understood implicitly that there are certain rules that must be honored and certain behaviors that threaten the stability of an essentially artificial system.

In the early 1950s, for instance, Swedish actress Ingrid Bergman was banned from coming to the United States because she had a "love child" with Italian director Roberto Rossellini. Today this may seem ridiculously quaint and prudish, but people knew full well that movie stars set standards for society and that if someone of Ingrid Bergman's stature could do it, others would as well. Today in a world where Hollywood offers up *Teen Mom* and *16 and Pregnant*, we can only cringe at how many teenage girls will become single mothers just because it looks so appealing on television.

Pornography is another area where public display is highly disruptive to monogamy. It tells married people that there are sexual adventures waiting for them out there and that they are foolish to be satisfied with their dull married lives. Thanks to the internet, pornography has never been more widespread than it is now.

But these are the negative instances. Is there anything positive that can be said about monogamy?

Where to begin? Monogamous marriage is the most thrilling adventure anyone ever undertakes—that perilous encounter with an individual who is so much like you yet so different, the other half of your humanity, without whom you are never a complete human being. It relies not on sex, which is easy, but on romance, falling in love and staying in love, which is the work of a lifetime. The Christian Right does a marvelous job of celebrating marriage, holding huge seminars in hotel ballrooms encouraging couples to pay attention to each other's needs and work out their differences. The secular Left does the same with its marriage counselors' offices and psychiatrists' couches. Yet it's hard to salvage any marriage without romance.

Wars between the sexes are common enough in nature. It is said that a dozen square yards of jungle are leveled when two panthers mate. But the story of humanity has been one of growing trust and cooperation between the sexes. It began in that moment when two chimpanzees sneaked off into the woods to build a nest in the trees so they could spend the night together some 5 million years ago. It triumphed in Victorian England and 1950s America, when the monogamous ideal became the universal standard to which everyone could aspire. There is no reason it cannot regain that same exalted place in today's society.

———

When I was in college, I went out with a girl who, in the parlance of the time, was "all screwed up." She was almost unbearably elusive, with fluttering eyelashes and a curtain of hair that always fell in front of her face whenever there was something important to say. Yet this elusiveness had an irresistible fascination for me and many of my classmates. And she would say things you would remember the rest of your life: "Sex obscures things," "It doesn't matter what you do with other people, it's what you do with the person that counts," "You make me realize there's a woman inside me."

We dated over a couple of months and then I visited her home in the Midwest. One night we found ourselves sitting alone together in her kitchen in the semi-darkness. Suddenly the curtain of hair was gone, the eyelashes were no longer fluttering and her face was a completely open book, searching me out saying, "I'm not afraid of you anymore. I want to know you. Tell me who you are."

I've only seen that look two or three times in my life but I've never forgotten it. In trying to write a novel about it years later, a phrase came into my head. "We were standing at the moment when civilizations are born, when two people trust each other." Well the romance didn't work out and I never managed to finish the novel either, but the phrase has always stayed with me, because I think it is true.

Civilizations are born when two people trust each other, namely a man and a woman. At that moment, we come out of the cold isolation of nature and begin to construct something that we call human society. It happened in the mists of time when the alpha couple decided to defy the code that everyone-belongs-to-everybody and formed a bond that excluded the others, creating a space in which human evolution could take place. It happened when Enkidu reminded Gilgamesh of the pact sealed by their ancestors that a bride and groom should be left alone on their wedding night. It happened when Odysseus decided he would rather return to his wife and family than live immortally with a goddess—and when Penelope fended off suitors every night awaiting his return. It happened when Lucretia decided she would rather die than live with the dishonor of being violated by a man who was not her husband. It happened when Pamela Andrews held out for something more permanent than a fleeting relationship with her aristocratic master. It happened when Suzanne decided she much preferred her humble Figaro to the powerful count who was trying to seduce her. It happened when Rani Padmini decided she would rather die on a funeral pyre than become the second or third wife of a sultan. And it happened when King Shahryar decided the woman lying next to him every night telling him stories was the woman with whom he wanted to spend the rest of his life.

And it happens over and over, every day, every year, every century to countless millions around the globe and across the span of human history. We need have no fear that boys will always be interested in girls and girls always interested in boys. Young people will always fall in love, over and over, time and again, and the world will once more be ready for renewal. It is as perennial as the grass. We only have to make sure that when they do, there is a reasonable chance there will be a girl for every boy and a boy for every girl, that they may once again join together to form yet another human family. Only then can we be certain we are living in a peaceful and prosperous society, a prosperous and peaceful world.

ACKNOWLEDGMENTS

My first acknowledgment must go to my wife, Stephanie. Ever since she came into my life, everything has been much easier. I doubt if this book ever would have been completed without her constant encouragement, support, and good advice.

I would also like to acknowledge Stephanie's father, David Gutmann, an accomplished field worker and author of *Reclaimed Powers*, a highly respected cross-cultural study of aging. Before his death at eighty-eight, we spent many a night at the dinner table arguing the pros and cons of the ideas presented here. And although he did not live to see the finished edition, I know exactly what his response would have been: "But you haven't done any field work!" We journalists just don't have the time to earn advanced degrees for everything we write about.

For a project on which I have been working for over twenty-five years, the list of people and institutions who have made contributions and helped move things along requires recollection. At one point in the deep distant past (around 1985), the Smith Richardson Foundation awarded me a grant to pursue this topic. Although I'm certain they have no institutional memory of this gift, it was extremely helpful and I would like to offer belated thanks. In 1989 the Hoover Institution invited me out for three months to work on the project, perhaps the first time it had funded a subject that didn't involve the domestic economy or foreign relations. The topic had very little resonance at the time. When I told people I was working on a book on "the family," they would ask, "Do you mean your family?"

Welfare reform was the focus of that era and I benefited greatly from the readings and conversations with George Gilder, who wrote with great wisdom on the subject. Allan Carlson and his tireless work at the Rockford Institute, from which the Howard Center for Family, Religion & Society developed, was also a constant source of insights. But it was the work of another friend and colleague, Lisa Schiffren, that really broke the ice. In 1992 she wrote a speech for Vice President Dan Quayle condemning the fatal lure that the fictional character Murphy Brown would have in glamorizing single motherhood for low-income teenagers. As might be expected, the speech was the subject of endless ridicule and condescension until a year later when Barbara Dafoe Whitehead wrote her landmark *Atlantic Monthly* article, "Dan Quayle Was Right" and the solemn facts of single motherhood and broken families became part of the public discussion. Had I had the time enough and a publisher, I definitely should have brought the book out then.

The events of September 11 gave this book new life. I had never thought of a connection between terrorism and polygamy but when I began applying the logic of the "women shortage" to other cultures, it opened an entirely new perspective. I had always wanted to extend my study of family formation to other societies and now it became an imperative. My son asks me, "Why did you miss the boat by not publishing in the 1990s?" but in retrospect I'm glad I did not. It gave me the chance to make the whole undertaking much more comprehensive.

Now I was trying to write a book about polygamy and terrorism. The subject seemed dramatic but the possibilities of finding a publisher willing to deal with such an unorthodox—and potentially dangerous—

subject were slim. At this point I am forever indebted to Theron Raines, one of New York's premier literary agents, who took an interest in the book, made several extremely helpful suggestions, and was making a valiant effort to sell the book when he died unexpectedly in 2010.

By some deus ex machina, Harry Crocker, a former editor of mine at Regnery, now entered the game and ran with the ball. He suggested abandoning the popularizing terrorism-and-polygamy scene and going back to the original subject of the book—the role that marriage and pair-bonding have played in the formation of human society. He also came up with the title, *Marriage and Civilization*, which finally brought the whole project into focus. His advice and encouragement have been critical throughout. I would also like to thank Maria Ruhl, managing editor at Regnery, for helping with the editorial process.

The last stages of this book have been written under very trying circumstances since I have contracted a rare condition that casts a shadow on my future. I would like to thank Dr. Matthew Lonberg at Nyack Hospital and Dr. Owen O'Connor at the Columbia Center for Lymphoid Malignancies for their help. If I am around to hand them signed copies, it will be because of their kind and expert care. I also have to thank two childhood friends, Nick Allis and Christine Van Lenten, for giving huge amounts of their time in helping me through this ordeal.

I also owe a debt of gratitude to my sons, Kevan, Fritz, and Dylan, who rarely ask for money anymore but have become fine, upstanding young gentlemen, and to Sarah for many long years of companionship and support. Also my sister Marcia and her husband Jeff and their daughter Mandy and sons Josh and Davey and grandchildren for their constant encouragement, and to Stephanie's brother Ethan, an accomplished writer in his own right, who has also been outstanding in his support.

But that brings me back to Stephanie, who is the beginning and end of it all.

BIBLIOGRAPHY

Part I: The Search for Origins

Chapter 1: Where Did the Family Come From?

Benedict, Ruth. *Patterns of Culture*. New York: Mentor, 1960.

Boas, Franz. *Anthropology and Modern Life*. New York: W.W. Norton & Company, 1962.

Briffault, Robert. *The Mothers: A Study of the Origins of Sentiments and Institutions*. New York: The Macmillan Company, 1927.

Bronowski, Jacob. *The Identity of Man*. Garden City, NY: Natural History Press, 1971.

Calverton, V. F., ed. *The Making of Man: An Outline of Anthropology*. New York: Modern Library, 1931.

Carreyett, Ray A. *Physical Anthropology*. London: W. & G. Foyle, 1954.

Carrington, Charles. *Man and His Nature*. Garden City, NY: Doubleday Anchor, 1953.

Carrington, Richard. *A Million Years of Man*. New York: Mentor, 1963.

Darwin, Charles. *The Descent of Man*. New York: P.F. Collier & Son, 1902.

De Waal Malefijt, Annemarie. *Images of Man: A History of Anthropological Thought*. New York: Alfred A. Knopf, 1974.

Engels, Friedrich. *The Origins of the Family, Private Property and the State*. New York: International Publishers, 1972.

Frazer, James George. *The Golden Bough*. New York: The Macmillan Company, 1975.

Freeman, Derek. *Margaret Mead and Samoa*. New York: Viking Penguin, 1984.

Freilich, Morris, ed. *The Pleasure of Anthropology*. New York: Signet, 1983.

Freud, Sigmund. *Moses and Monotheism*. New York: Vintage, 1967.

——. *Totem and Taboo*. New York: W.W. Norton & Company, 1950.

Fried, Morton H., ed. *Reading in Anthropology, Volume 1*. New York: Thomas Y. Crowell Company, 1968.

Frobeniu, Leo. *The Childhood of Man*. New York: Meridian Books, 1960.

Gould, Richard A., and *Natural History Magazine*. *Man's Many Ways*. New York: Harper & Row, 1973.

Huxley, Julian. *Evolution in Action*. New York: Mentor, 1957.

Jacobs, Melville, and Bernhard J. Stern. *General Anthropology*. New York: Barnes & Noble, 1960.

Johanson, Donald, and Edey Maitland. *Lucy: The Beginnings of Humankind*. New York: Warner Books, 1982.

Johanson, Donald, and James Shreeve. *Lucy's Child: The Discovery of a Human Ancestor*. New York: William Morrow & Company, 1981.

Kottak, Conrad Phillip. *Anthropology: The Exploration of Human Diversity, Fourth Edition*. New York: Random House, 1987.

Kropotkin, Peter. *Mutual Aid: A Factor of Evolution*. Forgotten Books, 2008.

Kuper, Adam. *The Invention of Primitive Society*. London: Routledge, 1988.

Levi-Strauss, Claude. *The Scope of Anthropology*. London: Jonathan Cape, 1971.

———. *Structural Anthropology*. New York: Basic Books, 1963.

Linton, Ralph. *The Tree of Culture*. New York: Vintage, 1959.

Lisitzky, Gene. *Four Ways of Being Human*. New York: Penguin, 1956.

Lowie, Robert. *Primitive Society*. New York: Harper Torchbooks, 1961.

Malinowski, Bronislaw. *A Scientific Theory of Culture and Other Essays*. Chapel Hill: The University of North Carolina Press, 1944.

———. *Sex, Culture, and Myth*. New York: Harcourt, Brace & Word, 1962.

Mead, Margaret. *Coming of Age in Samoa*. New York: New American Library, 1960.

Montague, Ashley. *Man: His First Million Years*. New York: Signet, 1962.

———. *Man in Process*. New York: Mentor, 1961.

Morgan, Lewis Henry. *Ancient Society*. Calcutta: Bharati Library, no date.

Nanda, Serena. *Cultural Anthropology*. Belmont, CA: Wadsworth Publishing Company, 1987.

Oliver, Douglas. *Invitation to Anthropology*. Garden City, NY: Natural History Press, 1964.

Pfeiffer, John E. *The Emergence of Man*. New York: Harper & Row, 1969.

Shapiro, Harry L., ed. *Man, Culture and Society*. New York: Oxford University Press, 1956.

Vlahos, Olivia. *Human Beginnings*. New York: Viking Press, 1966.

Wendt, Herbert. *In Search of Adam*. Boston: Houghton Mifflin Company, 1956.

Westermarck, Edward. *The History of Human Marriage (In Three Volumes)*. New York: The Allerton Book Company, 1922.

Chapter 2: The Primate Inheritance

Alee, W. C., *The Social Life of Animals*. Boston: Beacon Press, 1958.

Ardrey, Robert. *African Genesis*. New York: Dell Publishing, 1972.

———. *The Social Contract*. New York: Athenaeum, 1970.

———. *The Territorial Imperative*. New York: Dell Publishing, 1976.

Clark, W. E. LeGros. *History of the Primates: An Introduction to the Study of Fossil Man*. Chicago: Phoenix Books (University of Chicago Press), 1963.

Dawkins, Richard. *The Selfish Gene*. New York: Oxford University Press, 1976.

De Waal, Frans. *Peacemaking Among Primates*. Cambridge: Harvard University Press, 1989.

———, ed. *Tree of Origin: What Primate Behavior Can Tell Us about Human Social Evolution*. Cambridge: Harvard University Press, 2002.

Dubowski, Cathy East. *Great Apes*. New York: Parachute Press, 1991.

Fossey, Diane. *Gorillas in the Mist*. Boston: Houghton Mifflin Company, 1983.

Galdikas, Birute M. F. *Reflections of Eden: My Years with the Orangutans of Borneo*. Boston: Little, Brown and Company, 1995.

Haskins, Caryl P. *Of Societies and Men*. New York: Viking Press, 1960.

Leakey, Mary. *Disclosing the Past*. New York: McGraw-Hill, 1984.

Lorenz, Konrad. *On Aggression*. New York: Bantam, 1977.

Marais, Eugene. *The Soul of the Ape*. Middlesex, UK: Penguin, 1984.

Montgomery, Sy. *Walking with the Great Apes: Jane Goodall, Diane Fossey, Birute Galdikas*. Boston: Houghton Mifflin Company, 1991.

Morris, Desmond. *The Human Zoo*. New York: Dell, 1974.

Shaller, George B. *The Year of the Gorilla*. New York: Ballentine, 1964.

Southwick, Charles H., ed. *Primate Social Behavior*. Princeton, NJ: Van Nostrand, 1963.

Strum, Shirley C. *Almost Human: A Journey into the World of Baboons*. New York: W.W. Norton & Company, 1987.

Williams, Leonard. *Man and Monkey*. Philadelphia: J.B. Lippincott Company, 1968.

Wrangham, Richard, and Peterson, Dale. *Demonic Males: Apes and the Origin of Human Violence*. Boston: Houghton Mifflin, 1996.

Chapter 3: Chimp Sexual Communism

Caplan, Arthur L., ed. *The Sociological Debate*. New York: Harper & Row, 1978.

Ghiglieri, Michael P. *East of the Mountains of the Moon: Chimpanzee Society in the African Rain Forest*. New York: Free Press, 1988.

Goodall, Jane. *In the Shadow of Man*. New York: Dell Publishing, 1972.

———. *Through a Window: My Thirty Years with the Chimpanzees of Gombe*. Boston: Houghton Mifflin, 1990.

Peterson, Dale, and Jane Goodall. *Visions of Caliban: On Chimpanzees and People*. Boston: Houghton Mifflin, 1993.

Wickler, Wolfgang. *The Sexual Code: The Social Behavior of Animals and Men*. Garden City, NY: Anchor Books, 1973.

Chapter 4: The Alpha Couple and the Primal Horde

Axelrod, Robert. *The Evolution of Cooperation*. New York: Basic Books, 1984.

Becker, Gary. *The Economic Approach to Human Behavior*. Chicago: University of Chicago Press, 1976.

Chapais, Bernard. *Primeval Kinship: How Pair-Bonding Gave Birth to Human Society*. Cambridge: Harvard University Press, 2008.

De Waal, Frans. *Good Natured: The Origins of Right and Wrong in Humans and Other Animals*. Cambridge: Harvard University Press, 1996.

Evolutionary Game Theory. Hephaestus Books.

Fisher, Helen. *The Sex Contract: The Evolution of Human Behavior*. New York: William Morrow & Company, 1982.

Malinowski, Bronislaw. *The Sexual Life of Savages*. Boston: Beacon Press, 1987.

Sagan, Carl, and Ann Druyan. *Shadows of Forgotten Ancestors*. New York: Ballentine Books, 1992.

Schelling, Thomas C. *The Strategy of Conflict*. Cambridge: Harvard University Press, 1980.

Skyrms, Brian. *Evolution of the Social Contract*. New York: Cambridge University Press, 1996.

———. *The Stag Hunt and the Evolution of Social Structure*. Cambridge, UK: Cambridge University Press, 2004.

Smith, John Maynard. *Evolution and the Theory of Games*. New York: Cambridge University Press, 1982.

Sober, Elliott, and David Sloan Wilson. *Unto Others: The Evolution and Psychology of Unselfish Behavior*. Cambridge: Harvard University Press, 1998.

Tannahill, Reay. *Sex in History*. New York: Stein and Day, 1982.

Tiger, Lionel. *Men in Groups*. New York: Random House, 1969.

Tomasello, Michael. *Why We Cooperate*. Cambridge: The MIT Press, 2009.

Wilson, Edward O. *On Human Nature*. New York: Bantam, 1979.

Part II: The Emergence of Humanity

Chapter 5: Why We Didn't Remain Chimpanzees

Alland, Alexander. *Evolution and Human Behavior*. Garden City, NY: Doubleday Anchor, 1973.

Barash, David. *The Whispering Within: Evolution and the Origin of Human Nature*. New York: Penguin, 1985.

Becker, Gary S. *A Treatise on the Family*. Cambridge: Harvard University Press, 1981.

Bierstedt, Robert. *The Making of Society: An Outline of Sociology*. New York: Modern Library, 1959.

Calvin, William H. *The Ascent of Mind: Ice Age Climate and the Evolution of Intelligence*. New York: Bantam, 1991.

———. *The Throwing Madonna: Essays on the Brain*. New York: Bantam, 1991.

Dawkins, Richard. *The Blind Watchmaker*. Essex, England: Longman Scientific & Technical, 1986.

Degler, Carl N. *In Search of Human Nature: The Decline and Revival of Darwinism in American Social Thought*. New York: Oxford University Press, 1991.

De Waal, Frans. *The Ape and the Sushi Master*. New York: Basic Books, 2001.

Dunbar, Robin. *The Human Story*. London: Faber and Faber, 2004.

Errington, Frederick, and Deborah Gewertz. *Cultural Alternatives & a Feminist Anthropology*. Cambridge, UK: Cambridge University Press, 1990.

Fox, Robin. *The Red Lamp of Incest*. New York: E.P. Dutton, 1980.

———. *The Search for Society*. New Brunswick, NJ: Rutgers University Press, 1989.

Gibbons, Ann. *The First Humans*. New York: Anchor Books, 2007.

Goode, William J. *The Family*. Englewood Cliffs, NJ: Prentice-Hall, 1964.

Hawkes, Jacquetta. *Prehistory, Vol. 1, Part 1*. New York: Mentor, 1965.

Human Ancestors: Readings from Scientific American. San Francisco: W.H. Freeman and Company, 1979.

Kurten, Bjorn. *Not From the Apes*. New York: Vintage, 1972.

Leakey, Richard E. *People of the Lake*. New York: Avon Books, 1978.

Levi-Strauss, Claude. *Myth and Meaning*. New York: Schocken Books, 1979.

———. *The Savage Mind*. Chicago: University of Chicago Press, 1966.

Lewin, Roger. *Bones of Contention: Controversies in the Search for Human Origins*. New York: Simon & Schuster, 1987.

Malinowski, Bronislaw. *Magic, Science and Religion*. Garden City, NY: Doubleday Anchor, 1954.

Margulis, Lynn, and Dorion Sagan. *Mystery Dance: On the Evolution of Human Sexuality*. New York: Summit Books, 1991.

McCrone, John. *The Ape That Spoke*. New York: William Morrow & Company, 1991.

Mead, Margaret. *Sex and Temperament in Three Primitive Societies*. New York: New American Library, 1958.

Michod, Richard. *Eros and Evolution: A Natural Philosophy of Sex*. Reading, MA: Addison-Wesley, 1994.

Michod, Richard E., and Bruce R. Levin, eds. *The Evolution of Sex*. Sunderland, MA: Sinauer Associates, 1988.

Morgan, Elaine. *The Aquatic Ape*. New York: Stein and Day, 1982.

———. *The Descent of Woman*. New York: Bantam, 1973.

Morris, Desmond. *The Naked Ape*. New York: Dell Publishing, 1967.

Radin, Paul. *The World of Primitive Man*. New York: Grove Press, 1960.

Redfield, Robert. *The Little Community and Peasant Society and Culture*. Chicago: University of Chicago Press, 1989.

Ridley, Matt. *The Red Queen: Sex and the Evolution of Human Nature*. New York: Harper Perennial, 1993.

Ryan, Christopher, and Cacilda Jetha. *Sex at Dawn*. New York: Harper Perennial, 2010.

Smith, J. Maynard. *The Evolution of Sex*. Cambridge, UK: Cambridge University Press, 1978.

Symons, Donald. *The Evolution of Human Sexuality*. Oxford, UK: Oxford University Press, 1979.

Taylor, Timothy. *The Prehistory of Sex: Four Million Years of Human Sexual Culture*. New York: Bantam, 1997.

Tiger, Lionel, and Robin Fox. *The Imperial Animal*. New York: Holt, Rinehart and Winston, 1971.

Wade, Nicholas. *Before the Dawn: Recovering the Lost History of Our Ancestors*. New York: Penguin, 2007.

Wright, Robert. *The Moral Animal*. New York: Vintage Books, 1994.

Zak, Paul J. *The Moral Molecule*: *The Source of Love and Prosperity*. New York: Dutton, 2012.

Chapter 6: Hunter-Gatherer Monogamy

Ardrey, Robert. *The Hunting Hypothesis*. New York: Bantam, 1977.

Bicchieri, M. G. *Hunters and Gatherers Today*. Prospect Heights, IL: Waveland Press, 1972.

Burkitt, Miles. *The Old Stone Age*. New York: Atheneum, 1963.

Coon, Carleton S. *The Hunting Peoples*. Boston: Little, Brown and Company, 1971.

Dahlberg, Frances, ed. *Woman the Gatherer*. New Haven: Yale University Press, 1984.

Hallet, Jean-Pierre. *Congo Kitabu*. Greenwich, CT: Fawcett, 1966.

Hallet, Jean-Pierre, with Alexandra Pelle. *Pygmy Kitabu*. Greenwich, CT: Fawcett, 1975.

Holmberg, Allan. *Nomads of the Long Bow*. New York: Natural History Press, 1969.

Keeley, Lawrence H. *War before Civilization*: *The Myth of the Peaceful Savage*. New York: Oxford University Press, 1996.

Lee, Richard B. *The Dobe !Kung*. New York: Holt, Rinehart and Winston, 1984.

Lee, Richard B., and Irven DeVore, eds. *Man the Hunter*. Hawthorne, NY: Aldine Publishing Company, 1968.

Levi-Strauss, Claude. *The Raw and the Cooked*. New York: Harper Colophon, 1975.

MacGowan, Kenneth, and Joseph A. Herster Jr. *Early Man in the New World*. Garden City, NY: Doubleday Anchor, 1962.

Mowat, Farley. *People of the Deer*. Toronto: McClelland & Stewart-Bantam Limited, 1984.

Oakely, Kenneth. *Man the Tool-Maker*. Chicago: University of Chicago Press, 1964.

Thomas, Elizabeth Marshall. *The Harmless People*. New York: Vintage, 1959.

Turnbull, Colin M. *The Mbuti Pygmies*. New York: Holt, Rinehart and Winston, 1983.

Chapter 7: The End of Hunter-Gatherer Monogamy

Chagnon, Napoleon. *Noble Savages: My Life among Two Dangerous Tribes —The Yanomamo and the Anthropologists*. New York: Simon & Schuster, 2013.

———. *Yanomamö: The Fierce People*. New York: Holt, Rinehart and Winston, 1968.

———. *Yanomamö: The Last Days of Eden*. New York: Harcourt, Brace Jovanovich Publishers, 1992.

Cotlow, Lewis. *Amazon Head-Hunters*. New York: New American Library, 1954.

Donner, Florinda. *Shabono*. New York: Dell Publishing, 1982.

Ereira, Alan. *The Elder Brothers: A Lost South American People and Their Wisdom*. New York: Vintage, 1993.

Evans-Pritchard, E. E. *Kinship and Marriage among the Nuer*. Oxford: Clarendon Paperbacks, 1990.

Fox, Robin. *Kinship and Marriage*. Middlesex, England: Penguin, 1967.

Harris, Marvin, *Cannibals and Kings: The Origins of Culture*. New York: Vintage, 1978.

————. *Cows, Pigs, Wars and Witches*. New York: Vintage, 1975.

Hart, C. W. M., Arnold R. Philling, and Jane C. Goodale. *The Tiwi of North Australia*. New York: Holt, Rinehart and Winston, 1988.

Herdt, Gilbert H. *Guardians of the Flutes: A Study of Ritualized Homosexual Behavior*. New York: McGraw-Hill, 1981.

Keeley, Lawrence H. *War before Civilization: The Myth of the Peaceful Savage*. New York: Oxford University Press, 1996.

La Fontaine, J. S. *Initiation*. New York: Penguin, 1985.

Leslie, Charles, ed. *Anthropology of Folk Religion*. New York: Vintage, 1960.

Levi-Strauss, Claude. *Totemism*. Boston: Beacon Press, 1968.

Malinowski, Bronislaw. *Argonauts of the Western Pacific*. New York: E.P. Dutton, 1961.

Matthiessen, Peter. *Under the Mountain Wall*. New York: Ballentine Books, 1962.

Maybury-Lewis, David. *Akwe-Shavante Society*. New York: Oxford University Press, 1974.

Mead, Margaret. *Male and Female*. New York: William Morrow & Company, 1975.

Murphy, Yolanda, and Robert E. Murphy. *Women of the Forest*. New York: Columbia University Press, 1985.

Newman, Philip L. *Knowing the Gururumba*. New York: Holt, Rinehart and Winston, 1965.

Price, Sally. *Co-Wives and Calabashes*. Ann Arbor: University of Michigan Press, 1990.

Read, Kenneth. *The High Valley*. New York: Charles Scribner's Sons, 1965.

Schneebaum, Tobias. *Keep the River on Your Right*. New York: Grove Press, 1969.

Sherman, Harold M. *Tahara: Among African Tribes*. Chicago: The Goldsmith Publishing Company, 1933.

Siskind, Janet. *To Hunt in the Morning*. New York: Oxford University Press, 1973.

Turnbull, Colin M. *The Forest People*. New York: Simon & Schuster, 1962.

Weiner, Annette. *The Trobrianders of Papua New Guinea*. New York: Holt, Rinehart and Winston, 1987.

Chapter 8: Herding and Horticulture: The Two Roads to Polygamy

Banton, Michael. *West Africa City: A Study of Tribal Life in Freetown*. London: Oxford University Press, 1957.

Bensten, Cheryl. *Masai Days*. New York: Doubleday Anchor, 1989.

Boahen, Adu. *Topics in West African History*. London: Longman Group Limited, 1966.

Boserup, Ester. *Woman's Role in Economic Development*. New York: St. Martin's Press, 1970.

Bugul, Ken. *The Abandoned Baobab: The Autobiography of a Senegalese Woman*. Brooklyn: Lawrence Hill Books, 1991.

Davidson, Basil. *A Guide to African History*. Garden City, NY: Zenith Books, 1971.

Dinesen, Isak. *Out of Africa*. New York: Modern Library, 1992.

Drachler, Jacob, ed. *African Heritage*. New York: Collier Books, 1964.

Fox, Robin. *Kinship and Marriage*. Middlesex, England: Penguin, 1967.

Goody, Jack, and S. J. Tambiah. *Bridewealth and Dowry*. London: Cambridge University Press, 1973.

Hafkin, Nancy J., and Edna G. Bay. *Women in Africa: Studies in Social and Economic Change*. Stanford, CA: Stanford University Press, 1976.

Holder, Preston. *The Hoe and the Horse on the Plains*. Lincoln: University of Nebraska Press, 1970.

Kaplan, Flora Edouwaye S., ed. *Queens, Queen Mothers, Priestesses, and Power: Case Studies in African Gender*. New York: The New York Academy of Sciences, 1997.

Kenyatta, Jomo. *Facing Mount Kenya*. New York: Vintage Books, 1965.

Lamb, David. *The Africans*. New York: Vintage, 1987.

Laye, Camara, *The African Child*. London: Fontana Books, 1971.

———. *A Dream of Africa*. London: Collins Fontana Books, 1970.

Mead, Margaret. *Growing Up in New Guinea*. New York: Dell Publishing, 1968.

Njoh, Ambe J. *Tradition, Culture and Development in Africa*. Burlington, VT: Ashgate Publishing, 2006.

Pearce, Roy Harvey. *Savagism and Civilization*. Baltimore: Johns Hopkins University Press, 1965.

Schuster, Ilsa M. Glazer. *New Women of Lusaka*. Mountain View, CA: Mayfield Publishing Company, 1979.

Seabrook, William B. *Jungle Ways*. New York: Harcourt, Brace and Company, 1931.

Thomas, Elizabeth Marshall. *Warrior Herdsmen*. New York: Vintage, 1965.

Tudge, Colin. *Neanderthals, Bandits and Farmers: How Agriculture Really Began*. New Haven: Yale University Press, 1998.

Turner, V. W. *Schism and Continuity in an African Society: A Study of Ndembu Village Life*. Manchester, UK: Manchester University Press, 1968.

Van Gennep, Arnold. *The Rites of Passage*. Chicago: University of Chicago Press, 1960.

Part III: The Ancient World

Chapter 9: Marriage at the Dawn of Civilization

Ballou, Robert O., ed. *The Portable World Bible*. New York: Viking, 1975.

Cottrell, Leonard. *The Anvil of Civilization*. New York: New American Library, 1962.

Eliade, Mircea. *Cosmos and History*: *The Myth of the Eternal Return*. New York: Harper Torchbooks, 1969.

———. *Rites and Symbols of Initiation*: *The Mysteries of Birth and Rebirth*. New York: Harper Colophon Books, 1958.

Fairservis, Walter A., Jr. *The Threshold of Civilization*. New York: Charles Scribner's Sons, 1975.

Frankfort, Henri. *Ancient Egyptian Religion*. New York: Harper & Row, 1948.

———. *The Birth of Civilization in the Near East*. Garden City, NY: Doubleday Anchor, 1960.

Gaer, Joseph. *How the Great Religions Began*. New York: Signet, 1956.

Gardner, John, and John Maier, translators. *Gilgamesh*. New York: Alfred A. Knopf, 1984.

Gaster, Theodore. *The Oldest Stories in the World*. Boston: Beacon Press, 1952.

Goodrich, Norma Lorre. *The Ancient Myths*. New York: New American Library, 1960.

Howells, William. *Back of History*. Garden City, NY: Doubleday Anchor, 1963.

Kramer, Samuel Noah. *Sumerian Mythology*. Forgotten Books, 2007.

———. *The Sumerians*. Chicago: University of Chicago Press, 1971.

Mitchell, Steven, trans. *Gilgamesh*. New York: Free Press, 2004.

Moscati, Sabation. *The Face of the Ancient Orient*. Garden City, NY: Doubleday Anchor, 1962.

Stone, Merlin. *When God Was a Woman*. New York: Harcourt Brace Jovanovich, 1976.

Chapter 10: Egyptian and Hebrew Beginnings

Breasted, J. H. *Development of Religion and Thought in Ancient Egypt*. New York: Harper Torchbooks, 1959.

Ceram, C. W. *Gods, Graves and Scholars*. New York: Bantam, 1972.

Cottrell, Leonard. *Life under the Pharaohs*. London: Pan Books, 1960.

Ehrlich, Ernst Ludwig. *A Concise History of Israel*. New York: Harper Torchbooks, 1962.

Fairservis, Walter A., Jr. *The Origins of Oriental Civilization*. New York: Mentor, 1959.

Sandars, N. K. *Poems of Heaven and Hell from Ancient Mesopotamia*. London: Penguin, 1971.

Simpson, William Kelly. *The Literature of Ancient Egypt*. New Haven: Yale University Press, 2003.

Chapter 11: *The Iliad* and *The Odyssey*

Boer, Charles, trans. *The Homeric Hymns*. Chicago: The Swallow Press, 1970.

Bowra, C. M. *The Greek Experience*. New York: New American Library, 1957.

Homer. *The Iliad*. Translated by Richard Lattimore. Chicago: University of Chicago Press, 1951.

Homer. *The Odyssey*. Translated by Robert Fitzgerald. New York: Anchor Books, 1963.

Jaynes, Julian. *The Origins of Consciousness in the Breakdown of the Bicameral Mind*. Boston: Houghton Mifflin, 1990.

Rose, H. J. *Religion in Greece and Rome*. New York: Harper Torchbooks, 1959.

Chapter 12: Greece and the Birth of Monogamous Society

Auden, W. H., ed. *The Portable Greek Reader*. New York: Viking, 1977.

Euripides. *Alcestis/Hippoytus/Iphigenia in Taurus*. New York: Penguin, 1974.

Flaceliere, Robert. *Love in Ancient Greece*. New York: Crown Publishers, 1962.

Hadas, Moses, ed. *The Complete Plays of Aristophanes*. New York: Bantam, 1971.

Hamilton, Edith. *The Greek Way*. New York: Norton Paperback, 1964.

Hesiod and Theognis. New York: Penguin, 1973.

Muller, Herbert J. *The Loom of History*. New York: Oxford University Press, 1966.

Murray, Gilbert. *Euripides and His Age*. New York: Henry Holt and Company, 1913.

Chapter 13: The Rape of Lucretia and the Founding of Rome

Barrow, R. H. *The Romans*. New York: Penguin, 1987.

Cicero. *On the Good Life*. London: Penguin, 1971.

Davenport, Basil. *The Portable Roman Reader*. New York: Viking Press, 1951.

Dixon, Suzanne. *The Roman Family*. Baltimore: Johns Hopkins University Press, 1992.

Fowler, W. Warde. *Social Life at Rome in the Age of Cicero*. New York: The Macmillan Company, 1915.

Goldsworthy, Adrian. *How Rome Fell*. New Haven: Yale University Press, 2009.

Hadas, Moses. *A History of Rome*. Garden City, NY: Doubleday Anchor, 1956.

Hamilton, Edith. *The Roman Way*. New York: W.W. Norton & Company, 1993.

Horace. *The Odes*. New York: New American Library, 1973.

Laistner, M. L. W. *Christianity and Pagan Culture in the Later Roman Empire*. Ithaca, NY: Cornell University Press, 1967.

Ovid. *The Loves, The Art of Love, Love's Cure and The Art of Beauty*. Stillwell, KA: Digitreads.com Publishing, 2006.

Parkinson, C. Northcote. *East and West*. New York: New American Library, 1965.

Plautus. *The Pot of Gold and Other Plays*. London: Penguin, 1965.

———. *The Rope and Other Plays*. London: Penguin, 1965.

Plutarch. *Selected Essays on Love, the Family and the Good Life*, edited by Moses Hadas. New York: New American Library, 1956.

Saunders, Dero A., ed. *The Portable Gibbon: The Decline and Fall of the Roman Empire*. New York: Viking Penguin, 1978.

Segal, Eric, ed. *Classical Comedy*. London: Penguin, 1987.

Seneca. *Four Tragedies and Octavia*. London: Penguin, 1966.

Chapter 14: Christianity,
Droit du Seigneur, and the Virtuous Woman

Beroul. *The Romance of Tristan*. New York: Penguin, 1970.

Burckhardt, Jacob. *The Age of Constantine the Great*. Garden City, NY: Doubleday Anchor, 1949.

Gies, Frances, and Joseph Giles. *Marriage and the Family in the Middle Ages*. New York: Harper & Row, 1987.

Goody, Jack. *The Development of the Family and Marriage in Europe*. New York: Cambridge University Press, 1994.

Lewinsohn, Richard. *A History of Sexual Customs*. New York: Harper & Brothers, 1958.

Lope de Vega. *5 Plays*. New York: Hill and Wang, 1965.

Mitterauer, Michael, and Reinhard Sieder. *The European Family*. Chicago: University of Chicago Press, 1983.

Penman, Bruce, ed. *Five Italian Renaissance Comedies*. New York: Penguin, 1978.

Saint Augustine. *The City of God*. New York: Modern Library, 1950.

Chapter 15: The French Revolution and the End of Aristocracy

Beaumarchais, Pierre. *The Figaro Trilogy*. New York: Oxford University Press, 2008.

Burgierre, Andre, Christiane Klapisch-Zuber, Martine Segalen, and Francoise Zonabend, eds. *A History of the Family (Vols. 1 and 2)*. Cambridge: Belknap Press of Harvard, 1996.

Burke, Edmund. *Reflections on the Revolution in France*. New York: Holt, Rinehart and Winston, 1962.

Colman, George, and David Garrick. "The Clandestine Marriage," in *John Gay's "The Beggar's Opera" and Other 18th Century Plays*. London: J.M. Dent & Sons, 1962.

Congreve, William. *Complete Plays*. New York: Hill and Wang, 1956.

Shorter, Edward. *The Making of the Modern Family*. New York: Basic Books, 1977.

Chapter 16: The Victorian Era and the Triumph of Marriage

Adams, Brooks. *The Law of Civilization and Decay*. New York: Alfred A. Knopf, 1943.

Adams, William T. *Living Too Fast, or The Confessions of a Bank Officer*. Boston: Lee and Shepard, 1876.

Brinton, Crane. *The Shaping of the Modern Mind*. New York: New American Library, 1959.

Haight, Gordon, ed. *The Portable Victorian Reader*. New York: Penguin, 1972.

Himmelfarb, Gertrude. *The Demoralization of Society*. New York: Vintage, 1994.

Hunt, Morton M. *The Natural History of Love*. New York: Alfred A. Knopf, 1959.

Toynbee, Arnold. *"Civilization on Trial" and "The World and the West."* New York: Meridian Books, 1955.

Chapter 17: Mormonism: A Nineteenth Century Dissent from Monogamy

Brown, Christine, Janelle Brown, Kody Brown, Meri Brown, and Robyn Brown. *Becoming Sister Wives: The Story of an Unconventional Marriage*. New York: Gallery Books, 2012.

Jeffs, Brent W., with Maia Szalavitz. *Lost Boy*. New York: Broadway Books, 2009.

Jessop, Carolyn, with Laura Palmer. *Escape*. New York: Broadway Books, 2007.

Parkman, Francis. *The Oregon Trail*. New York: Signet Classic, 1963.

Schmidt, Susan Ray. *Favorite Wife*: *Escape from Polygamy*. Guilford, CT: Lyons Press, 2009.

Stenhouse, T. B. H. *Tell It All*: *The Story of a Life's Experience in Mormonism*. Hartford, CT: A.D. Worthington and Company, 1875.

Twain, Mark. *Roughing It*. New York: Signet Classic, 1965.

Wall, Elisa. *Stolen Innocence*. New York: Harper, 2009.

Part IV: The Non-Western World

Chapter 18: Nomadic Warriors and Islam

Ahmed, Leila. *Women and Gender in Islam*. New Haven: Yale University Press, 1992.

Ali, Nujood. *I Am Nujood, Age 10 and Divorced*. New York: Broadway Paperbacks (Random House), 2010.

Berger, Monroe. *The Arab World Today*. Garden City, NY: Doubleday Anchor, 1964.

Burman, Edward. *The Assassins*: *Holy Killers of Islam*. London: Crucible (The Aquarian Press), 1987.

Caner, Ergun Mehmet, and Emir Fethi Caner. *Unveiling Islam*. Grand Rapids, MI: Kregal, 2002.

Chambers, John. *The Devil's Horsemen*: *The Mongol Invasion of Europe*. New York: Atheneum, 1979.

Crimp, Susan, and Joel Richardson, eds. *Why We Left Islam*: *Former Muslims Speak Out*. Los Angeles: WND Books, 2008.

Esposito, John L. *What Everyone Needs to Know about Islam*. New York: Oxford University Press, 2002.

Faroqhi, Suraiya. *Subjects of the Sultan*: *Culture and Daily Life in the Ottoman Empire*. London: I.B. Tauris, 1995.

Fernea, Elizabeth Warnock. *Guests of the Sheik*. Garden City, NY: Doubleday, 1969.

FitzGerald, Edward. *Rubaiyat of Omar Khayyam*. Oxford, UK: Oxford University Press, 2009.

Gibb, Hamilton A. R. *Studies on the Civilization of Islam*. Boston: Beacon Press, 1962.

Gumley, Frances, and Brian Redhear. *The Pillars of Islam*. London: BBC Books, 1992.

Horrie, Chris, and Peter Chippindale. *What Is Islam? A Comprehensive Introduction*. London: Virgin Books, 2007.

Huntington, Samuel P. *The Clash of Civilizations and the Remaking of World Order*. New York: Simon & Schuster, 1997.

Ibn Khaldun. *The Muqaddimah*. Princeton, NJ: Princeton University Press, 1974.

Ibn Warraq. *Why the West Is Best: A Muslim Apostate's Defense of Liberal Democracy*. New York: Encounter Books, 2011.

The Koran. Middlesex, England: Penguin, 1974.

Lane, George. *Daily Life in the Mongol Empire*. Indianapolis: Hackett Publishing Company, 2006.

Lewis, Bernard. *The Middle East: A Brief History of the Last 2,000 Years*. New York: Scribner, 1995.

———. *Race and Slavery in the Middle East*. New York: Oxford University Press, 1990.

———. *What Went Wrong? Western Impact and Middle Eastern Response*. New York: Oxford University Press, 2002.

Mackintosh-Smith, Tim, ed. *The Travels of Ibn Battutah*. London: Picador, 2003.

Manji, Irshad. *The Trouble with Islam*. New York: St. Martin's Press, 2003.

Montesquieu. *Persian Letters*. New York: Penguin, 2004.

Morgan, David. *The Mongols*. Malden, MA: Blackwell Publishers, 2001.

Palmer, Alan. *The Decline and Fall of the Ottoman Empire*. New York: Fall River Press, 1992.

Patai, Raphael. *The Arab Mind*. New York: Charles Scribner's Sons, 1983.

Pryce-Jones, David. *The Closed Circle*: *An Interpretation of the Arabs*. Chicago: Ivan R. Dee, 2002.

Schuon, Frithjof. *Understanding Islam*. Baltimore: Penguin, 1972.

Smith, Wilfred Cantwell Smith. *Islam in Modern History*. Princeton, NJ: Princeton University Press, 1977

Spencer, Robert. *The Truth about Muhammad*. Washington: Regnery Publishing, 2006.

Tales from the Thousand and One Nights. London: Penguin, 1973.

Turnbull, S. R. *The Mongols*. London: Osprey, 1995.

Von Grunebaum, G. E. *Modern Islam*. New York: Vintage, 1964.

Chapter 19: Marriage in India

Beals, Alan R. *Gopalpur*: *A South Indian Village*. New York: Holt, Rinehart and Winston, 1980.

The Bhagavad-Gita. London: Penguin, 1962.

The Dhammapada. Middlesex, England: Penguin, 1973.

Embree, Ainsllie T., ed. *The Hindu Tradition*: *Readings in Oriental Thought*. New York: Vintage Books, 1972.

Goode, William. *World Revolution and Family Patterns*. New York: Free Press, 1965.

Kalildas. *The Loom of Time*: *A Selection of Plays and Poems*. New Delhi: Penguin, 1990.

Kautilya. *The Arthashastra*. New Delhi: Penguin, 1997.

Lal, P., trans. *Great Sanskrit Plays*. New York: A New Directions Book, 1964.

Mace, David, and Vera Mace. *Marriage East and West*. Garden City, NY: Doubleday, 1960.

Mayo, Katherine. *Mother India*. New York: Blue Ribbon Books, 1930.

Mukerji, Dhan Gopal. *A Son of Mother India Answers*. New York: E.P. Dutton, 1928.

Naipaul, V. S. *India: A Wounded Civilization*. New York: Vintage Books, 1977.

The Rig Veda. Cambridge, UK: Penguin, 1981.

Thackston, Wheeler M., trans. *The Baburnama: Memoirs of Babur, Prince and Emperor*. New York: Modern Library, 2002.

The Upanishads: Breath of the Eternal. New York: New American Library, 1957.

Wood, Ernest. *An Englishman Defends Mother India*. Nyack: Tantrik Press, 1930.

Yadav, K. P. *Child Marriage in India*. New Delhi: Adhyayan Publishers & Distributors, 2006.

Chapter 20: Marriage in China

Baker, Hugh D. R. *Chinese Family and Kinship*. New York: Columbia University Press, 1979.

Benedict, Ruth. *The Chrysanthemum and the Sword: Patterns of Japanese Culture*. New York: New American Library, 1974.

Bynner, Witter, trans. *The Jade Mountain: A Chinese Anthology*. New York: Vintage, 1957.

Che, Wai-Kin. *The Modern Chinese Family*. Palo Alto: R&E Research Associates, 1979.

Confucius. *The Wisdom of Confucius*. Edited and translated by Lin Yutang. New York: Modern Library, 1938.

Confucius and Ezra Pound, trans. *The Analects*. New York: New Directions, 1951.

Davis, Deborah, and Harrell, Steven, eds. *Chinese Families in the Post-Mao Era*. Berkeley: University of California Press, 1988.

Eastman, Lloyd E. *Family, Fields and Ancestors: Constancy and Change in China's Social and Economic History, 1550–1949*. New York: Oxford University Press, 1988.

Fenollosa, Ernest. *The Chinese Written Character as a Medium for Poetry*. San Francisco: City Lights Books, 1968.

Freedman, Maurice, ed. *Family and Kinship in Chinese Society*. Stanford, CA: Stanford University Press, 1970.

Giles, Herbert A. *A History of Chinese Literature*. New York: Grove Press, 1958.

Grousset, Rene. *The Rise and Splendor of the Chinese Empire*. Berkeley: University of California Press, 1962.

Hua, Cai. *A Society without Fathers: The Na of China*. New York: Zone Books, 2001.

Huc, Evariste Regis. *A Journey through the Chinese Empire, Vol. 1*. Forgotten Books, 2012.

———. *A Journey through the Chinese Empire, Vol. 2*. Port Washington, NY: Kennikat Press, 1970.

Hudson, Valerie M., and Andrea M. den Boer. *Bare Branches*. Cambridge: The MIT Press, 2004.

Hvistendahl, Mara. *Unnatural Selection: Choosing Boys over Girls, and the Consequences of a World Full of Men*. New York: Public Affairs, 2011.

Knapp, Ronald G., and Kai-Yin Lo, eds. *House Home Family: Living and Being Chinese*. Honolulu: University of Hawaii Press, 2005.

Lady Murasaki. *The Tale of Genji*. Garden City, NY: Doubleday Anchor Books, 1955.

Levenson, Joseph R. *Modern China and Its Confucian Past*. Garden City, NY: Doubleday Anchor, 1964.

Leys, Simon. *The Burning Forest: Essays on Chinese Culture and Politics*. New York: Henry Holt and Company, 1987.

McMahon, Keith. *Polygamy and Sublime Passion: Sexuality and Sublime Passion on the Verge of Modernity*. Honolulu: University of Hawaii Press, 2010.

McNeill, William H., and Jean W. Sedlar. *Classical China*. New York: Oxford University Press, 1970.

Mitamura, Taisuke. *Chinese Eunuchs*. Rutland, VT: Charles E. Tuttle Company, 1970.

Pa Chin. *Family*. Garden City, NY: Doubleday Anchor, 1972.

Parish, William, and Martin King Whyte. *Village and Family in Contemporary China*. Chicago: University of Chicago Press, 1978.

Pound, Ezra. *The Confucian Odes*. New York: New Directions, 1954.

Saso, Michael. *Velvet Bond: The Chinese Family*. Carmel, CA: New Life Center, 1999.

Tamura, Eileen H., Linda K. Menton, Noren W. Lush, and Francis K. C. Tsui, with Warren Cohen. *China: Understanding Its Past*. Honolulu: University of Hawaii Press, 1998.

Tsao Hsueh-Chin. *Dream of the Red Chamber*. Garden City, NY: Doubleday Anchor, 1958.

Van Gulik, Robert. *Sexual Life in Ancient China*. New York: Barnes & Noble Books, 1996.

Ware, James R., trans. *The Sayings of Confucius*. New York: New American Library, 1958.

Whyte, Martin King, and William L. Parish. *Urban Life in Contemporary China*. Chicago: University of Chicago Press, 1984.

Wu, Lucian. *New Chinese Writing*. Taipei: The Heritage Press, 1962.

Zhenman, Zheng. *Family Lineage Organization and Social Change in Ming and Qing Fujian*. Honolulu: University of Hawaii Press, 2001.

Part V: Modern Questions

Chapter 21: The Black Family and the Emergence of Single Motherhood

Banfield, Edward C. *The Unheavenly City*. Boston: Little, Brown and Company, 1970.

Brown, Claude. *Manchild in the Promised Land*. New York: Touchstone, 1965.

Clark, Kenneth B. *Dark Ghetto*: *Dilemmas of Social Power*. New York: Harper Torchbooks, 1965.

Cleaver, Eldridge. *Soul on Ice*. New York: Dell Publishing, 1992.

Glasgow, Douglas G. *The Black Underclass*. New York: Vintage, 1981.

Gutman, Herbert G. *The Black Family in Slavery and Freedom*: *1750–1925*. New York: Vintage, 1976.

Lemann, Nicholas. *The Promised Land*: *The Great Black Migration and How It Changed America*. New York: Alfred A. Knopf, 1991.

Liebow, Elliot. *Tally's Corner*: *A Study of Negro Streetcorner Men*. Boston: Little, Brown and Company, 1967.

Murray, Charles. *Losing Ground*. New York: Basic Books, 1984.

Sheehan, Susan. *A Welfare Mother*. New York: Mentor, 1977.

Chapter 22: What Is Happening to the Family Today?

Adler, Alfred. *Understanding Human Nature*. New York: Fawcett, 1965.

Bane, Mary Jo. *Here to Stay: American Families in the Twentieth Century*. New York: Basic Books, 1976.

Bednarik, Karl. *The Male in Crisis*. New York: Alfred A. Knopf, 1970.

Blankenhorn, David. *Fatherless America*. New York: Basic Books, 1995.

Blankenhorn, David, Steven Bayme, and Jean Bethke Elshtain, eds. *Rebuilding the Nest: A New Commitment to the American Family*. Milwaukee: Family Service America, 1990.

Bradshaw, John. *The Family: A Revolutionary Way of Self-Discovery*. Deerfield Beach, FL: Health Communications, 1988.

Cavan, Ruth Shonle, ed. *Marriage & Family in the Modern World, Third Edition*. New York: Thomas Y. Crowell Company, 1969.

Clinton, Hillary Rodham. *It Takes a Village*. New York: Simon & Schuster, 2006.

Dalrymple, Theodore. *Life at the Bottom: The Worldview That Makes the Underclass*. Chicago: Ivan R. Dee, 2001.

David, Deborah S., and Robert Brannon, eds. *The Forty-Nine Percent Majority: The Male Sex Role*. Reading, MA: Addison-Wesley, 1976.

Dinesen, Isak. *On Modern Marriage*. New York: St. Martin's Press, 1977.

Eberstadt, Mary. *Adam and Eve after the Pill: Paradoxes of the Sexual Revolution*. San Francisco: Ignatius Press, 2012.

Ember, Melvin, and Carol R. Ember. *Marriage, Family, and Kinship*. New Haven, CT: Human Relations Area Files, 1983.

Fisher, Helen. *Anatomy of Love*. New York: W.W. Norton & Company, 1992.

Gallagher, Maggie. *The Abolition of Marriage*. Washington: Regnery Publishing, 1996.

———. *Enemies of Eros*. Chicago: Bonus Books, 1989.

Gilder, George. *Men and Marriage*. Gretna, LA: Pelican Publishing Company, 1986.

Groves, Ernest R. *The American Family*. New York: J.B. Lippincott, 1934.

Henslin, James M. *Marriage and Family in a Changing Society*. New York: Free Press, 1985.

Humez, Alexander and Keith Fitzgerald Stavely. *Family Man: What Men Feel about Their Children, Their Parents, and Themselves*. Chicago: Contemporary Books, 1978.

Kammeyer, Kenneth C. W. *Marriage and Family*. Newton, MA: Allyn and Bacon, 1987.

Laing, R. D., *The Politics of the Family*. New York: Vintage, 1972.

Laing, R. D., and A. Esterson. *Sanity, Madness and the Family*. Middlesex, England: Penguin, 1964.

Lasch, Christopher. *Haven in a Heartless World: The Family Besieged*. New York: Basic Books, 1977.

Mount, Ferdinand. *The Subversive Family: An Alternative History of Love and Marriage*. New York: Basic Books, 1992.

Moynihan, Daniel Patrick. *Family and Nation*. New York: Harcourt Brace Jovanovich, 1987.

Murray, Charles. *Coming Apart: The State of White America, 1960–2010*. New York: Crown Forum, 2012.

Otto, Herbert A., ed. *The Family in Search of a Future*. New York: Appleton Century Crofts, 1970.

Rossi, Alice S., Jerome Kagan, and Tamara K. Hareven. *The Family*. New York: W.W. Norton & Company, 1978.

Santorum, Rick. *It Takes a Family*. Wilmington, DE: ISI Books, 2005.

Thompson, William Irwin. *At the Edge of History*. New York: Harper Colophon Books, 1971.

Tiger, Lionel. *The Decline of Males*. New York: Golden Books, 1999.

Truxal, Andrew G., and Francis E. Merrill. *The Family in American Culture*. New York: Prentice-Hall, 1947.

Waite, Linda J., and Maggie Gallagher. *The Case for Marriage*. New York: Doubleday, 2000.

Wilson, E. O. *The Social Conquest of the Earth*. New York: Liveright Publishing, 2012.

Young, Cathy. *Ceasefire! Why Women and Men Must Join Forces to Achieve True Equality*. New York: Free Press, 1999.

Young, Michael, and Peter Willmott. *The Symmetrical Family*. New York: Pantheon Books, 1973.

Chapter 23: What Do Women Want?

Brizendine, Louann. *The Male Brain*. New York: Three Rivers Press, 2010.

De Bouvoir, Simone. *The Second Sex*. New York: Bantam, 1961.

Decter, Midge. *The New Chastity*. New York: Berkley Medallion, 1972.

Eichenbaum, Luise, and Susie Orbach. *What Do Women Want*? New York: Berkley, 1984.

Firestone, Shulamith. *The Dialect of Sex*. New York: Bantam, 1971.

Fisher, Elizabeth. *Woman's Creation: Sexual Evolution and the Shaping of Society*. New York: McGraw-Hill, 1979.

Flam, Faye. *The Score: How the Quest for Sex Has Shaped the Modern Man*. New York: Penguin, 2008.

Friedan, Betty. *The Feminine Mystique*. New York: W.W. Norton & Company, 1997.

Gilder, George. *Naked Nomads: Unmarried Men in America*. New York: Quadrangle/The New York Times Book Co., 1974.

———. *Sexual Suicide*. New York: Bantam, 1975.

Goldberg, Steven. *The Inevitability of Patriarchy*. New York: William Morrow & Company, 1973.

Greer, Germaine. *The Female Eunuch*. New York: Harper Perennial, 1971.

Hrdy, Sarah Blaffer. *Mothers and Others*. Cambridge: Harvard University Press, 2009.

———. *The Woman Who Never Evolved*. Cambridge: Harvard University Press, 1981.

Koedt, Anne, Ellen Levine, and Anita Rapone, eds. *Radical Feminism*. New York: Quadrangle, 1973.

Lerner, Gerda. *The Creation of Patriarchy*. New York: Oxford University Press, 1986.

Lloyd, Elisabeth. *The Case of the Female Orgasm: Bias in the Science of Evolution*. Cambridge: Harvard University Press, 2005.

Mailer, Norman. *The Prisoner of Sex*. New York: New American Library, 1971.

Millett, Kate. *Sexual Politics*. London: Abacus, 1972.

Nickles, Elizabeth, with Laura Ashcraft. *The Coming Matriarchy*. New York: Berkley, 1982.

Rosaldo, Michelle Zimbalist, and Louise Lamphere, eds. *Women, Culture and Society*. Stanford: Stanford University Press, 1974.

Sapolsky, Robert M. *The Trouble with Testosterone*. New York: Scribner, 1997.

Shaw, Evelyn, and Joan Darling. *Female Strategies*. New York: Touchstone (Simon & Schuster), 1986.

Sherfey, Mary Jane. *The Nature and Evolution of Female Sexuality*. New York: Vintage, 1973.

Thompson, Clara M. *On Women*. New York: Signet, 1971.

Wassar, Samuel K., ed. *Social Behavior of Female Vertebrates*. New York: Academic Press, 1983.

Chapter 24: What Marriage Means for Civilization

Adler, Alfred. *Cooperation between the Sexes*. Garden City, NY: Doubleday Anchor, 1978.

INDEX